New Paradigms in Crowdfunding: Volume I

New Paradigms in Crowdfunding: Volume I

Scott Crowley

Larsen & Keller
www.larsen-keller.com

New Paradigms in Crowdfunding: Volume 1
Scott Crowley
ISBN: 979-8-88836-018-7 (Hardback)

Larsen & Keller
Published by Larsen and Keller Education,
5 Penn Plaza,
19th Floor,
New York, NY 10001, USA

Cataloging-in-Publication Data

New paradigms in crowdfunding : Volume 1 / Scott Crowley.
p. cm.
Includes bibliographical references and index.
ISBN 979-8-88836-018-7
1. Crowd funding. 2. Finance. I. Crowley, Scott.
HG4751 .N49 2023
658.152 24--dc23

For more information regarding Larsen and Keller Education and its products, please visit the publisher's website www.larsen-keller.com

Table of Contents

Preface

This book was inspired by the evolution of our times; to answer the curiosity of inquisitive minds. Many developments have occurred across the globe in the recent past which has transformed the progress in the field.

Crowdfunding is the practice of funding that involves the use of small amounts of capital from a large number of individuals to finance a new business venture. It exploits the easy accessibility of vast networks of people through social media and crowdfunding websites to bring together the investors and entrepreneurs. Crowdfunding aims to boost entrepreneurship activities by widening the pool of investors beyond the traditional circle of owners, relatives and venture capitalists. The two primary types of crowdfunding are rewards crowdfunding and equity crowdfunding. In rewards crowdfunding, entrepreneurs pre-sell a product or service to launch a business concept without incurring debt or sacrificing equity/shares. It can be used for several purposes such as album recording and motion-picture promotion, free software development, inventions development, scientific research, and civic projects. Equity crowdfunding or investment crowdfunding is a method of raising capital used by startups and early-stage companies. In this method, the entrepreneur offers the company's shares to investors who invest during the initial stages of the start-up company. This book provides a comprehensive overview of the new paradigms in crowdfunding. Those in search of information to further their knowledge will be greatly assisted by it.

This book was developed from a mere concept to drafts to chapters and finally compiled together as a complete text to benefit the readers across all nations. To ensure the quality of the content we instilled two significant steps in our procedure. The first was to appoint an editorial team that would verify the data and statistics provided in the book and also select the most appropriate and valuable contributions from the plentiful contributions we received from authors worldwide. The next step was to appoint an expert of the topic as the Editor-in-Chief, who would head the project and finally make the necessary amendments and modifications to make the text reader-friendly. I was then commissioned to examine all the material to present the topics in the most comprehensible and productive format.

I would like to take this opportunity to thank all the contributing authors who were supportive enough to contribute their time and knowledge to this project. I also wish to convey my regards to my family who have been extremely supportive during the entire project.

Scott Crowley

1

Fundamental Concepts and Dynamics of Crowdfunding

Rotem Shneor, Liang Zhao, and Bjørn-Tore Flåten

Crowdfunding is a method to obtain money from large audiences, where each individual provides a small amount, instead of raising large sums from a small group of sophisticated investors (Belleflamme et al. 2014). Such pooling of contributions from multiple backers (Short et al. 2017) is done via the Internet, and often without standard financial intermediaries (Mollick 2014). This phenomenon finds its origin in the application of crowdsourcing principles to the practices of fundraising while creating new community-enabled financing channels (Schwienbacher and Larralde 2012) for a wide variety of projects including commercial, cultural, humanitarian, social, political, environmental, and technological projects to name a few.

What started initially as sporadic independent fundraising initiatives, has transferred into a proliferation of crowdfunding-dedicated platforms, which served as market makers bringing fundraisers and funders to interact via a common trusted system. Indeed, research on the state of the

R. Shneor (✉) • L. Zhao • B.-T. Flåten
School of Business and Law, University of Agder, Kristiansand, Norway
e-mail: rotem.shneor@uia.no; liang.zhao@uia.no; bjorn-tore.flaten@uia.no

global industry, based on data collected from over a thousand platforms, shows that in 2017 global alternative finance volumes (covering all crowdfunding models) reached USD 371 billion, growing by 42% from 2016 volumes (Ziegler et al. 2019). Furthermore, when excluding the unique context of China, global volumes have grown by 28% from USD 47 billion in 2016 to USD 60 billion in 2017, growing by a further 48% to USD 89 billion in 2018 (Ziegler et al. 2020).

However, the term "crowdfunding" is an umbrella term reflecting a wide variety of fundraising models. At the most basic of levels, these models can be distinguished by their underlying logic either intermediating investments or non-investment financing. Thus far, research and practice have distinguished between four core models, including crowd-lending, equity, reward, and donation crowdfunding (Mollick 2014; Belleflamme et al. 2014). The first two capture the dominant investment types of models, and the latter the dominant non-investment types of models. Later in the book, we provide a detailed overview of crowdfunding models in use, their characteristics and unique aspects.

However, for introductory purposes one can highlight the four core models by building on the definitions provided by the Cambridge University Centre for Alternative Finance (hereafter "CCAF") in its annual reports (e.g. Ziegler et al. 2019): (1) *Crowd-lending* is when individual or institutional backers provide loans to borrowers while expecting the repayment of the principle and a set interest within a predefined timeframe. (2) *Equity crowdfunding* refers to backers buying an ownership stake in an organization. (3) *Reward crowdfunding* means that backers provide funding in exchange for non-monetary rewards, most frequently in the form of pre-purchased products or services. And, (4) *donation crowdfunding* is a provision of funding based on philanthropic or civic motivations without expectation of material rewards.

In this chapter, we introduce the fundamental concepts and dynamics of crowdfunding, which will serve as a common understanding for the discussions in the remaining chapters of this book. Here we present the key stakeholders in crowdfunding engagements, as well as the crowdfunding process and stages. This is followed by a brief introduction to each of the book's chapters while highlighting their main insights and contributions.

Crowdfunding Stakeholders

At the core of crowdfunding practice lies an expectation for a "win-win" game, where all parties enjoy various benefits from their involvement in the process, as highlighted in Fig. 1.1. The three main parties to crowdfunding transactions include the fundraiser, the backer, and the platform. Accordingly, in the context of crowdfunding, a *Fundraiser* can be defined as any individual or organization that makes a public call for the financing of project(s) with particular purpose(s). Literature has referred to them as either "fundraisers" (e.g. Wang et al. 2018), "creators" (e.g. Ryu and Kim 2018), or "campaigners" (e.g. Hobbs et al. 2016). Successful fundraisers may reap benefits from the money received, as well as from market validation outcomes that arise from wide public acceptance and support, establishing relations with prospective customers, engaging in cost-efficient marketing promotions, as well as collecting feedback that may inform further product development efforts (Frydrych et al. 2014; Thürridl and Kamleitner 2016; Wald et al. 2019).

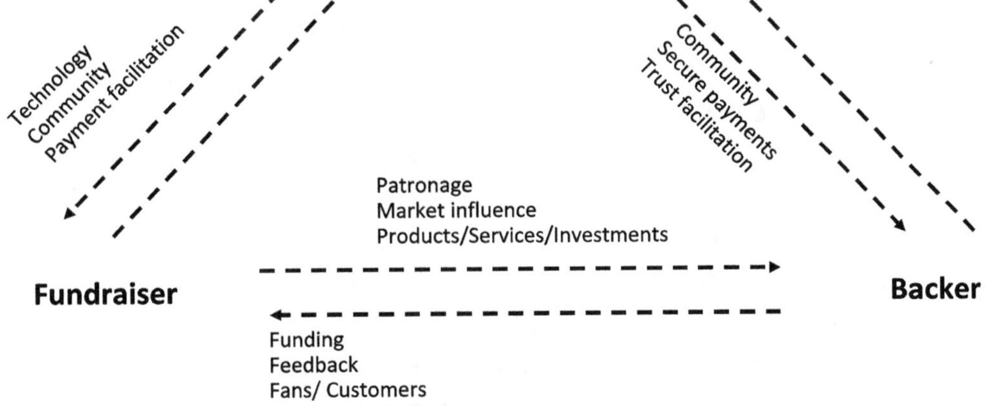

Fig. 1.1 Win-win dynamics in crowdfunding

Similarly, in the context of crowdfunding, a *Backer* can be defined as any individual or organization that provides finance while answering a public call for the financing of project(s) with particular purpose(s). Literature has labelled this group inconsistently as either "backers" (e.g. Shneor and Munim 2019), "funders" (e.g. Kang et al. 2016), "supporters" (e.g. Gerber and Hui 2013), as well as "donors" in donation crowdfunding (e.g. Carvajal et al. 2012), "sponsors" in reward crowdfunding (e.g. Ryu and Kim 2016), "investors" in equity and lending crowdfunding (e.g. Dorfleitner et al. 2018), as well as "lenders" in crowd-lending (e.g. Chemin and de Laat 2013). In terms of benefits from crowdfunding engagements, backers enhance their levels of customer empowerment by influencing the design of future market products, as well as their own future consumption opportunities, while strengthening their sense of belonging to certain groups and communities (Chaney 2019; Gerber et al. 2012; Steigenberger 2017).

A crowdfunding platform is defined as an Internet application linking fundraisers and their potential backers while facilitating the exchanges between them in accordance with pre-specified conditions (Shneor and Flåten 2015). Such intermediaries make their income in forms of campaign success fees and payments for supporting services (Belleflamme et al. 2015). However, at the same time, with each successful campaign completed, their own reputation is enhanced while making them more attractive facilitators for future fundraising initiatives and contribution behaviour. Furthermore, each campaign helps the platform build its own user base (Thies et al. 2018), both in terms of attracting new fundraisers, as well as expanding the value of new users that registered for the purpose of supporting a specific campaign, and converting them into prospective funders of future campaigns as well.

An additional stakeholder, namely the public authorities, while not directly involved in each transaction, do carry great influence on the way the industry develops, and how each party to the crowdfunding transaction interacts with the other. More specifically, regulation sets the rules under which different models of crowdfunding may be practiced by defining compliance requirements primarily aimed at consumer and investor protection. However, at the same time, authorities also have vested interests in supporting new channels for the financing of small and medium sized businesses in their jurisdictions (as job creators and tax payers), as well as enabling greater public contributions to civic, cultural, educational, and environmental initiatives that may align with government policies and agenda. Research here has both theorized about (Kshetri 2015) and empirically showed a clear positive association between perceived adequacy of national crowdfunding regulation and crowdfunding volumes per capita both globally and regionally (Ziegler et al. 2019, 2020).

The Crowdfunding Process

Crowdfunding is not a quick or short-term activity and involves a process with multiple stages, requiring different activities and focus. One earlier conceptualization of this process has identified two stages relevant for backers, including pre-investment and post-investment (Macht and Weatherston 2015). Pre-investment involves due-diligence efforts and investment decision making based on relevant motivations. The post-investment stage relates to additional involvement of backers in a project at later stages either in value adding activities, or additional investments. From a fundraiser perspective, earlier conceptualization referred to three stages simply defined as before, during, and after the campaign (Gerber and Hui 2013).

Taking into consideration additional insights that have emerged in recent years, we propose a more detailed process model including seven distinct stages that while corresponding with earlier conceptualization, do provide some additional clarity. Figure 1.2 presents the three core stages and their sub-stages, while listing related activities fundraisers should engage in during these stages. In this respect, the suggested model represents both descriptive and normative aspects of best practice that fundraisers are encouraged to follow for enhancing the likelihood of their success.

First, before the campaign is formally published and open for money collection, fundraisers usually should engage in (1) *campaign planning*. During this stage, the objectives and goals of the campaign are defined, different platforms are evaluated, one is chosen, campaign materials such

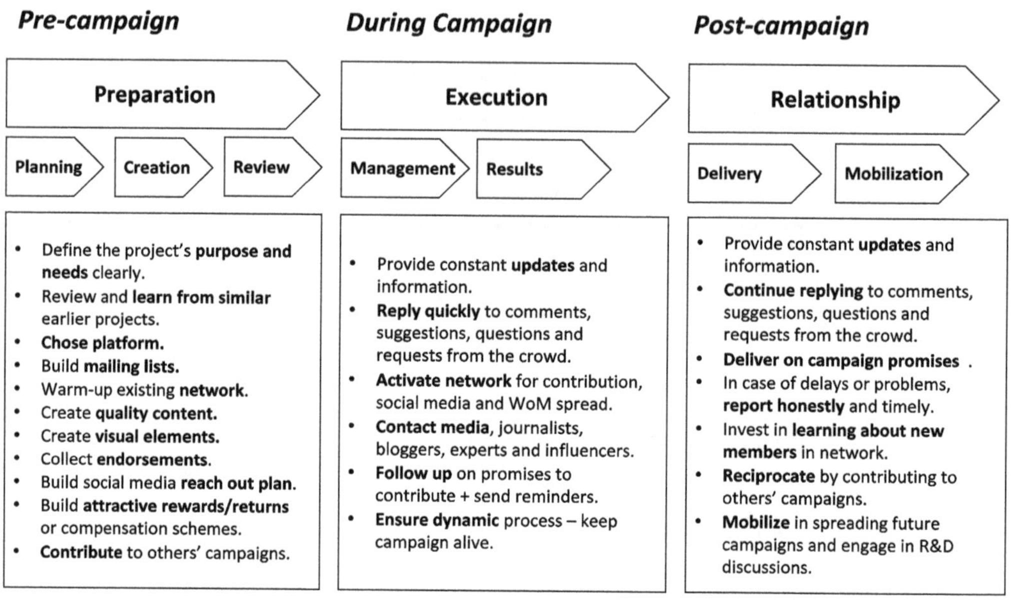

Fig. 1.2 The crowdfunding campaign process

as texts and visual media elements are prepared, promotional strategies are devised, and an execution plan with action points and deadlines can be outlined. Next, fundraisers engage in (2) *campaign creation*—where materials are uploaded to the selected platform, presence in social media is established (e.g. Facebook page, Instagram page, Twitter account, etc.), and initial feedback is collected from first pilot viewers. Lastly, the (3) *campaign review* takes place when the submitted materials are reviewed by platform operators, which ensures compliance with regulation, verification of fundraiser identity, and in some cases quality of the materials provided. When meeting requirements, the platform then approves the campaign for publication, its information is made publicly available, and the collection of funding is enabled.

Second, once approved, the campaign is live and during a set period defined for the campaign, fundraisers engage in (4) *campaign management* which includes promotional efforts both offline and online, and especially via social media platforms, mobilization of network relations takes place, and new information and updates are gradually provided to fans and followers. At this stage, fundraisers need to focus on availability and responsiveness to comments, suggestions, and questions from the crowd for signalling trustworthiness as well as avoiding the loss of prospective contributors. In this sense, during this stage, the backers' decision-making process is both triggered and supported.

This phase ends when the campaign reaches its end date, and (5) *campaign results* are finalized. The results may vary by the scheme under which the campaign was run (Cumming et al. 2019). Campaigns which ran under the "all-or-nothing" schemes are paid out to fundraisers after deduction of platform fees only if they met the minimum stated sum goal. If this goal was not met, payments made are returned to the backers that made them. Campaigns which ran under "keep-it-all" schemes are paid out to fundraisers after deduction of platform fees regardless of whether they have met their minimum stated goals or not. While the former models are relevant for non-investment crowdfunding models, in the case of investment models only the "all-or-nothing" scheme is available. However, some platforms allow campaigns to publish a range rather than a specific sum goal, but in such cases the sum which defines the minimum threshold of the range applies as the basis for "all-or-nothing" pay-out to campaigners.

Finally, once the campaign is finished, a post-campaign stage unfolds. During this period fundraisers must first (6) *deliver on campaign promises* in sending promised products, services, or information, pay back loans with stated interest, or inform investors about firm growth and finances in case of equity investments. In case changes occur to original plans that were specified in campaigns, and informed financial contribution decisions by backers, fundraisers need to honestly inform their backers about such changes and their implications in terms of delays or when surpassing expectations by meeting goals earlier than planned. Furthermore, the backers constitute a network of supporters the fundraisers can and should (7) *develop further relations* with. Such backers are assets that can be mobilized and tapped into in future activities, may they be additional rounds of fundraising or business development activities such as spreading promotional campaigns, or engagement in product development initiatives. In this context, research indeed shows that fundraiser track record and experience can lead to the creation of social capital that supports additional successful fundraising in following campaigns, however it does have its limitations and depreciates over time if excessively used (Butticè et al. 2017).

Towards Advances in Crowdfunding Research and Practice

During the past decade interest in crowdfunding among academic scholars has increased dramatically. Indeed, research has been identified as one of the key pillars that can support both industry development and policy making (De Buysere et al. 2012). An initial mapping of core themes in early crowdfunding research (Moritz and Block 2016) has identified several streams of inquiry including: analyses of fundraisers' motivations to adopt crowdfunding, the determinants of successful crowdfunding campaigns, legal compliance, and challenges primarily with respect to investment crowdfunding models, factors impacting backer behaviour, the role of social networks in crowdfunding, applications of signalling theory in crowdfunding, as well as typologies of crowdfunding models. Here, while initial strides have been made, various authors have suggested that a gap between the available research on crowdfunding (Short et al. 2017) and the increasing academic and public interest in it (Martínez-Climent et al. 2018) remains wide. Lists outlining relevant directions for future research opportunities have been outlined in several literature reviews (e.g. McKenny et al. 2017; Moritz and Block 2016; Shneor and Vik 2020).

Accordingly, in this book, we aim to contribute to improved understanding of crowdfunding by both taking stock of existing knowledge, as well as presenting new aspects and insights that help us advance it. The book includes contributions from a wide range of influential authors and thought leaders from across the globe, representing a range of significant research institutions. In the remainder of this chapter we provide a brief overview of each of the chapters to follow while highlighting their main contributions.

In the first chapter, *Shneor* unravels the diversity of models through which crowdfunding manifests itself. He does so by laying a detailed review of the characteristics of the different crowdfunding models currently in use, as well as the key premises for the use of each. Furthermore, he suggests some of the first frameworks developed for guiding prospective fundraisers in choosing between models. Each of the frameworks is designed for a different type of fundraisers may they be organizations or consumers. In this respect, he provides a useful tool for guiding relevant decision making by practitioners, and at the same time presents a framework that can be tested and fine-tuned in research about such decision making.

In Chap. 2, *Ziegler and colleagues* take a macro level view on crowdfunding market development dynamics and present insights from research on the factors impacting such development trajectories highlighting the roles of economic development, adequate regulation, and IT infrastructure, among others. They present facts and figures from national and regional markets in a comparative manner, while accounting for the diversity of crowdfunding models, growth trajectories, and geographical variations. The chapter shows that crowdfunding is no longer a fringe activity but gradually moving mainstream with substantial volumes recorded nationally, regionally, and globally. Furthermore, it illustrates the dominance of crowd-lending models across regions, as well as their sub-model variations within regions.

The following four chapters examine each of the core models in greater detail. Chapter 3 picks up from the previous chapter and delves deeper into the understanding of the crowd-lending variant of crowdfunding. Here, *Ziegler & Shneor* present the brief history of crowdlending, its diversity of models, the current state of the industry, as well as the underlying mechanisms and principles guiding platform operations including risk assessment and the matching of borrowers and lenders. These discussions are supported with evidence from recent research and highlights the benefits and risks for both lenders and borrowers while assessing the industry development vis-à-vis earlier practices via traditional financial institutions.

In Chap. 4, *Lukkarinen* provides a review of research on equity crowdfunding. She describes the typical equity crowdfunding process, investor characteristics, and investor motivations. Recognizing the limited due diligence efforts of the crowd, Lukkarinen refers to the role of platforms in evaluating and preselecting target ventures. She highlights the importance of rapidly observable campaign features and signals of venture quality in investor decision making, while also emphasizing the relevance of experienced investors and the herding tendency of crowd investors. These discussions are supplemented by a comparison of equity crowdfunding investors with traditional providers of early-stage equity financing enhancing our understanding of the commonalities and differences among these groups of investors.

In Chap. 5, *Zhao & Ryu* present the reward-based crowdfunding model and its unique aspects. This discussion is based on a four-dimensional framework of the crowdfunding process accounting for the fundraisers, the backers, the campaigns, and the platforms. In addition, the development of reward-based crowdfunding is reviewed in a comparative manner across different global regions, highlighting regional variances in terms of developing trends, R&D priorities, female participation, internationalization of platforms, and risks involved. This is supplemented by a literature review of the academic research with a focus on the two main research streams of campaign success drivers, as well as consumer behaviour in reward crowdfunding.

Next, in Chap. 6, *Zhao & Shneor* address the current state and particularities of donation-based crowdfunding, as primarily driven by philanthropic motivations without expectation of monetary or material rewards. In this model intrinsic motivations dominate, and a form of impure altruism characterizes backers that seek satisfaction, joy, and sense of belonging to be achieved with their donations. They suggest that despite accounting for only a marginal share of global crowdfunding volumes, donation crowdfunding is a unique model for supporting a wide range of prosocial and charitable causes, while allowing fundraisers to leverage benefits afforded by ICT solutions for more effective and efficient fundraising. The chapter provides an overview of the limited research available in the context of donation crowdfunding while highlighting donor motivations and behaviour, as well as drivers of success in donation campaigns.

Once the various models are outlined in detail, and the state of both research and practice concerning each are presented, the two chapters that follow shift towards the normative view of crowdfunding. Here, in Chap. 7, *Shneor & Torjesen* present one of the first discussions of ethical issues in crowdfunding practice from multiple stakeholders' perspective. Here, the authors draw on ethical principles outlined in both classical and business-specific approaches and discuss whether crowdfunding presents an ethical solution or a source of ethical problems. To further anchor the discussion, a framework classifying potential ethical dilemmas and pitfalls in crowdfunding practice, as well as potential means for addressing them, is developed for each relevant stakeholder. This framework may both guide practitioner's practice, as well as serve as a theoretical basis for research on ethical practices in crowdfunding.

Furthermore, in Chap. 8, *Cai and colleagues* acknowledge that since financial crowdfunding involves a range of risks, it requires comprehensive governance mechanisms. In this chapter, the authors build a three-level stylized model to explain how legal institutions and social capital at the macro, meso, and micro levels affect the performance of crowdfunding campaigns and the development of the financial crowdfunding market. Such discussion results in highlighting the critical roles of platforms in enforcing laws and building social capital at both the meso and micro levels are highlighted.

In the second part of the book, readers are encouraged to take a step back in order to look forward with two chapters reviewing crowdfunding in a historical perspective. Chapter 9 examines crowdfunding development in the context of the financial industry. Here, *Kallio & Vuola* build on the view that the history of financial markets is marked by continuous fluctuations between economic cycles, which are often caused by structures that enable opportunism and moral hazards. Every crisis contains the seeds of change, but also risks for regulative overreactions. Accordingly, crowdfunding as a form of financing is part of this series of innovations in financial markets. Hence, this chapter gives a historical overview of crowdfunding as part of the history of the ever-changing modern financial markets.

A different perspective, more anchored in the historical evolution of technology, places crowdfunding in the context of Financial Technology (FinTech). Such narrative is outlined in Chap. 10, where *Griffiths* gives an overview of how the financial services sector, especially banking, was a driver for ICT development in the last quarter of the twentieth century, and early years of this century. The chapter examines the conditions that have led banks to "get their eyes off the ball" and open the window for a whole new industrial sector to emerge, namely—Fintech. Furthermore, a framework consisting of a double-entry table where one dimension is financial services functionality and the other technological applications, is suggested for helping readers understand the diversity within the industrial organization of the sector. More specifically, crowdfunding occupies two positions on the functional dimension of this framework: Alternative Finance, and Investment Opportunities.

In the third part of the book, a series of chapters geographically contextualize the crowdfunding industry development while considering relevant drivers, barriers, and growth trajectories, as well as highlighting context particularities. In Chap. 11, *Zhao & Li* discuss the unique conditions and development trends of crowdfunding in China, the world's largest crowdfunding market by far. The authors discuss crowdfunding in China from the perspectives of different stakeholders (platforms, fundraisers, funders, and regulators) and crowdfunding models (reward-based, equity-based, loan-based, and donation-based). Overall, they suggest that while the Chinese crowdfunding market has developed rapidly such development is contrasted with a reality of a relatively underdeveloped regulatory system and availability of personal credit, which are likely to limit further growth. Accordingly, some solutions for addressing these challenges are proposed in this chapter.

Chapter 12 examines crowdfunding market development in the Indian subcontinent, which represents somewhat of a contrast to rapid dynamics that characterized the Chinese crowdfunding market development. Here, *Suresh and colleagues* explore the history, ongoing activity, and future prospects of crowdfunding in the new emerging markets of India and Bangladesh. Overall, they observe that India is largely dominating the crowdfunding activity in the South Asian region, which is otherwise limited in its neighbouring countries. Such discussion highlights the social, cultural, and regulatory conditions influencing such developments.

Chapter 13 veers further afield to the African continent. Here, *Chao and colleagues* present the current state of crowdfunding research and practice in Africa while outlining opportunities and challenges associated with them. The authors suggest that the growing popularity of digital and mobile finance, low penetration of traditional financial institutions, and a long cultural heritage of communal support may enhance crowdfunding uptake in this region. On the other hand, conditions of unclear regulation, relatively low levels of Internet access, and societies characterized by low social trust may all hinder such uptake. Accordingly, African crowdfunding is at its infancy and involves transitory hybrid practices of early adoption, often involving reliance on foreign contributors via donations and pro-social lending platforms.

In Chap. 14, *Efrat and colleagues* present the crowdfunding market in Israel, representing a unique national context that despite adversities has emerged as a regional leader, as well as one of the global leaders, in terms of both general entrepreneurial finance market, and crowdfunding market in particular. The authors argue that crowdfunding has its roots deep in the Israeli entrepreneurship ecosystem. The characteristics of which include collective individualism combined with flat hierarchies, low degree of separation, mandatory army service that enforces innovative thinking and improvisation, Chutzpah, and finally high tolerance for failure, all provide fertile ground for entrepreneurship and facilitate innovative approaches to entrepreneurship funding such as crowdfunding.

Chapter 15 ventures further north and reviews the crowdfunding market in Europe, while highlighting the various facets of its fragmented nature. Here, *Wenzlaff and colleagues* present current market conditions and argue that fragmentation is mostly caused by differences in national regulations, which represent an obstacle to industry growth. At the same time, the European Union has recently introduced the European Crowdfunding Service Provider (ECSP) regime aiming towards harmonized regulations. This regime is expected to facilitate platform growth via easier cross-border transactions and international expansion of platforms operating under the business lending and equity investment models.

In part four of the book, three chapters provide insights into unique aspects of crowdfunding applications for concrete types of campaign objectives. Chapter 16 focused on using crowdfunding for financing sustainable projects, that is projects aiming to extend their goal beyond market success and provide benefit to the larger part of society. Here, *Maehle and colleagues* discuss the definition and dimensions of sustainable development and entrepreneurship. The chapter provides an overview of the existing literature on crowdfunding of sustainable projects. The authors also review four European sustainability-oriented crowdfunding platforms representing different crowdfunding models. This review reveals that sustainable projects have rather high success rates in crowdfunding and may address important dimensions of sustainable development. And while the environmental dimension gets the most attention, pro-social crowdlending seems to have the highest success rates. Hence, the focus on a certain sustainability dimension may influence the choice of the crowdfunding model employed.

Chapter 17 discussed crowdfunding applications in the cultural industries. In this chapter, *Rykkja and colleagues* trace the early adoption of crowdfunding by cultural industries to a comprehensive value chain reconfiguration in the cultural sector, which were triggered by the advent of digitalization on the one hand and the downsizing in public funds in many countries on the other. The authors highlight the importance of studying crowdfunding in the cultural sector, as it presses creators to strike a balance between the commercial and the non-commercial, the economic and the cultural outcomes, as well as the authentic and independent versus the mass dictated and dependent. Accordingly, they review earlier research on cultural crowdfunding, identify core themes that attracted research attention, and outline an agenda for future research.

In Chap. 18, *Wenzlaff* discusses civic crowdfunding, as when crowdfunding campaigns are used for funding the creation or provision of a semi-public good. Unlike other crowdfunding practices, civic crowdfunding creates benefits for people outside of the group of supporters as well. Such a situation creates unique dilemmas as well as motivations for participation. This chapter analyses the literature on civic crowdfunding and proposes to view this through four perspectives: the project, the supporter, the project owner, and the platform. The chapter argues that the platform is central to understanding the self-positioning of projects, supporters, and project owners within civic crowdfunding.

Finally, the concluding fifth part of the book includes two chapters addressing future considerations for crowdfunding research and practice. Chapter 19 highlights the importance of education about crowdfunding highlighting both its benefits and advantages, as well as its risks and challenges. Here, *Shneor & Flåten* argue on the need for crowdfunding education, and present a concrete program developed at the University of Agder as a credit awarding course named the "UiA Crowdfunding Lab". This chapter outlines course objectives, content, pedagogy, and assessment issues, while presenting opportunities for further development.

The book concludes with Chap. 20 which is dedicated to a critical reflection on current crowdfunding research and practice. Here, *Shneor and colleagues* present eight dilemmas that are expected to influence and shape the future of crowdfunding. Each of which is critically discussed and followed by suggestions for future research. These dilemmas include (1) the need to strike a balance between idealism and pragmatism; (2) the extent to which crowdfunding platforms should cooperate with traditional financial institutions; (3) how should we measure crowdfunding success and performance in both financial and socio-economic terms; (4) the need to strike a balance between quantity and quality in campaigns approved for publication on platforms; (5) understanding the conditions and implications of domestic versus international growth of crowdfunding platforms; (6) the responsibility of manoeuvring between facilitation of collective decisions as crowd wisdom while avoiding crowd madness, as well as intentional and unintentional harmful crowd behaviour; (7) whether should platforms focus their technological development on efficiency gains versus community support; as well as (8) how to best inform the public through educational efforts without constraining our understanding of the crowdfunding phenomenon too early.

At this stage, we wish to express our gratitude to all contributors, and invite readers to explore the rest of the book in greater detail.

References

Belleflamme, P., Lambert, T., & Schwienbacher, A. (2014). Crowdfunding: Tapping the Right Crowd. *Journal of Business Venturing, 29*(5), 585–609.

Belleflamme, P., Omrani, N., & Peitz, M. (2015). The Economics of Crowdfunding Platforms. *Information Economics and Policy, 33*, 11–28.

Butticè, V., Colombo, M. G., & Wright, M. (2017). Serial Crowdfunding, Social Capital, and Project Success. *Entrepreneurship Theory and Practice, 41*(2), 183–207.

Carvajal, M., García-Avilés, J. A., & González, J. L. (2012). Crowdfunding and Non-profit Media. *Journalism Practice, 6*(5-6), 638–647.

Chaney, D. (2019). A Principal–Agent Perspective on Consumer Co-production: Crowdfunding and the Redefinition of Consumer Power. *Technological Forecasting and Social Change, 141*, 74–84.

Chemin, M., & de Laat, J. (2013). Can Warm Glow Alleviate Credit Market Failures? Evidence from Online Peer-to-Peer Lenders. *Economic Development and Cultural Change, 61*(4), 825–858.

Cumming, D. J., Leboeuf, G., & Schwienbacher, A. (2019). Crowdfunding Models: Keep-It-All vs. All-Or-Nothing. *Financial Management,* https://doi.org/10.1111/fima.12262

De Buysere, K., Gajda, O., Kleverlaan, R., et al. (2012). A Framework for European Crowdfunding. Retrieved from https://www.fundraisingschool.it/wp-content/uploads/2013/02/European-Crowdfunding-Framework-Oct-2012.pdf.

Dorfleitner, G., Hornuf, L., & Weber, M. (2018). Dynamics of Investor Communication in Equity Crowdfunding. *Electronic Markets, 28*(4), 523–540.

Frydrych, D., Bock, A. J., Kinder, T., et al. (2014). Exploring Entrepreneurial Legitimacy in Reward-Based Crowdfunding. *Venture Capital, 16*(3), 247–269.

Gerber, E. M., & Hui, J. (2013). Crowdfunding: Motivations and Deterrents for Participation. *ACM Transactions on Computer-Human Interaction, 20*(6), 1–32.

Gerber, E. M., Hui, J. S., & Kuo, P.-Y. (2012). Crowdfunding: Why People Are Motivated to Post and Fund Projects on Crowdfunding Platforms. Retrieved from http://www.juliehui.org/wp-content/uploads/2013/04/CSCW_Crowdfunding_Final.pdf.

Hobbs, J., Grigore, G., & Molesworth, M. (2016). Success in the Management of Crowdfunding Projects in the Creative Industries. *Internet Research, 26*(1), 146–166.

Kang, M., Gao, Y., Wang, T., et al. (2016). Understanding the Determinants of Funders' Investment Intentions on Crowdfunding Platforms: A Trust-Based Perspective. *Industrial Management & Data Systems, 116*(8), 1800–1819.

Kshetri, N. (2015). Success of Crowd-Based Online Technology in Fundraising: An Institutional Perspective. *Journal of International Management, 21*(2), 100–116.

Macht, S. A., & Weatherston, J. (2015). Academic Research on Crowdfunders: What's Been Done and What's to Come? *Strategic Change, 24*(2), 191–205.

Martínez-Climent, C., Zorio-Grima, A., & Ribeiro-Soriano, D. (2018). Financial Return Crowdfunding: Literature Review and Bibliometric Analysis. *International Entrepreneurship and Management Journal, 14*(3), 527–553.

McKenny, A. F., Allison, T. H., Ketchen, D. J., et al. (2017). How Should Crowdfunding Research Evolve? A Survey of the Entrepreneurship Theory and Practice Editorial Board. *Entrepreneurship Theory and Practice, 41*(2), 291–304.

Mollick, E. (2014). The Dynamics of Crowdfunding: An Exploratory Study. *Journal of Business Venturing, 29*(1), 1–16.

Moritz, A., & Block, J. H. (2016). Crowdfunding: A Literature Review and Research Directions. In D. Bruntje & O. Gajda (Eds.), *Crowdfunding in Europe: State of the Art in Theory and Practice*. London: Springer.

Ryu, S., & Kim, Y.-G. (2016). A Typology of Crowdfunding Sponsors: Birds of a Feather Flock Together? *Electronic Commerce Research and Applications, 16*, 43–54.

Ryu, S., & Kim, Y.-G. (2018). Money Is Not Everything: A Typology of Crowdfunding Project Creators. *The Journal of Strategic Information Systems, 27*(4), 350–368.

Schwienbacher, A., & Larralde, B. (2012). Crowdfunding of Small Entrepreneurial Ventures. In D. Cumming (Ed.), *The Oxford Handbook of Entrepreneurial Finance*. New York, NY: Oxford University Press.

Shneor, R., & Flåten, B.-T. (2015). Opportunities for Entrepreneurial Development and Growth Through Online Communities, Collaboration, and Value Creating and Co-creating Activities. In H. R. Kaufmann & S. M. R. Shams (Eds.), *Entrepreneurial Challenges in the 21st Century*. Basingstoke: Palgrave Macmillan.

Shneor, R., & Munim, Z. H. (2019). Reward Crowdfunding Contribution as Planned Behaviour: An Extended Framework. *Journal of Business Research, 103*, 56–70.

Shneor, R., & Vik, A. A. (2020). Crowdfunding Success: A Systematic Literature Review 2010–2017. *Baltic Journal of Management, 15*(2), 149–182.

Short, J. C., Ketchen, D. J., McKenny, A. F., Allison, T. H., & Ireland, R. D. (2017). Research on Crowdfunding: Reviewing the (Very Recent) Past and Celebrating the Present. *Entrepreneurship Theory and Practice, 41*(2), 149–160.

Steigenberger, N. (2017). Why Supporters Contribute to Reward-Based Crowdfunding. *International Journal of Entrepreneurial Behavior & Research, 23*(2), 336–353.

Thies, F., Wessel, M., & Benlian, A. (2018). Network Effects on Crowdfunding Platforms: Exploring the Implications of Relaxing Input Control. *Information Systems Journal, 28*(6), 1239–1262.

Thürridl, C., & Kamleitner, B. (2016). What Goes Around Comes Around? Rewards as Startegic Assets in Crowdfunding. *California Management Review, 58*(2), 88–110.

Wald, A., Holmesland, M., & Efrat, K. (2019). It Is Not All About Money: Obtaining Additional Benefits Through Equity Crowdfunding. *The Journal of Entrepreneurship, 28*(2), 270–294.

Wang, T., Liu, X., Kang, M., et al. (2018). Exploring the Determinants of Fundraisers' Voluntary Information Disclosure on Crowdfunding Platforms: A Risk-Perception Perspective. *Online Information Review, 42*(3), 324–342.

Ziegler, T., Shneor, R., Wenzlaff, K., et al. (2019). *Shifting Paradigms—The 4th European Alternative Finance Benchmarking Report.* Cambridge: Cambridge Centre for Alternative Finance.

Ziegler, T., Shneor, R., Wenzlaff, K., et al. (2020). *The Global Alternative Finance Benchmarking Report.* Cambridge, UK: Cambridge Centre for Alternative Finance.

Part I

Crowdfunding: The Current Situation

2

Crowdfunding Models: Characteristics and Diversity

Rotem Shneor

Introduction

During the last decade, the emergence and growing popularity of crowdfunding were manifested and promoted through the proliferation of thousands of online crowdfunding platforms worldwide. A crowdfunding platform is "an internet application bringing together project owners and their potential backers, as well as facilitating exchanges between them, according to a variety of business models" (Shneor and Flåten 2015, p. 188). According to Méric et al. (2016) most platforms have the following characteristics in common: first, providing fundraisers with campaign presentation formats for their project, which is accessible to all online users; second, allowing small to medium sized financial transactions that enable widespread participation while keeping risks within reasonable limit; and, third, provide relevant financial information about

R. Shneor (✉)
School of Business and Law, University of Agder, Kristiansand, Norway
e-mail: rotem.shneor@uia.no

the campaign and its progress, as well as communication tools for interaction between prospective backers and fundraisers. In addition, some platforms also provide advice, social media PR functionalities, as well as referrals to other supporting services (ibid.).

The operation of platforms is overseen by regulation in each national jurisdiction (Gajda 2017). In addition, self-regulation is also evident through codes of conduct developed by industry associations for their member platforms (Wenzlaff and Odorovic 2020), as well as in rules and procedures developed by platforms themselves for own campaign approval and user verification. Nevertheless, dependency on legal compliance often results in a more constrained scope of operation both in geographical and functional terms. Here, while some platforms have developed into global giants (i.e. Kickstarter, Indiegogo, Gofundme, etc.) or regional actors (i.e. Latvia-based Mintos covering Eastern Europe, Finland-based Investor covering the Nordic countries, etc.), thus far, most platforms remain local and have a domestic focus or very limited international scope of activities (regulatory and international aspects of platform operations will be covered in greater detail in later chapters).

At this stage, it is also worth noting that in addition to platforms, crowdfunding activity also exists in the form of 'individual crowdfunding campaigns' (Belleflamme et al. 2013), which are individual- or organization-specific fundraising efforts carried outside formal platform control and oversight. However, due to the latter's sporadic nature, non-systematic approach, and limited scope within private networks, most research documents crowdfunding with respect to platform activities and not with respect to individual campaigning efforts.

In the current chapter we present crowdfunding model types and their different characteristics. This will be followed by a discussion of how fundraisers may choose the best crowdfunding model for their own project's fundraising needs. The chapter will then conclude by highlighting its main contributions, limitations, as well as implications for research and practice.

Crowdfunding Models: A Typology

Earlier studies have suggested a number of typologies for capturing the differing value propositions, practice patterns, funder motivations, risks and legal compliance needs of crowdfunding platforms (i.e. Haas et al. 2014; De Buysere et al. 2012; Méric et al. 2016; Belleflamme and Lambert 2016). We build on these earlier references but use the most-comprehensive typology currently employed by the Cambridge Centre for Alternative Finance (CCAF) in its annual industry reports (Ziegler et al. 2018b, b, d, 2019; Zhang et al. 2018) and further elaborate on it. This typology is outlined in Table 2.1.

The first model of online crowdfunding to emerge was debt-based, in what is known as peer-to-peer (P2P) or marketplace lending, with the establishment of platforms like Zopa in the UK and Prosper in the USA in 2005. In the CCAF typology, debt-based models include non-deposit taking platforms that facilitate online credit (both in the form of a secured and unsecured loan) to individuals or business borrowers from individuals or institutional investors. In this respect, the platform functions as an intermediary. In some cases, known as balance sheet lending, one can observe a departure from original conceptualization of debt-based crowdfunding, where the platform serves as the loan-provider, drawing upon funds in a dedicated platform balance-sheet. In this respect, the platform goes beyond the role of intermediary facilitating exchanges between lenders and borrowers, and actively funds and services the loan.

A unique sub-set of lending included in the above is what is referred to as 'pro-social lending', which may, but not necessarily, take the form of micro-finance. Here, pro-social lending happens when lenders evaluate prospective borrowers on both traditional financial lending criteria and prosocial, charitable criteria (Allison et al. 2015). Prosocial loans relate to either consumer or business loans and may involve high as well as low sums, while catering projects with social welfare, human development, or environmental well-being and sustainability objectives. Thus, micro-finance can be considered as a sub-set of prosocial loans specifically when loans involve small sums catering to economically disadvantaged and

Table 2.1 An extended CCAF global crowdfunding typology

Generic model		Specific model	Definition
Investment	Debt	P2P / Marketplace Consumer Lending	Individuals or institutional funders provide a loan to a consumer borrower.
		Balance Sheet Consumer Lending	The platform entity provides a loan directly to a consumer borrower.
		P2P / Marketplace Business Lending	Individuals or institutional funders provide a loan to a business borrower.
		Balance Sheet Business Lending	The platform entity provides a loan directly to a business borrower.
		P2P / Marketplace Property Lending	Individuals or institutional funders provide a loan secured against a property to a consumer or business borrower
		Balance Sheet Property Lending	The platform entity provides a loan secured against a property to a consumer or business borrower
		Micro-Finance	Individuals or institutional funders provide a low sum loan to entrepreneurs who are often economically disadvantaged and marginalized.
	Invoice trading	Invoice Trading	Individuals or institutional funders purchase invoices or receivable notes from a business at a discount.
	Equity	Equity Crowdfunding	Individuals or institutional funders purchase registered securities or equity from a business, mostly early stage firms.
		Real Estate Crowdfunding	Direct investment into a property by individuals or institutional funders, usually through the sale of a registered security or subordinated-debt financing through a special purpose vehicle (SPV).
		Debt-based Securities	Individuals or institutional funders purchase debt-based securities (typically a bond or debenture) at a fixed interest rate. Lenders receive full repayment plus interest paid at full maturity.
		Mini Bonds	Individuals or institutions purchase securities from companies in the form of unsecured retail bonds.

		Profit-sharing Crowdfunding	Individuals or institutions purchase securities from a company, such as shares or bonds, and share in the profits or royalties of the business.
		Community Shares	Individuals purchase a withdrawable share capital in cooperative and community benefit societies.
Non-investment	Reward	Reward Crowdfunding	Backers provide funding to individuals, projects or companies in exchange for non-monetary rewards or products. Most commonly in the form of pre-purchase of products prior to their production.
	Donation	Donation Crowdfunding	Donors provide funding to individuals, projects or companies based on philanthropic or civic motivations with no expectation of monetary or material benefit.
		Patronage	Donors make subscription-like payments to individuals to fund an ongoing occupation or career. Most commonly used by artists.

financially marginalized individuals aiming "to improve the well-being of the poor through better access to savings services and loans" (Schreiner 2001).

Equity-based models, including equity crowdfunding, relate to activities where individuals or institutions invest in unlisted shares or debt-based securities issued by a business, typically an SME. Here, entrepreneurs make an open call to sell a specified amount of equity or bond-like shares via the internet in the hope of attracting a large number of investors (Ahlers et al. 2015). As equity-based models have advanced, more diversified applications have emerged beyond venture funding. Here, subsets of the model like Real Estate and Property-based crowdfunding have flourished, with investors able to acquire ownership of a property asset via the purchase of property shares.

Another interesting variant of the equity model relates to community shares, also referred to as the cooperative model. Under this model, funders' investments are collected to support a community project. And while some revenue-generating community projects have the potential of repaying backers wishing to cash-in their shares, most funders are motivated by investing in their local community rather than in financial returns (Gray and Zhang 2017).

A more recent addition to the crowdfunding models has been invoice trading, which is considered as a "fast and easy way in which small and medium sized enterprises (SMEs) can raise short-term debt by pre-financing their outstanding invoices through individual or institutional investors" (Dorfleitner et al. 2017, p. 56.). Such a short-term supply of financing, in which companies sell their accounts receivables at a discount in exchange for immediate cash, helps in alleviating cash-flow challenges that often affect SMEs. Hence, unlike other crowdfunding models, this specific model is less about fundraising per se, and more about cash-flow management that is financed through crowd investments.

Finally, the reward and donation crowdfunding models, are arguably the models most commonly recognized by the public. In the case of these two models, individuals provide funding to a project, an individual, or a business without expectations of monetary returns for the funds raised. Here, while reward models often represent pre-sales of products and services, which funders expect to receive within a certain time frame, in donation, there are no tangible rewards, and funders are likely to have a sense of satisfaction from contributing to something they deem important and are passionate about. One interesting variant of donation crowdfunding captured above is patronage, which involves subscription-like payments (rather than a one-time donation) to individuals to fund an ongoing occupation or career and is of particular relevance for artists (Swords 2017), despite being relatively marginal in the overall crowdfunding sphere thus far.

While the above list of models presents a clear distinction between them, it is important to acknowledge that some platforms offer combinations of models, either as experiment or extensions of their services. These have been labelled as 'Hybrid Models' (De Buysere et al. 2012), and while not representing main stream practice, may offer extra benefits to funders and fundraisers alike. One example here may be a combination of equity and rewards campaign, where an equity investment may also incorporate special benefits for investors as consumers of the products produced by the firm that they are investing in.

In an attempt to simplify matters, and at the most basic of levels, Belleflamme and Lambert (2016) suggest a distinction between 'investment models' and 'non-investment models' defined based on the nature of compensation promised to, and expected by, funders. Accordingly, non-investment models include reward and donation crowdfunding, while investment models include lending and equity models (including royalty models such as profit or income sharing). In addition, one should add the relatively newer model of invoice trading to investment models of crowdfunding.

An additional, simple distinction between platforms is that distinguishing between two types of fundraising strategies. One, labelled as the 'all or nothing' (AON) approach, where fundraisers receive the funds raised only if the campaign has reached its stated minimum goal, otherwise funds are either returned or not charged from backers. The second, labelled as the 'take it all' (TIA) approach, where fundraisers receive the funds raised regardless of whether the campaign reached its stated minimum sum goal or not. The prevailing approach across models is the former, as it may signal greater levels of commitment and seriousness. Nevertheless, the latter is a popular approach in donation and pro-social lending, where some welfare improvement is preferable to none.

Interestingly, research examining the two approaches in the specific context of reward crowdfunding has shown that AON forces fundraisers to bear greater risk but serves as a signal of commitment, which in turn yields higher quality campaigns and greater success rates (Cumming et al. 2019b).

A different typology suggested by Haas et al. (2014), identifies three archetypes of crowdfunding intermediaries by their different value propositions—Hedonism, Altruism, and For-Profit. *Hedonism* platforms are those where backers pledge for innovative or creative products or projects with consumption in mind, all while addressing individuals' interests and sense of joy. These are mostly associated with the Reward crowdfunding model. *Altruism* platforms are those where backers pledge for a 'greater good' or 'enhanced welfare' and are mostly associated with donation or pro-social lending platforms but can also relate to community shares. *For-profit* platforms are those where backers pledge for a profit-oriented return and are associated with equity, royalty (profit sharing), and lending platforms to which one can also add invoice trading.

Nevertheless, the most popular generic classification of crowdfunding models has thus far included—equity, lending, reward and donation (Méric et al. 2016). We suggest adding invoice trading to this generic classification, as it presents a unique new model that only in recent years became significant in volumes in multiple markets, accounting for 22% of the 2017 annual crowdfunding volumes in Latin America (Ziegler et al. 2018b), 18% in the UK (Zhang et al. 2018), and 16% in mainland Europe (Ziegler et al. 2019).

Crowdfunding Models: Key Characteristics

Once the models have been defined, it is important to establish an understanding of their characteristics. Table 2.2 summarizes the key characteristics of each model while providing illustrative figures whenever available from earlier research and industry reports.

Equity models are associated with the highest levels of funds raised, while involving projects with a long time horizon and some of the highest levels of risk, although the latter remains uncertain as available data capture ventures that have entered the equity crowdfunding market at its

Table 2.2 Main crowdfunding model characteristics

	Equity	Lending	Invoice trading	Reward	Donation
Sum raised Europe 2016 figures[a] (value of average campaign)	Relatively high Equity CF: € 302K Real Estate: € 453K Profit Sharing: € 94K	Varies among sub-models Debt-based securities: € 275K P2P Property: € 119K P2P Business: € 111K P2P Consumer: € 6.3K	Medium € 27K	Medium € 15K	Low € 4.6K
Risk (Default rates in loans, non-delivery rates in reward)	High CrowdCube (UK)—10%[b]	Low-Medium Lending Club (USA)—4.6%[c]; Kiva (USA/Global)—1.22%[d]; Yooly (China)—9.95%[e]; Unspecified (China)—11.56%[f]	Medium-Low MarketInvoice (UK)—2%[g]	Medium Kickstarter (USA/Global)—9% Non-delivery and 75.1% delayed delivery[h] 3% Non-delivery, Fraud—0.01%[i]	Medium N/A
Fulfillment time-horizon	Multiple years	Few months to few years	Few months to few weeks	Multiple months	Immediate/short-term
Funder benefits	Ownership of a share in firm or future revenue/profit streams Sense of patronage	Interest payment on loans Sense of patronage	Profit margins between invoice purchase sum and claim value	Consumption Sense of joy Sense of patronage	Sense of joy Sense of mission fulfilment Sense of patronage
Fundraiser benefits	Funding Market validation promotion	Funding Cash-flow remedies Market validation in business loans	Cash-flow remedies	Funding Market validation, Initial sales Initial customers Promotion	Funding Alleviating hardships Improving welfare

(*continued*)

Table 2.2 (continued)

	Equity	Lending	Invoice trading	Reward	Donation
Onboarding rates Europe 2017 figures[j] (value of average campaign)	Very Low (less than 10%)	Low in P2P Consumer, P2P business, and debt-based securities (ca. 17%-22%)	High (ca. 61%)	Medium (ca. 47%)	Very High (ca. 74%)
Successful funding Europe 2017 figures[k] (value of average campaign)	High (ca. 81%)	Low in consumer (ca. 29%) High in business (ca. 83%) Very High in debt-based securities (ca. 95%)	High (ca. 88%)	Medium (ca. 66%)	Medium (ca. 69%)

[a]Ziegler et al. (2018c)
[b]Signori and Vismara (2016)
[c]Emekter et al. (2015)
[d]Dorfleitner and Oswald (2016)
[e]Lin et al. (2017)
[f]Wang et al. (2018)
[g]Dorfleitner et al. (2017)
[h]Mollick (2015a)
[i]Cumming et al. (2019a)
[j]Ziegler et al. (2019)
[k]Ibid.

very early stages. Well-reflective of the risk levels involved, as well as strict regulations governing this model, platforms employ high levels of filtering efforts, with only a small minority of suggested projects being approved for publication and live campaigning (otherwise known as onboarding rate). However, as a result, equity models also present some of the highest success rates among campaigns approved for publication across all models.

The characteristics of lending models are more diverse based on the model employed and the target audience served. Debt-based securities involve the highest volumes raised on average per campaign, low onboarding rates, and very high success rates. On the other hand, P2P consumer lending involves relatively low sums, and despite low onboarding rates, has some of the lowest success rates across all models, as well as some of the highest recorded default rates. An exception here are micro-finance loans exhibiting some of the lowest default rates among all lending models.

Invoice trading is characterized by low default rates, relatively high onboarding, and very high success rates. This may be related to the relative novelty of the model, where platforms need to achieve legitimacy in the market, as well as the fact that transactions tend to involve relatively modest sums in a grander business financing context.

Reward crowdfunding, however, involves more modest sums and is associated with medium onboarding rates and levels of success. Here, while outright fraud is extremely rare, and non-delivery levels remain low, late delivery is a major aspect of fulfilment on reward crowdfunding campaign promises. Delays were frequently associated with either very small sums or very large sums raised (Mollick 2015b). In the former, entrepreneurs are likely to face higher costs than expected, which may delay production and delivery. And in the latter, entrepreneurs may face overfunding and high demands which generate complexities requiring more time to overcome by relatively small businesses (Hainz 2018).

Finally, donation crowdfunding is associated with the lowest sums raised per campaign on average, and is characterized by relatively high onboarding rates, and medium success rates in comparison to other models. However, being one of the least studied crowdfunding models and offering no tangible benefit in return for funds raised, it is more difficult to assess the extent of non-delivery or fraudulent activities under this model.

Fundraiser Model Choice

Once the models have been defined and outlined, and their characteristics presented, prospective fundraisers need to choose the best fitting model for their respective projects. In the current section decision-making frameworks are suggested to guide fundraisers through key considerations when making such choices, based on establishing a good fit between funding needs and each model's characteristics. In total, three frameworks are presented. Figure 2.1 presents the 'Generic Organizational Fundraiser Model Choice Framework'. Figure 2.2 presents its more elaborate version labelled as the 'Extended Organizational Fundraiser Model Choice Framework'. Here, the extended framework incorporates the generic framework. The former is provided for simplification purposes as it covers the most familiar crowdfunding models, while the latter also incorporates newer or less familiar models. In any case, the focus here is on organizations without limitations on size (from micro-entrepreneurs to large businesses) or sectoral affiliation. In addition, Fig. 2.3 presents the "Consumer Fundraiser Model Choice Framework", reflecting individuals with fundraising for non-business private consumption needs.

First, from the perspective of the organizational fundraiser, both the generic and the extended frameworks present relevant guidelines. Here,

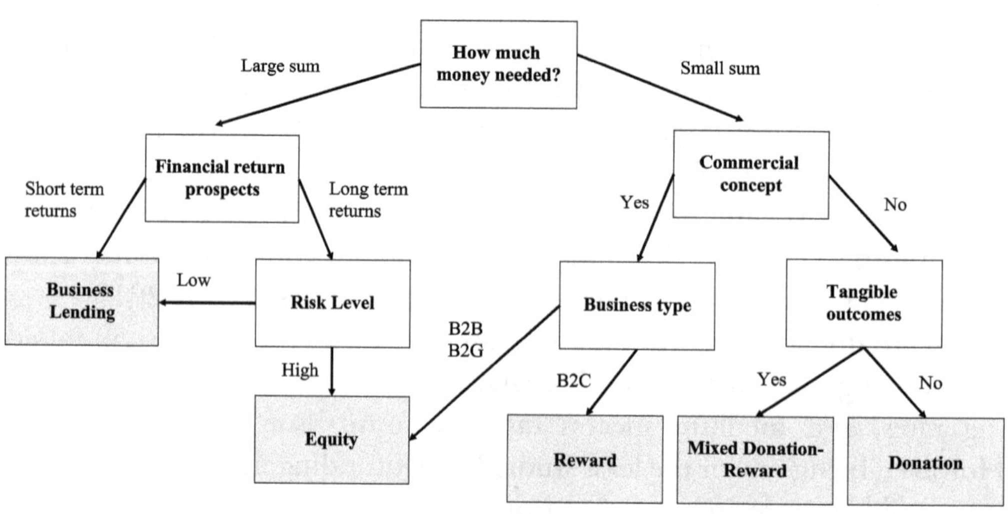

Fig. 2.1 Generic organizational fundraiser model choice framework

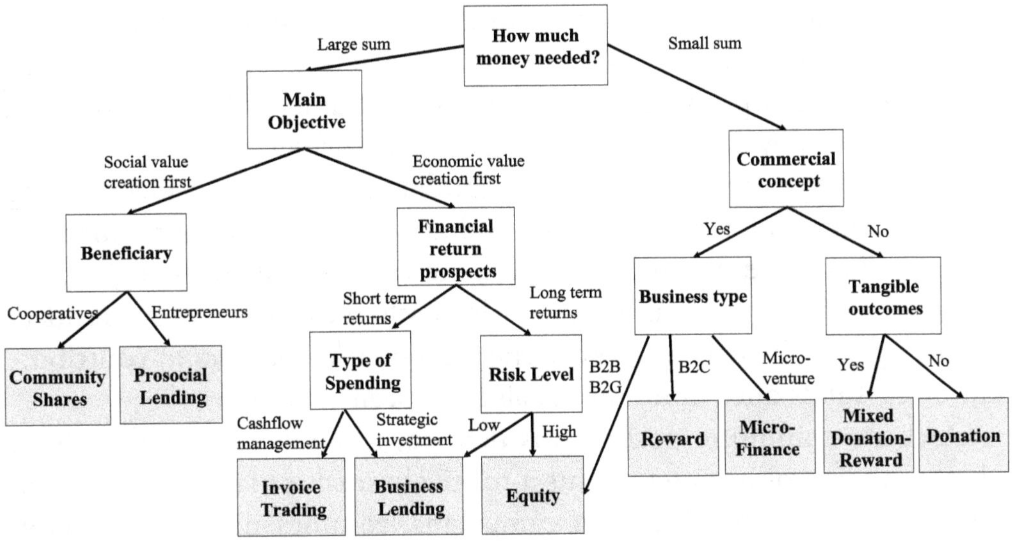

Fig. 2.2 Extended organizational fundraiser model choice framework

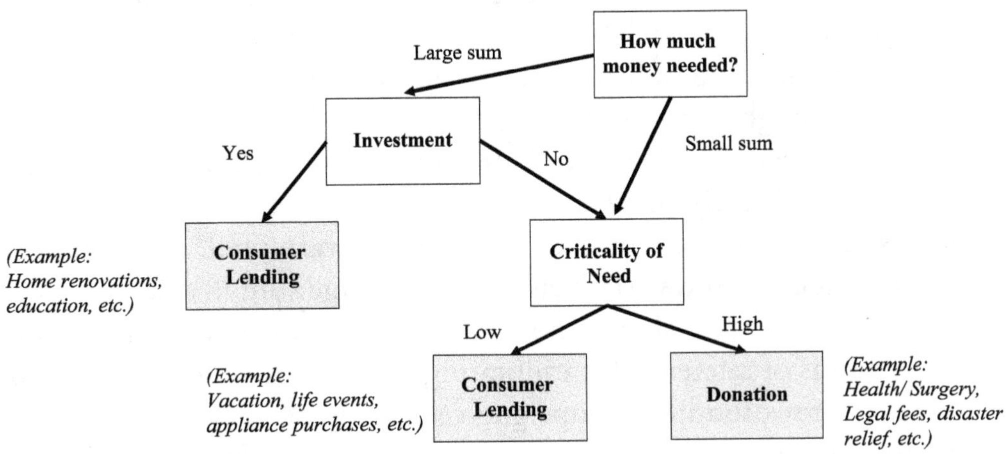

Fig. 2.3 Consumer fundraiser model choice framework

the first issue that requires addressing is an understanding of the sum needed to be raised in the campaign. Establishing such a sum should be based on a detailed project plan and budget that includes all costs expected for the execution of the project itself, the crowdfunding campaigning efforts, and a necessary buffer margin for unexpected costs. Prospective fundraisers should also consider all sources of finances necessary for project execution and the relative share of crowdfunding among these.

Furthermore, how to use the funds raised should be meticulously planned, so that it would be easier to convey what is expected to be achieved by a successful campaign in concrete terms (i.e. number of units produced, number of employees recruited, IPR protections achieved, number of people helped, etc.). Once this is clarified, fundraisers should consider defining both their minimum goals for the fundraising efforts without which the project will not be executed, as well as some 'stretch goals' referring to what can be achieved, beyond minimum goals should the project get overfunded. Specifying stretch goals helps encouraging potential backers to contribute additional funds once minimum goals have been achieved.

Once the minimum goal sum is defined, fundraisers should evaluate whether their ambition represents a relatively small or large sum in comparison to other crowdfunding campaigns' volumes in their respective national market. Such thresholds are imprecise, vary by country, and continue to change annually as the industry develops. Hence, to best understand current local dynamics, fundraisers are encouraged to both consult experts and do some research bench-marking their own goal against earlier campaigns in the same industrial sector and country during the last few years. In very rough terms, and in most countries during 2017–2018, the threshold was between $25K and $50K, where sums below this range can be regarded as relatively small, and above it as relatively large.

In this respect, some words of caution are warranted. First, understanding what constitutes relatively small and large sum in a certain context and point in time should not be considered as solid barriers, but rather as points of reference for calibrating expectations about likelihood of success. Crowdfunding campaigns constantly set new records, and higher sums under various models are being achieved. However, the more ambitious a campaign is, the riskier it is and the more likely it is to require additional campaigning efforts and resources.

Small Sum Campaigns

If the minimum goal sum that was set by the fundraiser falls within the range of relatively small sums, the next consideration is the very nature of the project to be funded. If the project is of a commercial nature, where, simply put, someone is expected to earn financially from, it is considered a business campaign. If the project is non-commercially oriented, and no one is expected to earn financially from its execution, it can be considered as a non-profit project.

Next, if the project is of a non-profit nature, the question becomes whether backers are offered tangible outcomes or benefits in the form of rewards, products or services. If no such benefits are offered, the campaigner should consider using the donation crowdfunding model. If tangible benefits are offered in a non-profit context, the fundraiser may consider a mixed reward and donation model. In such cases, funding is primarily oriented for some 'greater good' but may offer backers tangible benefits in the form of promotional goodies (e.g. caps, cups, or t-shirts promoting the project for attracting further support and funding), or products created by the individuals benefiting from the project being funded (e.g. handcraft, consumer goods, or food and drink experiences created by members of disadvantaged or marginalized social groups whose training, livelihood, or employment is created via funds raised).

However, if the project is business-oriented, the question becomes what type of products and services it is offering to produce or provide. If the products or services cater to certain segments of private consumers, in most cases the reward crowdfunding model will be recommended. Here, the fundraisers can pre-sell their products or services before incurring the costs in their actual production. Such pre-sales, through the offering of different rewards, may also help identify consumer preferences in advance in terms of design, feature inclusion, and pricing. An exception here is when the fundraiser is from an economically disadvantaged and financially marginalized background, and when the project involves a modest micro-venture with limited capacities for delivery of rewards long-distance. In such cases, online micro-finance may be the preferred crowdfunding model, and instead of products supporters can receive modest or no financial returns (which in most cases they reinvest in similar cases).

If the project is business-oriented and the products and services being crowdfunded cater to business or government customers, fundraisers should consider equity campaigning. Since industrial and institutional buyers are concerned with bulk purchases rather than individual rewards, as well as in economic viability encouraging them to contribute via equity crowdfunding may be more relevant than reward crowdfunding. Here, such buyers may enjoy both preferential rates in procurement, as well as potentially earning money indirectly from their own consumption of these products and services via holding an ownership stake in the supplier company.

Large Sum Campaigns

If the minimum goal sum that was set by the fundraiser falls within the range of relatively large sums, the next consideration is the very nature of the project to be funded. If the project funded is primarily expected to generate non-financial returns, it is considered as offering social returns. 'Social returns' is used here as an umbrella term for social, humanitarian and environmental benefits. If the project funded is primarily aimed at generating financial returns, it is considered as offering an investment opportunity.

When projects primarily offer social returns, the question becomes who the main beneficiary of such benefits is. If the project is likely to benefit a group of people with a common social mission and need (for example—village installing windmills or solar panels for resident electricity consumption), they may organize themselves as a cooperative society, while selling ownership shares in the cooperative to its prospective members. However, if the project is likely to benefit entrepreneurs creating social ventures that are primarily concerned with social returns, and financial returns represent secondary concerns, such fundraisers may consider various formats of pro-social lending (e.g. start-up for plastic collecting and recycling that employs unemployed people while cleaning up natural reserves and waterbodies).

When projects primarily offer financial returns from a pure commercial activity, the question becomes what the expected time horizon until backers receive such benefits is likely to be. If the project entails long-term investments, the question again becomes what level of risk is involved. If risks are relatively low, and sufficient cashflows from the project are highly likely, the fundraising venture should consider using a business lending model. However, if risks are relatively high, and cashflow timing and volumes are more uncertain, fundraisers should consider using an equity crowdfunding model by selling ownership stakes in the venture.

Alternatively, if the project entails short-term investments for potential backers, the question becomes how the funding raised will be spent. If funding is used for a strategic investment towards firm enhanced capacities and growth, fundraisers should consider using a business lending model. However, if the funding is used for managing healthier cash-flows, and the firm already has sales, fundraisers should consider using invoice trading.

Consumption-Oriented Campaigns

In addition to organizational fundraisers, a large proportion of crowdfunding volumes is associated with financing consumers. In this context, the model options are more limited, but the volumes are substantial, as shown in the CCAF reports (Ziegler et al. 2018a, b, 2019; Zhang et al. 2018) throughout recent years. However, it is worth noting that while a large portion of such loans is indeed associated with consumption, some of it also camouflages early-stage venturing by single entrepreneurs taking consumer loans to fund their business startup activities.

Here, again, the first aspect to be considered is the amount of money sought. Consumers need to plan for costs associated with the consumption activity they are planning to engage in, as well as the costs associated with the crowdfunding activity. Once such costs are clarified in advanced, a minimum goal sum for a campaign may be set. Once such a sum is defined, fundraisers should evaluate whether their ambition represents a relatively small or large sum in comparison to other consumer crowdfunding campaigns' volumes in their respective national market. As in organizational crowdfunding, such thresholds are imprecise, vary by country, and continue to change annually as the industry develops. Here as well, fundraisers are encouraged to both consult experts and do some research bench-marking their own goal against earlier campaigns with similar goals, which took place in the same country and during the last few years. In very rough terms, and in most countries during 2017–2018, the threshold was between \$5K and \$10K, where sums below this range can be regarded as relatively small, and above it as relatively large.

If the minimum goal sum that was set by the fundraiser falls within the range of relatively small sums, the next consideration is how critical the funding is to the well-being of the fundraiser. If the funding is very critical for the well-being of the fundraisers (e.g. health or surgery emergencies, payment of legal fees, disaster relief), they should consider a donation crowdfunding model. However, if the funding is not critical to the well-being of the fundraiser as in the cases of regular consumption (e.g. life events such as weddings or birthdays, purchase of home appliances, home renovations and upgrades), fundraisers should consider consumer lending models.

If the minimum goal sum that was set by the fundraiser falls within the range of relatively large sums, the next consideration is how would the funds raised be used. If the funding will be used for investment in physical or human capital (e.g. home renovations and upgrades, education procurement), fundraisers should consider using a consumer lending model. If large sums will be used for consumption rather than investment, the concern for the criticality of funding for the fundraiser's well-being emerges again, and the choice of models follows that described earlier.

Conclusion

In the current chapter all crowdfunding models that have been employed in recent years have been defined and their characteristics outlined. Furthermore, the chapter presents novel frameworks guiding both organizations (including those involving one-man operations) and consumers through a decision-making process towards choosing the model that best fits their funding needs and characteristics. In this sense, the chapter's main contributions are in both presenting one of the most elaborate, up-to-date, and detailed typologies for crowdfunding models currently in use, and in being the first to suggest frameworks for systematic choice-making between models by fundraisers.

Nevertheless, the current chapter has some limitations that also present opportunities for further research. First, the characterization of models that were presented in terms of success rates, onboarding rates, and risk levels capture current dynamics, understanding, and knowledge.

However, since the industry is young and dynamic, and since some evidence for regional differences does exist, these should be revisited and tested empirically in future studies capturing the state of the market at more advanced levels of maturation, and across national and regional markets. Second, the suggested frameworks that were outlined follow a prescriptive and normative nature based on the accumulated experience of working with the industry from its early days til now. However, as such, it represents a certain set of heuristics that may guide prospective fundraisers, but it is not the only relevant set of such heuristics. Accordingly, future studies may seek to both empirically validate the decision process outlined, as well as further develop and amend it in a systematic data collection and analysis efforts (both qualitatively and quantitatively). Third, the organizational model choice frameworks suggested do not differentiate between different kinds of organizations in terms of size, age, or popular awareness. Accordingly, it may be interesting for future researchers to investigate whether model choice heuristics differs by such organizational characteristics.

Finally, the information and frameworks presented in this chapter also have several implications for practice. In this context, prospective fundraisers may consult the typology, model characteristics, and the outlined model choice frameworks and use them in their own fundraising decision making efforts. Furthermore, these may also be used by educators and trainers that wish to introduce crowdfunding to both students and practitioners as roadmaps for navigating through the multiple models available, while providing initial guidance into choosing between them for different project purposes.

References

Ahlers, G. K. C., Cumming, D., Günther, C., et al. (2015). Signaling in Equity Crowdfunding. *Entrepreneurship Theory and Practice, 39*(4), 955–980.

Allison, T. H., Davis, B. C., Short, J. C., et al. (2015). Crowdfunding in a Prosocial Microlending Environment: Examining the Role of Intrinsic Versus Extrinsic Cues. *Entrepreneurship Theory and Practice, 39*(1), 53–73.

Belleflamme, P., & Lambert, T. (2016). An Industrial Organization Framework to Understand the Strategies of Crowdfunding Platforms. In J. Méric, I. Maque, & J. Brabet (Eds.), *International Perspectives on Crowdfunding: Positive, Normative, and Critical Theory*. Bingley: Emerald Group Publishing Limited.

Belleflamme, P., Lambert, T., & Schwienbacher, A. (2013). Individual Crowdfunding Practices. *Venture Capital, 15*(4), 313–333.

Cumming, D. J., Leboeuf, G., & Schwienbacher, A. (2019a). Crowdfunding Models: Keep-It-All vs All-Or-Nothing. *Financial Management*, https://onlinelibrary.wiley.com/doi/abs/10.1111/fima.12262.

Cumming, D. J., Hornuf, L., Karami, M., et al. (2019b). Disentangling Crowdfunding from Fraud Funding, May 16, 2019. Retrieved from https://onlinelibrary.wiley.com/doi/abs/10.1111/fima.12262.

De Buysere, K., Gajda, O., Kleverlaan, R., et al. (2012). A Framework for European Crowdfunding. Retrieved from https://www.fundraisingschool.it/wp-content/uploads/2013/02/European-Crowdfunding-Framework-Oct-2012.pdf.

Dorfleitner, G., & Oswald, E.-M. (2016). Repayment Behavior in Peer-to-Peer Microfinancing: Empirical Evidence from Kiva. *Review of Financial Economics, 30*, 45–59.

Dorfleitner, G., Rad, J., & Weber, M. (2017). Pricing in the Online Invoice Trading Market: First Empirical Evidence. *Economics Letters, 161*, 56–61.

Emekter, R., Tu, Y., Jirasakuldech, B., et al. (2015). Evaluating Credit Risk and Loan Performance in Online Peer-to-Peer (P2P) Lending. *Applied Economics, 47*(1), 54–70.

Gajda, O. (Ed.). (2017). *Review of Crowdfunding Regulation: Interpretations of Existing Regulation Concerning Crowdfunding in Europe North America and Israel*. Brussels: European Crowdfunding Network AISBL.

Gray, M., & Zhang, B. (2017). Crowdfunding: Understanding Diversity. In R. Martin & J. Pollard (Eds.), *Handbook on the Geographies of Money and Finance*. Cheltenham: Edward Elgar Publishing.

Haas, P., Blohm, I., & Leimeister, J. M. (2014). An Empirical Taxonomy of Crowdfunding Intermediaries. In *International Conferences of Information Systems 2014*, Auckland, New Zealand.

Hainz, C. (2018). Fraudulent Behavior by Entrepreneurs and Borrowers. In D. Cumming & L. Hornuf (Eds.), *The Economics of Crowdfunding: Startups, Portals and Investor Behavior*. Cham: Springer International Publishing.

Lin, X., Li, X., & Zheng, Z. (2017). Evaluating Borrower's Default Risk in Peer-to-Peer Lending: Evidence from a Lending Platform in China. *Applied Economics, 49*(35), 3538–3545.

Méric, J., Maque, I., & Brabet, J. (2016). A Cartography of the Academic Literature on Crowdfunding. In J. Méric, I. Maque, & J. Brabet (Eds.), *International Perspectives on Crowdfunding: Positive, Normative and Critical Theory*. Bingley: Emerald Group Publishing Limited.

Mollick, E. (2015a). Delivery Rates on Kickstarter, December 4, 2015. Retrieved from https://ssrn.com/abstract=2699251.

Mollick, E. (2015b). *The Kickstarter Fulfillment Report* [Online]. Kickstarter.com. Retrieved April 30, 2019, from https://www.kickstarter.com/fulfillment.

Schreiner, M. (2001). Informal Finance and the Design of Microfinance. *Development in Practice, 11*(5), 637–640.

Shneor, R., & Flåten, B.-T. (2015). Opportunities for Entrepreneurial Development and Growth Through Online Communities, Collaboration, and Value Creating and Co-creating Activities. In H. R. Kaufmann & S. M. R. Shams (Eds.), *Entrepreneurial Challenges in the 21st Century*. Basingstoke: Palgrave Macmillan.

Signori, A., & Vismara, S. (2016). Returns on Investments in Equity Crowdfunding, April 10, 2016. Retrieved from https://ssrn.com/abstract=2765488.

Swords, J. (2017). Crowd-Patronage—Intermediaries, Geographies and Relationships in Patronage Networks. *Poetics, 64*, 63–73.

Wang, Z., Jiang, C., Ding, Y., et al. (2018). A Novel Behavioral Scoring Model for Estimating Probability of Default Over Time in Peer-to-Peer Lending. *Electronic Commerce Research and Applications, 27*, 74–82.

Wenzlaff, K. & Odorović, A. (2020). Joint Production of Confidence—Self-Regulation in European Crowdfunding Markets. *Baltic Journal of Management, 15*(2), https://doi.org/10.1108/BJM-04-2019-0119.

Zhang, B., Ziegler, T., Mammadova, L., et al. (2018). *The 5th UK Alternative Finance Industry Report*. Cambridge: Cambridge Centre for Alternative Finance.

Ziegler, T., Johanson, D., Zhang, B., et al. (2018a). *The 3rd Asia Pacific Region Alternative Finance Industry Report*. Cambridge: Cambridge Centre for Alternative Finance.

Ziegler, T., Johanson, D., King, M., et al. (2018b). *Reaching New Heights: The 3rd Americas Alternative Finance Industry Report*. Cambridge: Cambridge Centre for Alternative Finance.

Ziegler, T., Shneor, R., Garvey, K., et al. (2018c). *Expanding Horizons: The 3rd European Alternative Finance Industry Report*. Cambridge: Cambridge Centre for Alternative Finance.

Ziegler, T., Suresh, K., Garvey, K., et al. (2018d). *The 2nd Annual Middle East & Africa Alternative Finance Industry Report*. Cambridge: Cambridge Center for Alternative Finance.

Ziegler, T., Shneor, R., Wenzlaff, K., et al. (2019). *Shifting Paradigms—The 4th European Alternative Finance Benchmarking Report*. Cambridge: Cambridge Centre for Alternative Finance.

3

Crowdfunding Market Development: Key International Trends

Tania Ziegler, Rotem Shneor, and Bryan Zheng Zhang

Introduction

The advancing pace of technology-enabled innovation is rapidly transforming the financial services industry (Kotarva 2016; Zavolokina et al. 2016). Across the world, developments in financial technology (FinTech) are revolutionizing the way people interact with financial services—allowing faster payments, more secure transactions, user-friendly interfaces, and reducing costs. Crowdfunding represents one category of FinTech developments, addressing needs in capital raising through innovative and digital solutions (Haddad and Hornuf 2019). Specifically,

T. Ziegler (✉) • B. Z. Zhang
Cambridge Centre for Alternative Finance, Judge Business School, University of Cambridge, Cambridge, UK
e-mail: t.ziegler@jbs.cam.ac.uk; b.zhang@jbs.cam.ac.uk

R. Shneor
School of Business and Law, University of Agder, Kristiansand, Norway
e-mail: rotem.shneor@uia.no

fund- and capital-raising crowdfunding, and its related activities, can potentially enable and widen financial access in previously underserved or unserved areas and populations, as well as offer new solutions in areas currently served by traditional financial institutions (Bruton et al. 2015; Lehner 2013).

This chapter will discuss several key international trends as related to crowdfunding market development, as well as provide some insights into the limited research done to date at the macro level attempting to explain such developments. Specifically, the facts and figures presented throughout the chapter are drawn from the research efforts undertaken by the Cambridge Centre for Alternative Finance (CCAF) and its partners culminating in a series of annual industry bench-marking reports. Hence, for full disclosure and avoidance of repetitive referencing, all statistics presented in the current chapter are adopted from the CCAF's recent reports covering the Americas (Ziegler et al. 2018a), the Asia-Pacific (Ziegler et al. 2018b), Europe (Ziegler et al. 2019), the UK (Zhang et al. 2018), and the Middle East and Africa (Ziegler et al. 2018c), unless otherwise indicated.

In the next sections we first present global trends, total volumes, as well as volumes by model. These findings are linked to some explanations that have been suggested in the limited research that has sought to explain macro-level developments. We then present market status at regional level for highlighting commonalities and differences across regions. Finally, we conclude with some implications for research and practice.

A Global Snapshot: Market Volumes and Growth

The global alternative finance market volume is estimated based upon platform data collected from over 3000 unique platforms in 161 countries during the period 2015–2017. A crowdfunding platform is "an internet application bringing together project owners and their potential backers, as well as facilitating exchanges between them, according to a variety of business models" (Shneor and Flåten 2015, p. 188). All platforms are restricted to online, peer-to-peer or crowd-led marketplaces that are open, at least partially, to individual backers and retail investors (the "crowd"). As such, it does not include what are known as 'individual crowdfunding' initiatives (Belleflamme et al. 2013), which are individual- or organization-specific fundraising campaigns carried outside the control and oversight by a formal crowdfunding platform.

The total global alternative finance volume has grown from $11.06 billion in 2013 to $418.52 billion in 2017. Overall, while growth rates are gradually slowing down on an annual basis, total volumes have increased substantially. The slowing of growth rates may signal maturation, at least among early adopters of crowdfunding services, but is more likely to be associated with a growth trajectory that started with a very low absolute base and reached substantial volume in just five years. Figure 3.1 illustrates that despite the slowing of year-on-year growth rate, between 2016 and 2017 global crowdfunding market volume grew by 44% from $290 billion to reach $418 billion. The extent of future growth remains uncertain, but given the head room for growth in more advanced markets, as well as the fact that many developing and emerging markets are still considerably underdeveloped in terms of online capital raising, the global industry is likely to maintain momentum in coming years.

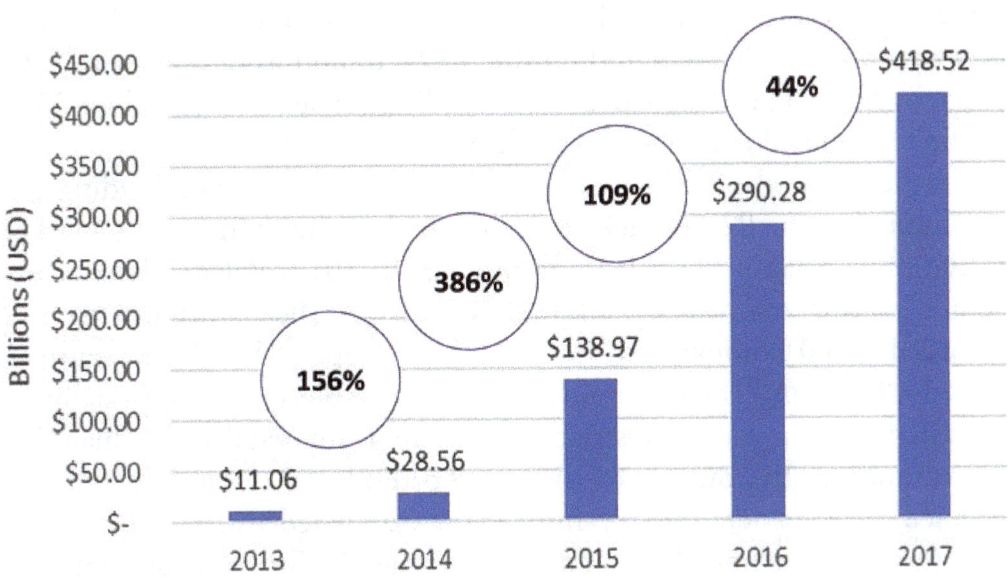

Fig. 3.1 Global volumes 2013–2017 (USD)

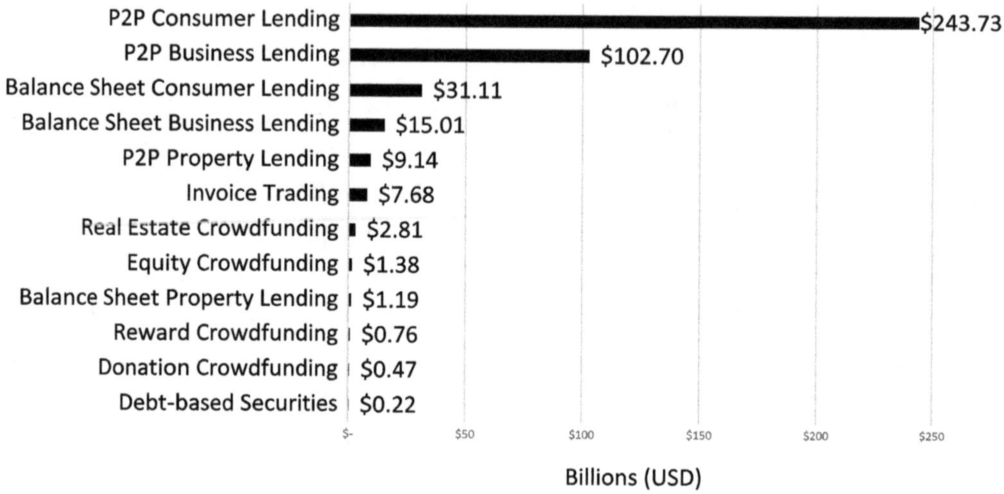

Fig. 3.2 Global volumes by top models 2017 (USD)

When breaking overall volumes into the various crowdfunding models, substantial differences emerge among the models. Figure 3.2 presents the 2017 global volumes by model. In 2017, peer-to-peer (P2P) consumer lending emerged as the leading model with a volume of $243.73 billion, accounting for 58% of global alternative finance volumes. This was closely followed by P2P business lending with $102.7 billion. Indeed, since 2013, these two models have continued to rank first and second every year. Overall, when adding the $9.14 billion associated with P2P property lending, the share of all P2P-lending models accounted for 85% of the total global crowdfunding volumes.

Furthermore, the popularity and pervasiveness of crowd lending are not limited to the P2P models. Since 2016, data shows increasing market activities in Balance Sheet lending models. In 2017, Balance Sheet consumer lending reached $31.11 billion, Balance Sheet business lending recorded $15.01 billion, and Balance Sheet property lending accounted for $1.19 billion. These demonstrate considerable growth especially in jurisdictions that largely restrict investment from retail individuals for crowdfunding. In contrast to the more orthodox P2P-lending models, balance sheet lenders directly fund loans originated on their platforms and therefore assume the credit risk associated. They operate with an intermediation model that is more akin to bank lending, by financing loans with equity and debt on their own balance sheet and, also like banks, periodically refinancing by securitizing pools of the loans they have funded. Unlike regulated bank lenders, however, these balance sheet lenders do not have access to deposits to fund their lending activity. When brought together, all P2P and Balance Sheet models jointly accounted for 96% of global crowdfunding volume in 2017, demonstrating that lending-based models dominate the global crowdfunding landscape.

The remaining volumes were accounted for by other investment models including invoice trading (1.8% of total volumes), real-estate investment crowdfunding (0.6% of total volumes), and equity crowdfunding (0.3% of total volumes). All investment crowdfunding models accounted for 99.8% of global volume. This stands in stark contrast to popular belief often associating crowdfunding with non-investment models such as reward and donation crowdfunding, which collectively only registered a little over $1 billion, representing just 0.2% of total global crowdfunding volume (Fig. 3.3).

Great differences are also observed when breaking global volumes down geographically both at regional and country levels. Here, while volumes of crowdfunding transactions are recorded in some 161 countries, three countries dominated the scene by accounting for 97% of the

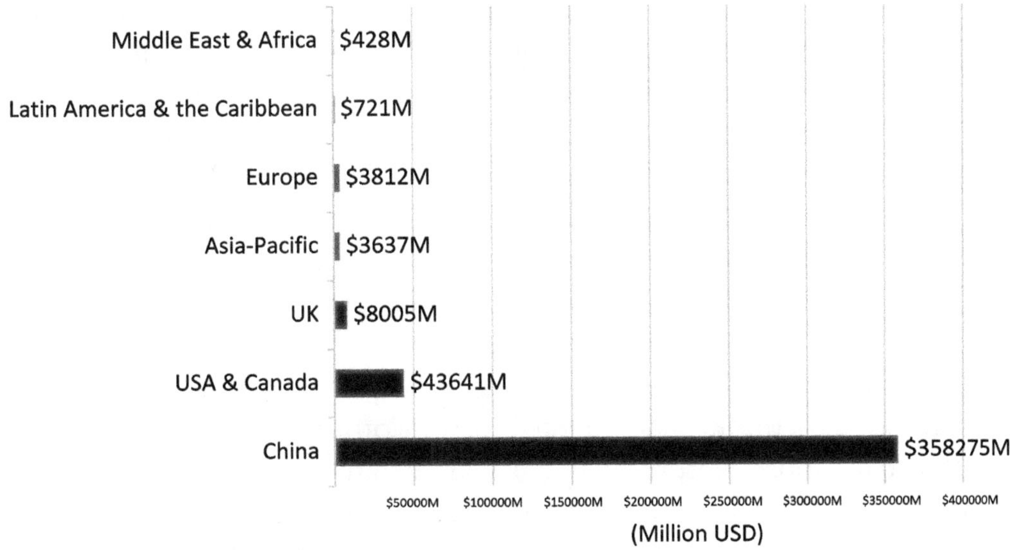

Fig. 3.3 Total 2017 volumes by region (million USD). (Source: Ziegler et al. 2020)

entire global crowdfunding volumes. These three countries are China, the United States, and the UK, representing the regional leaders for the Asia-Pacific region, the Americas and Europe respectively. China is the single largest contributor across all years observed. In 2017, China generated $358.275 billion, representing 86% of the 2017 global figure. The United States and Canada accounted for $43.641 billion (or 10%), and the United Kingdom $8.01 billion (2%) of the 2017 global crowdfunding volume respectively.

In addition to the three global leaders, other important markets are identified and ranked by their respective 2017 volumes as listed in Table 3.1. When we exclude the top three performers, this group includes 14 jurisdictions from Europe, 8 from the Asia-Pacific region, 4 from the Americas, and only 1 from the Middle East and Africa region among the global top 30. This includes both developed (e.g. Canada, Australia, Germany, Netherlands, and Japan) and emerging economies (e.g. India, Brazil, and Indonesia), G8 countries (e.g. France, and Italy) and smaller economies (e.g. Estonia, Latvia, and Georgia), countries that have pioneered the concept of online crowdfunding (e.g. the UK and the United States) as well as relative newcomers to the crowdfunding scene (e.g. Poland and Chile).

However, when examining the 2017 volumes per capita, one can identify a strong correlation between economic development (represented by GDP per capita) and crowdfunding market volumes per capita, indicating that the greater levels of economic development tend to be associated with larger per capita crowdfunding volumes. Figure 3.4 presents this significant correlation among the leading markets (excluding China as a considerable outlier). Such analysis identifies strong market performers such as Estonia, Latvia and Georgia that may represent small open economies that have endorsed crowdfunding and other forms of alternative finance as part of wider market liberalization and economic digitization efforts, and where such services may meet capital needs in markets not fully fulfilled by traditional financial institutions. Other strong performers that have more mature financial markets are countries such as New Zealand, Australia, Finland, Israel, and South Korea. The list also includes countries such as Switzerland, Germany, and Japan which all have well developed financial markets, as well as emerging markets such as India,

Table 3.1 Top thirty national markets by volume in 2017

Rank	Region	Country	Total volume (in USD)	Volumes per Capita (in USD)
1	China (Asia)	China	$358,275,377,038.89	$258.08
2	Americas	United States	$42,773,174,202.50	$131.02
3	UK (Europe)	United Kingdom	$8,004,783,637.55	$122.19
4	Asia	Australia	$1,148,515,565.00	$46.61
5	Asia	South Korea	$1,129,918,098.00	$22.28
6	Americas	Canada	$867,577,549.42	$23.69
7	Europe	France	$747,274,513.52	$11.51
8	Europe	Germany	$672,751,878.90	$8.34
9	Asia	Japan	$348,650,302.00	$2.77
10	Europe	Netherlands	$316,287,611.90	$18.57
11	Middle East	Israel	$295,455,044.29	$35.50
12	Europe	Italy	$271,919,936.14	$4.55
13	Asia	India	$268,579,820.00	$0.20
14	Asia	New Zealand	$261,621,933.00	$56.81
15	Europe	Finland	$222,314,696.19	$38.92
16	Europe	Sweden	$221,890,190.29	$22.37
17	Americas	Brazil	$216,357,244.21	$1.02
18	Europe	Georgia	$195,784,289.95	$49.28
19	Asia	Singapore	$190,821,714.00	$32.99
20	Europe	Spain	$181,620,894.27	$3.94
21	Europe	Poland	$160,967,488.70	$4.17
22	Americas	Mexico	$153,756,417.15	$1.18
23	Americas	Chile	$150,695,263.44	$8.23
24	Europe	Ireland	$120,666,518.06	$25.41
25	Europe	Latvia	$108,236,669.08	$55.66
26	Asia	Taiwan	$103,502,237.00	$4.42
27	Europe	Belgium	$102,704,518.28	$8.97
28	Europe	Estonia	$91,794,107.14	$70.30
29	Europe	Switzerland	$87,114,373.27	$10.30
30	Asia	Indonesia	$80,114,824.00	$0.30

Indonesia, Mexico, and Brazil, where crowdfunding and other forms of online alternative finance are expected to grow more substantively given that financing gaps in these jurisdictions are not well served by incumbents.

Why are some countries more developed in crowdfunding than others?—The limited research to date has pointed to several influential factors. Dushnitsky et al. (2016) found that levels of new crowdfunding

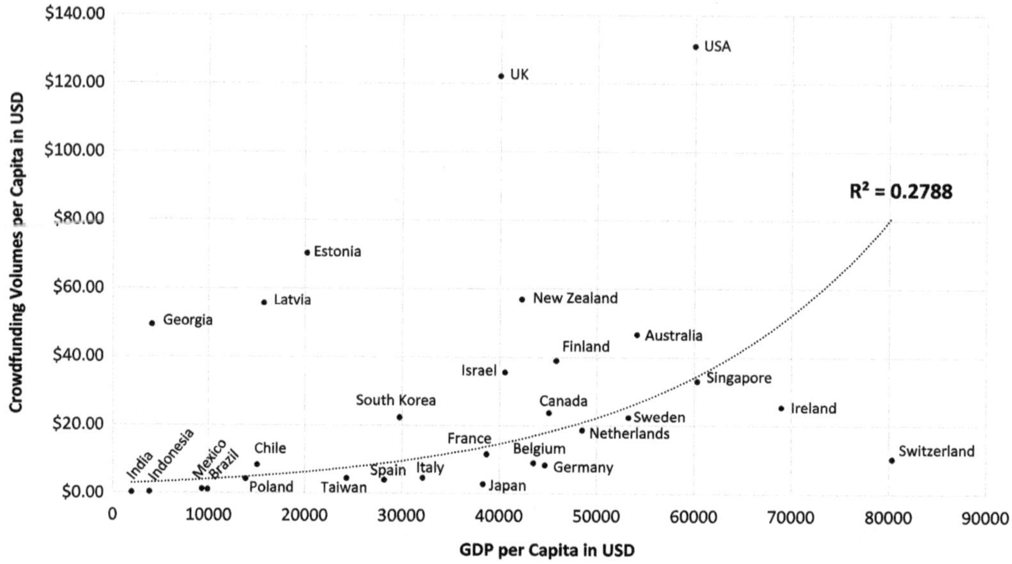

Fig. 3.4 Crowdfunding per capita volumes by GDP per capita 2017—Lead markets

platform creation in the early days of the industry in Europe were positively associated with population size. It was also positively associated with new business ownership levels and the share of platforms operated by a financial operator, but only in the case of reward, donation, and equity platforms (not with respect to creation of lending platforms). The strength of legal rights in terms of borrower and lender protection was found to be positively associated with lending platform formation, but negatively associated with donation and equity platform formation. Economic development was only positively associated with the formation of reward platforms.

Hadded and Hornuf's (2019) analysis of FinTech start-up formation level by country, using the Crunchbase database, showed that it is positively associated with economic development, availability of venture capital, ease of access to loans, availability of labour, good IT infrastructure as captured by number of secure servers, and mobile infrastructure as represented by mobile subscription numbers. In addition, specifically with respect to start-up formation in the financing category (e.g. crowdfunding), the study also finds a positive association with severity of in-country impact from the global financial crisis, less stringent financial regulation, and the strength of legal rights (as represented by the extent of borrower and lender protection).

Finally, a study by Rau (2019), using the CCAF database, shows that national volumes of crowdfunding are positively associated with the rule of law in the country, its quality of regulation, control of corruption, presence of explicit or bespoke crowdfunding regulations, ease of setting up business, and financial profitability of existing financial intermediaries (e.g. the banking sector). Interestingly, neither levels of social trust in strangers nor the adventure seeking tendency of the populace were significantly associated with national crowdfunding volumes.

The following section presents trends in the main national and regional markets. First, since the top three national markets, namely—China, the United States, and the UK, jointly represent 97% of the global market volumes, they are analysed separately. This is followed by a presentation of regional-trends in the three major regions, namely—the Asia-Pacific region, Europe and Latin Americas.

China

China is by far the global market leader, alone accounting for 85% of the 2017 global volumes. It is dominated by P2P consumer-lending activities, responsible for 63% of the total national market volume, and when the Balance Sheet consumer-lending activities are included, the consumer-lending proportion grows to 67% of China's total volume in 2017. Business-lending platforms also play a significant role in the Chinese crowdfunding ecosystem. All consumer and business-lending activities across models (both P2P and Balance Sheet) accounted for 98% of the entire national market volume. In this sense, there is a considerable lack of model diversity in China, with the remaining volume heavily concentrated in property lending or equity crowdfunding.

The prominence of crowd-lending activities in China may stem from continued uncertainty and lagged implementation of Chinese crowdfunding regulation. At present, there is no clear regulatory body at national level responsible for regulating an supervising equity crowdfunding activities (BOP Consulting 2017). Regulatory clarity and framework were lacking for the P2P-lending sector, which has witnessed increasing scrutiny and challenges in recent years. Late in 2016, the China Banking Regulatory Commission issued interim rules for regulating the P2P lending industry, in an effort to curtail credit risk (Chorzempa 2018). Unlike the orthodox P2P-lending model, where the platform serves as an informed intermediary, in many instances across China platforms were acting more like deposit takers with creation of a 'capital pool', with retail investors effectively lending to the platform rather than funding specific loans or loan-parts.

In an effort to properly regulate this sector, Chinese regulators created a '1+3 system' (e.g. one method, three guidelines') to monitor, manage and mitigate industry risks (Ziegler et al. 2018b). As a result of strengthened oversight, the Chinese P2P industry has begun to grapple with liquidity problems, credit risk issues and reconciling new best-practices. Additionally, as regulation has developed, the Chinese marketplace lenders have started to collaborate with traditional banks to a greater extent through partnerships, with 28% having a fund depository relationship with a bank by the end of 2017 (BOP Consulting 2017). Accordingly, it is likely that the 2018 market data will reflect the changing dynamics in China, where volumes are likely to temporarily decline with increasing regulatory oversight.

Unites States of America

In the United States, Balance Sheet consumer lending and P2P consumer lending garnered first and second places respectively in 2017, which together made up 70% of the US market volume. Despite the significant concentration in these two models, the remaining 30% of the market share is far more diversified when compared to China. In the United States, a greater diversity within the crowdfunding industry is manifested by significant volumes of business-lending models, real estate and property-focused activities, equity crowdfunding, and non-investment activities such as reward crowdfunding. Indeed, all fourteen models included in the CCAF reports' taxonomy were present in the United States.

The crowdfunding industry ecosystem in the United States has been shaped significantly by its regulatory frameworks. Specifically, US firms are heavily reliant upon institutional investment, with strict guidelines on marketing and promotions towards retail (unaccredited/accredited) investors. The Jobs Act, the over-arching regulation dictating this landscape, was very much geared towards a broker/intermediary model (Ziegler et al. 2017). As a result, it is not surprising that models which rely upon institutional investment make up a greater proportion of this alternative finance landscape, while models which are more suited towards retail investors (such as Equity Crowdfunding) have seen slower paced growth.

Similarly, a major trend entrenched in the United States, but also evident globally, is the increasing proportion of volume funded by institutional investors via alternative financing platforms. Institutional investors include but are not limited to banks, pension funds, mutual funds, asset management firms, family offices and VC/PE firms. In the United States, 88% of market volume originated from institutional investors—a total of $37.6 billion in 2017. Though the dominance of institutional investment varies by model type, it was most prominent in P2P consumer lending ($14.21 billion, or 97% of the model's total volume), Balance Sheet consumer lending (88% or $11.98 billion) and P2P business lending (76% or $1.1 billion) (Ziegler et al. 2018a).

United Kingdom

The crowdfunding landscape in the United Kingdom is markedly different in composition when compared to China and the United States. P2P business lending is the dominant model in the UK, closely followed by P2P consumer lending. Unlike the United States, Balance Sheet lending activities were significantly lower, and are often blended with other activities on a platform. Typically, a firm can operate a predominantly P2P model with a component that relies upon balance sheet funding.

The UK P2P-lending arena has seen an increase in institutionalization in recent years, though not to the same degree as in the United States. While retail investment remained the main driving force of alternative finance volumes in 2017, 40% of the P2P business-lending volume came from institutional investors, a sharp increase from the 28% in 2016. The corresponding figure for P2P consumer lending was 39%.

Furthermore, the UK also exemplifies a diverse ecosystem, with strong market activities for each of the models within the CCAF reports' taxonomy. Specifically, it is worth noting that in 2017 the UK had the highest volume of equity crowdfunding of any other country in the world valued at $430 million.

The UK has been the pioneering country in Europe venturing into crowdfunding with the establishment of the world's first P2P-lending platform Zopa in 2005. Since then, it has led the European countries in crowdfunding activities and the advancement of regulatory reform in crowdfunding regulations (Gajda 2017). However, like many other aspects of the British economy, future development of the crowdfunding industry is likely to suffer from uncertainties related to the BREXIT process and pending agreement with the European Union, especially with respect to cross-border flows and international operations of platforms (ibid.).

Asia-Pacific, Europe, and the Americas

When excluding the top three performing countries (i.e. China, the United States, and the UK), the annual market volume of Europe and the Asia-Pacific (APAC) region, were quite similar, while those of Latin America and the Caribbean (LAC) were much smaller in 2017. The APAC region grew by 81% in 2017 against the previous year, while Europe saw a 63% annual increase. Growth in the APAC was driven predominantly by two key countries, Australia ($1.15 billion) and South Korea ($1.13 billion), both of which crossed the $1 billion thresholds in 2017. In contrast, there is no single mainland European country that has yet crossed the $1 billion mark. For a fifth year in a row, France ($747.27 million), Germany ($672.75 million), and the Netherlands ($316.28 million) ranked amongst the top three performing European countries. Though smaller, the LAC market has grown rapidly in a relatively short period of time, while achieving 111% year-on-year growth rate between 2016 and 2017. Here, the key national markets include Brazil ($216.36

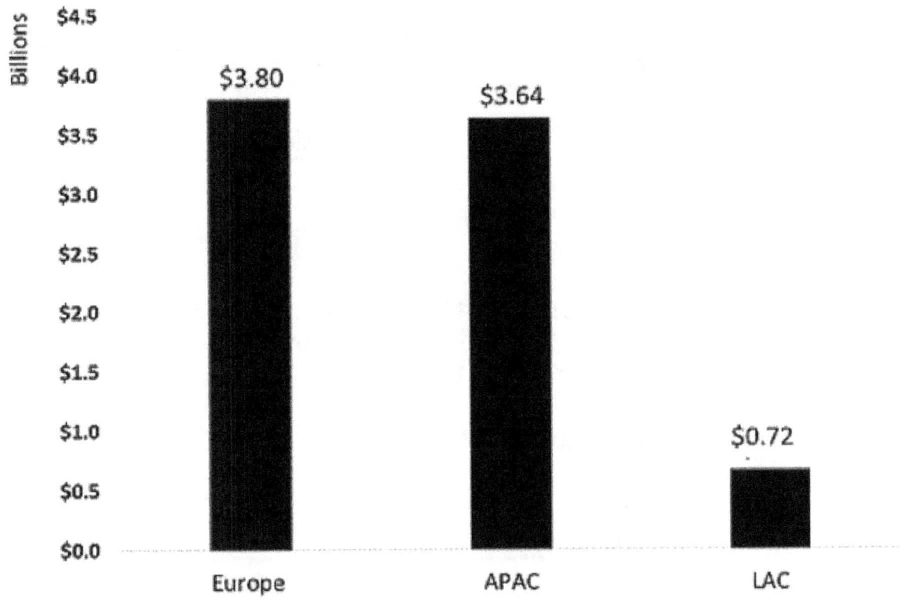

Fig. 3.5 Regional volumes—Europe, Asia-Pacific, and Latin America & the Caribbean (USD). (Source: Ziegler et al. 2020)

million), Mexico ($153.76 million) and Chile ($150.70 million) (Fig. 3.5).

When reviewing the leading six crowdfunding models for each region, making up 90% or more of their respective markets, more regional dissimilarities are evident than similarities, as presented in Table 3.2. In all three regions, P2P Consumer lending is the top-ranking model, but that is where most similarities end.

Though retail investors still contributed the majority of total funding, the APAC region has seen a higher level of institutionalization in 2017 than previous years. Specifically, 98% of Balance Sheet business lending, 43% of the P2P consumer lending and 42% of the Invoice Trading model are driven by institutional investment. With respect to countries with the most active institutional investors, the Indian market took the lead with 74% of its annual funding coming from institutional investors in 2017, followed by Australia (65%) and Indonesia (61%). The pattern of institutionalization correlates heavily with markets that have strong Balance Sheet and P2P/Marketplace-lending sectors.

Table 3.2 Top crowdfunding models by region

Europe		Asia Pacific		Latin America and Caribbean	
Model	Share (%)	Model	Share (%)	Model	Share (%)
P2P Consumer	41	P2P Consumer	23	P2P Consumer	25
Invoice Trading	16	BS Business	19	Invoice Trading	22
P2P Business	14	P2P Property	19	Balance Sheet Consumer lending	17
Real Estate CF	8	P2P Business	17	P2P Business	10
Equity CF	6	Real Estate CF	10	Balance Sheet Business lending	5
Reward CF	5	Invoice Trading	5	Donation CF	4

The European landscape is far more varied, with the representation of debt, equity and non-investment models among the six top ranked market segments. Far more retail investor-oriented, institutionalization has not yet taken root in Europe to the same degree that it has in Asia, or most other regions. P2P consumer lending, the largest single market segment in Europe, only saw 12% of its volume financed by institutional investors. Although the proportion of institutional investment is slightly higher for invoice trading (46%) and P2P business lending (24%), by and large most models were financed by retail investors. This is likely because regulations in most European countries include permissions related to solicitation of retail investors, however, marketing and promotions to retail investors are normally restricted by wealth and previous investment experience.

Following the global trend, in LAC, P2P consumer lending is the largest model within the region and accounted for nearly a quarter of the regional market. Considerable number of platforms operate both P2P and Balance Sheet consumer-lending models. In Mexico, Balance Sheet consumer lending accounted for nearly 45% of the country's overall volume. While consumer lending is the largest model within the region, the overall landscape in LAC is marked by a variety of models, with a focus on business financing activities.

Business-focused funding activities have been viewed as a key priority when considering the usefulness of crowdfunding. Over the past few years, crowdfunding has grown to become a viable funding source for entrepreneurs and small and medium-sized enterprises (SMEs) globally. In 2017, crowdfunding market volume attributed to business financing amounted to $153.2 billion globally, while showing an average annual growth rate of 155% since 2013. China, the United States and the UK provided the bulk of business funding, contributing 32%, 2%, and 1% respectively.

Though in absolute terms business volumes in LAC are dwarfed by comparable figures elsewhere, the dominance of alternative business funding is a key characteristic of the region. In LAC, $565.7 million can be attributed to business-specific fundraises, accounting for nearly 80% of total volume across the region. The top three contributing countries towards business finance were Chile ($150.6 million), Mexico ($73 million), and Brazil ($57 million). Not surprisingly, the majority of business-based alternative finance derived from debt models (92%), such as P2P business lending, invoice trading, etc. Interestingly, a significant proportion of consumer-driven volumes were attributed to business-borrowers too, typically in the form of sole-traders utilizing personal credit to fund their business (Ziegler et al. 2018a). Equity-driven models, such as equity crowdfunding, real-estate crowdfunding and profit-sharing accounted for 7% of all LAC business financing.

When considering the role of institutional investment, 51% of the regional volume was financed by institutional investors ($330.9 million), with the highest levels of institutional investment recorded with respect to Balance Sheet consumer lending (75%, or $84.36 million), invoice trading (73%, or $112.70 million) and P2P consumer lending (47% or $75.95 million).

Conclusion

This chapter has provided a review of the recent status of the global crowdfunding industry while presenting key international trends, as well as presenting some insights from the limited research done at the macro level explaining such developments.

Overall, one can conclude that crowdfunding is no longer a 'fringe' activity but instead has moved into the mainstream. On a global level, growth while slowing down, still represents fast-paced development in comparison to most other industries and financial sectors. At the same time, this slowing of year-on-year growth may indicate initial signs towards market stabilization and consolidation. As incumbent firms begin to consolidate their positions within their respective markets, crowdfunding is gradually maturing, at least among early market movers and adopters.

Furthermore, the market dynamics presented earlier illustrated that crowd-lending models are the most popular form of crowdfunding across the globe. This is closely linked to growing efficiencies thanks to digitization driving greater access to finance and investment opportunities to an ever-larger pool of both lenders and borrowers. The combination of new online credit channels, easy-to-use interfaces and widened access, in parallel with continued scepticism towards traditional financial institutions and their ability and/or willingness to serve all segments of the business community, has created a market opportunity that has been seized by online platforms through a variety of crowd-lending models.

Finally, our review also shows that a thriving crowdfunding market may emerge in both developed economies and emerging markets, regardless of the size of the economy or history of crowdfunding adoption. Limited empirical research also suggests that appropriate regulations, good levels of IT infrastructure, and a generally well-functioning economy may present favourable conditions for the development of crowdfunding industry.

Accordingly, in terms of implications for practice, our findings suggest that countries can benefit from the diversification of financing channels. To achieve this, industry actors and government agencies should work closely together in developing responsible, appropriate, and proportionate regulatory frameworks and policies that both support industry growth, as well as ensure consumer and investor protection, may they be fundraisers (i.e. investees, borrowers, sellers, donation collectors, etc.) or funders (i.e. investors, lenders, backers, buyers, donors, etc.).

When considering implications for research, it becomes clear that opportunities are abundant. There are very few earlier studies that aimed to capture and explain the macro-level growth of the crowdfunding industry, and those that are available mostly capture the industry's early days. Similar studies are necessary for capturing current market dynamics and reflect more mature market conditions. Researchers are encouraged to explore further which factors may impact the trajectory of market development in various settings and given different socio-economic conditions. Such studies may compare emerging and developed markets, as well as markets characterized by high levels of e-readiness and larger scale of digital economy versus those with more modest levels of both.

Future studies may also focus more on the role played by regulations and policies in market development. Insights from such studies can further enhance our understanding about necessary policy components that need to be in place in order to support technology-enabled financial innovation. Research may also expand our understanding of market dynamics by delving deeper into its specific market characteristics, including the extent of institutionalization, international scope of activity and dependencies, as well as default and failure rates at more granular levels.

Finally, as the industry matures, it becomes even more valuable to study the medium- to long-term impacts of crowdfunding activity on real economies. For instance, it would be particularly helpful to capture and measure the impact of the crowdfunding industry on economic development, innovation levels, employment, entrepreneurial venture activity and growth, as well as social impact in terms of access to finance for underserved or unserved social groups and geographical areas in various countries. Such insights are much needed for a better assessment of the crowdfunding industry and its socio-economic impact.

References

Belleflamme, P., Lambert, T., & Schwienbacher, A. (2013). Individual Crowdfunding Practices. *Venture Capital, 15*(4), 313–333.

BOP Consulting. (2017). China UK Equity Crowdfunding Regulatory and Market Comparison Study. Retrieved from http://bop.co.uk/assets/others/China_UK_Crowdfunding_Regulatory_and_Market_Report_Final_24072017.pdf.

Bruton, G., Khavul, S., Siegel, D., et al. (2015). New Financial Alternatives in Seeding Entrepreneurship: Microfinance, Crowdfunding, and Peer-to-Peer Innovations. *Entrepreneurship Theory and Practice, 39*(1), 9–26.

Chorzempa, M. (2018). Massive P2P Failures in China: Underground Banks Going Under. *China Economic Watch* [Online]. Retrieved from https://www.piie.com/blogs/china-economic-watch/massive-p2p-failures-china-underground-banks-going-under2019.

Dushnitsky, G., Guerini, M., Piva, E., et al. (2016). Crowdfunding in Europe: Determinants of Platform Creation Across Countries. *California Management Review, 58*(2), 44–71.

Gajda, O. (Ed.). (2017). *Review of Crowdfunding Regulation: Interpretations of Existing Regulation Concerning Crowdfunding in Europe North America and Israel.* Brussels: European Crowdfunding Network AISBL.

Haddad, C., & Hornuf, L. (2019). The Emergence of the Global Fintech Market: Economic and Technological Determinants. *Small Business Economics, 53*(1), 81–105.

Kotarva, M. (2016). New Factors Including Changes in the Retail Banking Customer Relationship Management (CRM) and Their Exploration by the Fintech Industry. *Foundations of Management, 9*, 69–78.

Lehner, O. M. (2013). Crowdfunding Social Ventures: A Model and Research Agenda. *Venture Capital, 15*(4), 289–311.

Rau, R. (2019). Law, Trust, and the Development of Crowdfunding, 31 May 2019. Retrieved from https://ssrn.com/abstract=2989056.

Shneor, R., & Flåten, B.-T. (2015). Opportunities for Entrepreneurial Development and Growth Through Online Communities, Collaboration, and Value Creating and Co-creating Activities. In H. R. Kaufmann & S. M. R. Shams (Eds.), *Entrepreneurial Challenges in the 21st Century.* Basingstoke: Palgrave Macmillan.

Zavolokina, L., Dolata, M., & Schwabe, G. (2016). The FinTech Phenomenon: Antecedents of Financial Innovation Perceived by the Popular Press. *Financial Innovation, 2*(1), 16.

Zhang, B., Ziegler, T., Mammadova, L., et al. (2018). *The 5th UK Alternative Finance Industry Report*. Cambridge: Cambridge Centre for Alternative Finance.
Ziegler, T., Johanson, D., King, M., et al. (2018a). *Reaching New Heights: The 3rd Americas Alternative Finance Industry Report*. Cambridge: Cambridge Centre for Alternative Finance.
Ziegler, T., Johanson, D., Zhang, B., et al. (2018b). *The 3rd Asia Pacific Region Alternative Finance Industry Report*. Cambridge: Cambridge Centre for Alternative Finance.
Ziegler, T., Suresh, K., Garvey, K., et al. (2018c). *The 2nd Annual Middle East & Africa Alternative Finance Industry Report*. Cambridge: Cambridge Center for Alternative Finance.
Ziegler, T., Reedy, E. J., Le, A., et al. (2017). *The 2nd Americas Alternative Finance Industry Report*. Cambridge: Cambridge Centre for Alternative Finance.
Ziegler, T., Shneor, R., Wenzlaff, K., et al. (2019). *Shifting Paradigms—The 4th European Alternative Finance Benchmarking Report*. Cambridge: Cambridge Centre for Alternative Finance.
Ziegler, T., Shneor, R., Wenzlaff, K., et al. (2020). *The Global Alternative Finance Benchmarking Report*. Cambridge, UK: Cambridge Centre for Alternative Finance.

4

Crowdlending: History and Classification of Models

Tania Ziegler and Rotem Shneor

Introduction

The crowdfunding phenomenon has entered the world stage with the advent of lending-based crowdfunding in the mid-2000s as two new platforms emerged from both sides of the Atlantic. Zopa was established in the UK in 2005, and briefly afterwards Prosper was established in the United States in 2006. Both broke grounds by mediating between private

T. Ziegler (✉)
Cambridge Centre for Alternative Finance, Judge Business School, University of Cambridge, Cambridge, UK
e-mail: t.ziegler@jbs.cam.ac.uk

R. Shneor (✉)
School of Business and Law, University of Agder, Kristiansand, Norway
e-mail: rotem.shneor@uia.no

lenders and borrowers via dedicated websites, which bypassed traditional financial institutions while benefiting from fees on successful transactions (Bachmann et al. 2011).

The new phenomenon was labelled as Peer-to-Peer (hereafter 'P2P') Lending. Since its emergence, P2P lending has offered good returns to investors and lower cost of capital to borrowers (Hollas 2013). Such model allowed borrowers to receive a loan without a financial institution involvement and a possibility of receiving better conditions than those offered by traditional credit providers (Bachmann et al. 2011). For lenders, the new model presented a new investment and portfolio diversification opportunities, where risk was coupled with credit ratings of loans, and which offered better returns than some of the existing products (ibid.).

The phenomenon received a further push following the global financial crisis as a consequence of the drying up of traditional financing (Bruton et al. 2015). Such development was part of a wider Financial Technology (FinTech) industry development in which technological changes enabled new practices and business models disrupting traditional financial services while building on a degree of user distrust towards traditional institutions following the financial crisis (Haddad and Hornuf 2019). Furthermore, alternative finance models carried the potential to unlock access to finance for individual and business borrowers who might have previously been excluded or marginalised by traditional lending practices (Serrano-Cinca et al. 2015). For both borrowers and investors, the crowdlending space offers unprecedented access, as the barrier to entry is often low, with some platforms offering a minimum investment as little as $1, while the minimum and maximum loan amounts on platforms range from a few dollars, to several million dollars. Hence, overall, crowdlending can offer more diverse sources of funding for the real economy in countries that have previously over-relied on bank lending for growth.

During the last decade, the industry has seen a proliferation of debt-based crowdfunding models from P2P lending to Balance Sheet lending, Invoice Trading, and Debt-based Securities, jointly referred to from now onwards as 'Crowdlending'. Such models have dominated the crowdfunding industry throughout its brief history, with crowdlending almost doubling in size every year. In 2018, crowdlending models accounted for 97% of the USD 300 billion global crowdfunding industry, while exhibiting an average year-on-year growth rate of 93% since 2014 (Ziegler et al. 2020).

Unsurprisingly, in light of this impressive growth, and thanks to its related efficiency gains, some began suggesting that crowdlending represents a real challenge to traditional finance (Hollas 2013; Kotarba 2016). However, others suggest that FinTech solutions may both complement existing financing channels as well as fill market needs from which traditional institutions have withdrawn (Haddad and Hornuf 2019). Indeed, recent empirical evidence clearly shows that traditional financial institutions actively participate in crowdlending and represent an important portion of related volumes (Ziegler et al. 2020).

In this chapter we review the current state of crowdlending. First, we present important milestones in its brief history followed by a detailed classification of the crowdlending model types that have emerged in this period. Next, we present facts and figures reflecting the current state of crowdlending both at global and regional levels. This is followed by a brief review of the mechanisms underlying crowdlending platform operations, supported by insights from current knowledge and existing research. Our chapter then concludes with suggestions for future research, as well as some implications for practice.

A Brief History of Crowd Lending

Crowdlending originated from the emergence of P2P Lending with the launching of ZOPA (Bachmann et al. 2011). Being the first P2P lending platform, ZOPA began its operation in 2005, while originating personal loans to British consumers through funds provided by retail investors. In this respect, individual investors would be matched to borrowers as related to their own lending criteria and appetite, bypassing conventional lending processes. Nearly 15 years on, Zopa was set to become the first 'Unicorn' of the Digital Lending era (Armstrong 2018).

Within a year, the US-based platform Prosper was launched and closely followed up by Lending Club, both focusing on the consumer lending market as well as on refinancing of student loans. P2P lending activities in the United States have some critical contextual differences that should be highlighted. The first relates to how the industry self-identifies. In the United States, firms have broadly adopted the moniker of 'marketplace' instead of 'peer-to-peer' largely to reflect the difference of stakeholders that utilise their services. The United States tends to rely heavily on sale of full or partial loans to institutional or professional investors, rather than focusing on matching retail individuals to borrowers (Milne and Parboteeah 2016). In this respect, the firms act more in a syndicate manner, creating a mechanism for matching loan-notes to interested investors.

As this marketplace began to grow quickly within the United States, concerns over how to best regulate it also emerged. By 2008, the Securities and Exchange Commission of the United States began to require P2P Lending firms (marketplace lenders) to register the loans executed on their platform as a security (Barry 2019). Specifically, investors would be purchasing non-recourse notes representing fractional interests in specific underlying consumer loans (Popescu 2016). Though this was the first example of regulating the P2P Lending industry, regulation of alternative finance activities in the United States is arguably still in flux. Notably, the JOBS Act was not signed into law until 2012, with a slow roll-out of legislation and regulatory guidance that persists in the United States as of today.

By 2010, examples of P2P Lending FinTech firms began to emerge worldwide, with some of the first examples of P2P lending focused on the Small and Medium-sized Enterprises (hereafter 'SME') or Business borrower space. Since their launch in 2010, Funding Circle became one of the first FinTech firms to apply the P2P lending model specifically to business loans (Milne and Parboteeah 2016). Though the consumer lending model remains the single largest iteration of P2P Lending, the asset class has expanded significantly, with firms now offering business loans, property loans, mortgages, and an array of other debt-facilities.

In 2011, the first P2P Lending-focused trade-body emerged in the form of the UK's "Peer-to-Peer Finance Association". Though this trade-body has since ceased its activities, its emergence came at a critical point for the advancement of the landscape in the UK (Nixon 2020). This association implemented a code of conduct, effectively creating rules for 'self-regulation' in advance of formal regulation of the industry. By 2013, the UK's Financial Conduct Authority launched its first consultation on Crowdfunding, which included digital lending activities referred to as 'loan-based crowdfunding'. Since 2014, the P2P lending market in the UK has fallen under the remit of the FCA. By 2016, examples of proposed or existing regulation of P2P/Marketplace activities was apparent globally.

By the end of the decade, crowdlending has become a global and mainstream activity, with platforms operating in nearly every country in the world. However, nowhere as prominently as in China, which grew to be the world's largest crowdlending market, estimated at USD 356 billion in 2017 (Ziegler et al. 2018). More specifically, China presents an interesting evolution path in a unique context characterized by relatively undeveloped regulatory environment, where loans are riskier than in the United States or the United Kingdom, the credit referencing system is not fully developed, and where loans are financed primarily by households (Milne and Parboteeah 2016).

However, recent years have seen growing concerns with fraud in the Chinese crowdlending space, especially following the collapse of platforms such as Ezubao, which was found to be operating as a "Ponzy scheme" (Zhang and Miller 2017). Late in 2016, the China Banking Regulatory Commission issued interim rules for regulating the P2P lending industry, in an effort to limit credit risk (Chorzempa 2018). This was necessary to address problems where Chinese platforms were acting more like deposit takers with creation of a 'capital pool', with retail investors effectively lending to the platform rather than funding specific loans or loan-parts intermediated by the platforms, as elsewhere. This crackdown has led to a course correction, with the Chinese crowdlending market seeing a 34% decline in market volume between 2017 and 2018 (Ziegler et al. 2020). Following regulatory crackdown and the exit of platforms suspected of questionable practices, it is expected that the market may gradually recover in the future, but it remains unclear how quickly and to what extent such recovery will occur. Despite this decline, China remains the largest crowdlending market in the world with a volume of close to USD 215 billion in 2018 (ibid.).

A Continually Evolving Classification of Models

While the concept of private individuals lending money without mediation is not new or revolutionary, what makes crowdlending a new phenomenon is the conduct of such transactions over the Internet while using online platforms (Bachmann et al. 2011). Most importantly, these are non-deposit taking platforms that facilitate online credit (through either secured or unsecured loans) to individuals or business borrowers, with capital lent by individuals or institutional investors. These platforms, and the models they represent, have evolved as a response to the gaps in the traditional credit market dominated by banks, and live outside of the incumbent or traditional debt ecosystem.

Crowdlending, also referred to as 'FinTech Credit', can be defined as all credit activity facilitated by platforms that match borrowers with lenders (investors) and includes activities referred to as "P2P lending", "loan-based crowdfunding" or "marketplace lending" and also may include platforms that use their own balance sheet to intermediate between borrowers and lenders (Bank for International Settlements and Financial Stability Board 2017).

This chapter will adopt the classification used and developed by the Cambridge Centre for Alternative Finance (CCAF) in its annual industry bench-marking reports (e.g. Ziegler et al. 2020). This classification includes a variety of alternative finance lending models that fall under the broader scope of FinTech Credit. In the text that follows, definitions and terms provided are adopted from the CCAF reports, unless stated otherwise.

First, *Peer-to-peer (P2P) Lending*—is a model in which a group of individual or institutional investors provide a loan (secured or unsecured) to a consumer or business borrower. In its most orthodox form, the P2P lending platform acts as a marketplace that connects the borrower and investor(s) such that the risk of financial loss if the loan is not repaid is with the investor and not with the platform. Depending upon the jurisdiction, this model may be referred to as Loan-based Crowdfunding, Marketplace Lending, or Collaborative Financing.

The mechanics, as graphically presented in Fig. 4.1, are as follows. The P2P lending firm provides potential borrowers with an easily accessible

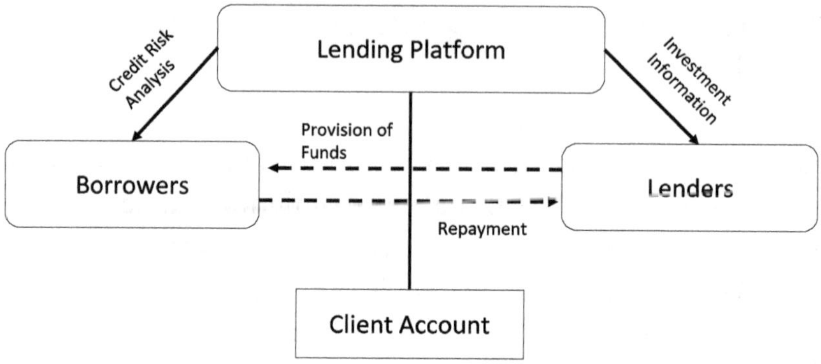

Fig. 4.1 Traditional P2P lending model. (Source: Bank for International Settlements and Financial Stability Board (2017). Market structure, business models and financial stability implications Bank for International Settlements. The full publication is available on the BIS website free of charge: www.bis.org)

and low-cost loan application, which is processed on an online platform. In most cases, the P2P lending firm will rely upon traditional credit scoring facilities and borrower-provided financial information in order to assess the borrower's affordability, loan price, and rating, while verifying the information provided within the loan application. Nevertheless, in-house methodologies used for platforms' own loan risk assessment are difficult to ascertain, as these are proprietary and disclosure is limited (Bank for International Settlements and Financial Stability Board 2017). With the advent of Open Banking, APIs to connect to individualized financial data is on the rise, but this is largely occurring within the constraints of the European Union.

In the early days of P2P lending, investors would review individual loan applications and make the decision to lend their funds against their own assessment. In this respect, the P2P Lending firm would function only as an intermediary, executing the loan once self-matched by lenders. As the model has developed, it is now far more common for the lending platform to automatically match individual lenders against pre-selected loan criteria. Regardless, the platform is typically responsible for communicating appropriate credit grades, setting a pre-fixed interest rate (a shift away from auction models that were more popular at the inception of P2P lending) and servicing the loan once it has been originated.

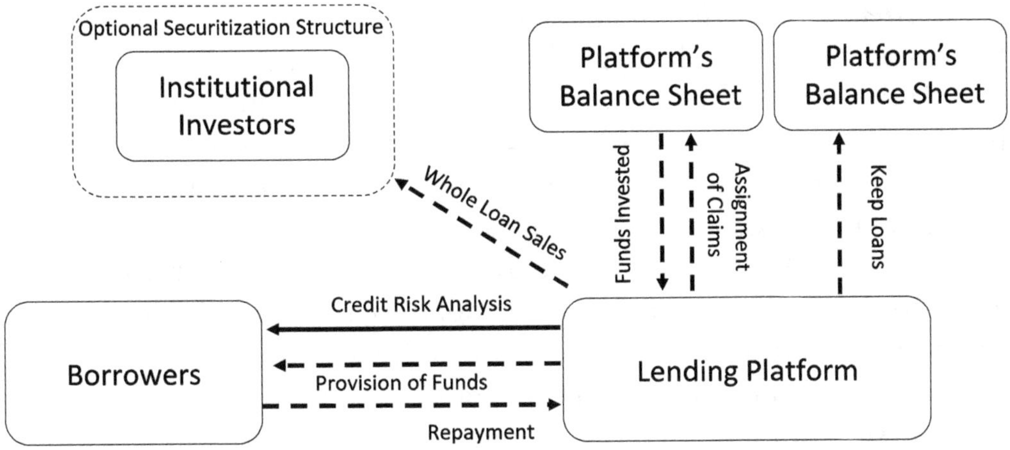

Fig. 4.2 Balance sheet lending model. (Source: Bank for International Settlements and Financial Stability Board (2017). Market structure, business models and financial stability implications Bank for International Settlements. The full publication is available on the BIS website free of charge: www.bis.org)

Second, *Balance Sheet Lending*—refers to a model in which a digital lending platform directly retains consumer or business loans (either whole loans or partial loans), using funds from the platform operator's balance sheet. These platforms therefore function as more than just intermediaries, originating and actively funding loans, so the risk of financial loss if the loan is not repaid is with the platform operator. In this respect, the platform operator looks more like a non-bank credit intermediary (Bank for International Settlements and Financial Stability Board 2017). The mechanics of this model are described in Fig. 4.2.

While the above represent the largest share of crowdlending volumes, as well as the most common practice. Recent years have seen the emergence of additional models such Invoice Trading, Debt-based Securities and Mini Bonds. Here, *Invoice Trading*, one of the fastest growing models, refers to an online marketplace where businesses can sell partial or whole receivables (invoices) at a discount. Individual lenders or institutional investors may serve as the counterparty in the sale transaction, again opening a new investment opportunity to a wider public of investors. This model is of particular importance for SMEs for raising short-term debt by pre-financing their outstanding invoices through individual or institutional investors (Dorfleitner et al. 2017).

Debt-based Securities are models where individuals or institutional funders purchase securities, typically a bond or debenture, at a fixed interest rate. And *Mini Bonds* refer to a model in which individuals or institutions purchase securities from companies in the form of an unsecured bond which is 'mini' because the issue size is much smaller than the minimum issue amount needed for a bond issued in institutional capital markets. Furthermore, Mini Bonds are not always transferable, either because the issue size is too small to provide secondary market liquidity or because prospectus exemptions require investors to hold the bond until maturity. Other terms can be very similar to traditional corporate bonds, such as being subject to early call provisions allowing the issuer to repay prior to maturity if its prospects improve.

Extended Services and Functionalities

As FinTech credit markets mature and the number of players increases, extended services and functionalities emerge. One type of such extensions may be identified in the emergence of aggregator platforms, which are tools that compile data from a range of platforms to allow borrowers to find suitable loan products from several crowdlending platforms in a centralised location. Aggregators offer an opportunity for lenders to compare loan products efficiently across platforms and better understand their different financing options. Aggregators may also act as brokers and potentially receive commission on referred business.

A second type of extension is associated with the establishment of secondary markets. In response to the largely illiquid nature of loan parts or traches held by investors, some platforms (or third-parties) have established secondary markets. In crowdlending, a secondary market acts as a marketplace that allows lenders to sell their loan parts before the loan reaches maturity. Here, the purchaser may be another lender or even the platform itself (in balance sheet lending). Loans may be sold at—a discount or premium, or they might be sold at par, assuming the loan is amortizing or repaid in accordance with the loan schedule. Where secondary markets are highly automated and the platform has discretion to buy and sell on behalf of investors, it is common for a standard valuation algorithm to assign values to each loan in real time, so that the platform can ensure it is swapping one loan for another of equivalent value. However, secondary markets for P2P loans are a relatively new development, not all platforms offer secondary markets, and many secondary markets are highly illiquid.

The State of the Crowdlending Market

In the current section we present the most up-to-date market data from the 2019 CCAF Global Alternative Finance Report (Ziegler et al. 2020). In 2018, the global alternative finance volumes amounted to just over $300 billion, 97% of which derived from models that would fall under lending activities.

Since starting to track the alternative finance industry, the P2P Consumer Lending model has remained the single largest volume driver, accounting for 66% of all alternative lending volumes. This was followed by P2P Business Lending (17%) and Balance Sheet Business Lending (7%). Individual borrowers, or consumers, are the largest group of borrowers as illustrated in Fig. 4.3, driving Fintech Credit activities globally. Consumers are individuals, typically receiving an unsecured loan. Although loan size varies significantly by jurisdiction, individuals tend to borrow between USD $2,500–30,000, with annual percentage rates ranging typically between 7% and 20%. Borrowers use these loans to consolidate their debt or refinance credit on their credit cards; to purchase a vehicle, repay a student loan, pay utility bills or wedding expenses, or to cover the costs associated with illness or unexpected hardship. More specifically, it should be noted that research conducted by the CCAF suggests that borrowers using P2P or Balance Sheet Consumer Lending are increasingly seeking loans to support their business (sole-traders, micro-business, early stage capital).

Table 4.1 presents the annual development in crowdlending volumes. While the industry has experienced a dramatic growth year-on-year since 2013 (when data was first collected), a notable drop can be observed in five of the eight applicable models between 2017 and 2018. This drop can be explained by market dynamics in China, while the rest of the world has seen continued healthy growth.

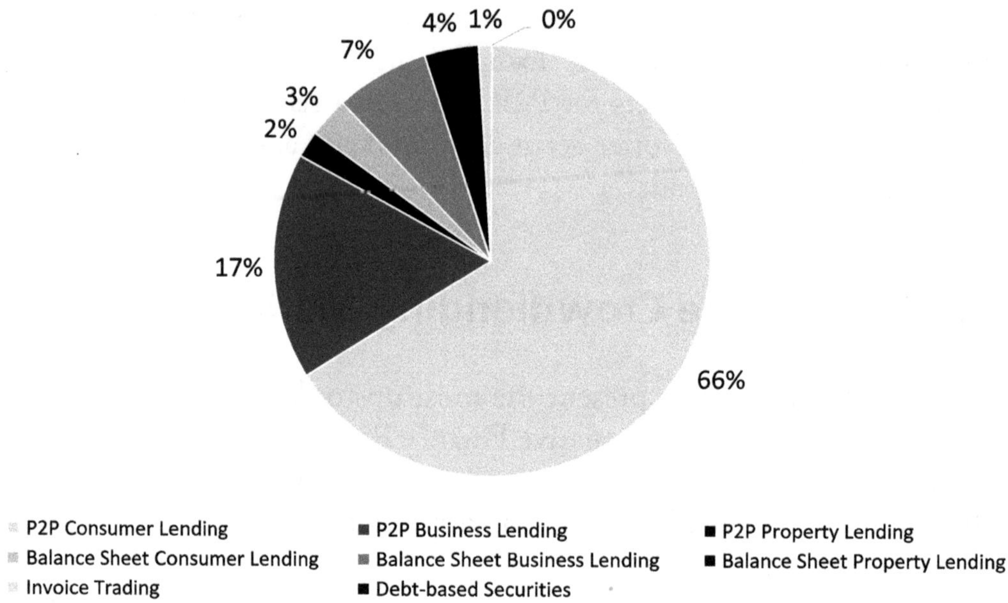

Fig. 4.3 Proportion of global volume from key crowdlending models

Table 4.1 Global alternative lending in USD billion (inclusive of China figures)

	2018	2017	2016	2015	2014	2013
P2P Consumer Lending	$195.29	$243.80	$157.60	$73.09	$21.78	$6.62
P2P Business Lending	$50.33	$103.59	$61.59	$43.70	$10.50	$2.20
Balance Sheet Business Lending	$21.08	$16.02	$33.99	$2.97	$1.30	$0.51
Balance Sheet Property Lending	$11.02	$1.19	$0.57	$0.00	$0.00	$0.00
Balance Sheet Consumer Lending	$9.78	$31.17	$12.43	$3.21	$0.72	$0.09
P2P Property Lending	$5.73	$9.14	$11.40	$7.12	$1.62	$0.26
Invoice Trading	$3.22	$7.68	$3.38	$2.20	$0.75	$0.18
Debt-based Securities	$0.85	$0.22	$0.47	$0.03	$0.02	$0.01

As mentioned earlier, despite China remaining as the global market leader in alternative lending, wide-spread closures of P2P and balance sheet lending platforms have occurred due to the implementation of increasingly strict regulations. Since July 2018, the absolute number of firms, as well as the trading volume of China's P2P lending platforms, have shown a continuing downward trend month by month. According

Table 4.2 Global alternative lending in USD billion (exclusive of China figures)

	2018	2017	2016	2015	2014	2013
P2P Consumer Lending	$31.99	$19.30	$24.40	$27.77	$9.44	$3.49
Balance Sheet Business Lending	$14.95	$8.14	$6.71	$2.40	$1.16	$0.50
Balance Sheet Property Lending	$11.02	$1.19	$0.57	$0.00	$0.00	$0.00
Balance Sheet Consumer Lending	$9.40	$15.34	$3.05	$3.09	$0.69	$0.09
P2P Business Lending	$7.59	$5.27	$4.93	$4.60	$2.46	$0.77
P2P Property Lending	$3.88	$3.20	$4.36	$1.56	$0.14	$0.02
Invoice Trading	$2.53	$2.07	$1.10	$0.74	$0.48	$0.15
Debt-based Securities	$0.84	$0.22	$0.22	$0.03	$0.02	$0.01

to the data from WDZJ (P2P online loan industry portal in China), as of November 30, 2019, the number of operating marketplace lending platforms in China was 456, a decrease of 87.24% compared to 3574 (historical peaks) in December 2015; the monthly trading volume in November 2019 dropped to 50.623 billion, having fallen by almost 80% compared to its peak in 2017.

When we remove China from the alternative finance equation (Table 4.2), we see considerable annual growth across seven of the eight applicable alternative finance models. As expected, P2P Consumer Lending is the largest model even when China's activity is removed, and we note a 66% annual growth from $19.3 billion in 2017 to $31.99 billion in 2018. Balance Sheet Business Lending ($14.95 billion) and Balance Sheet Property Lending ($11.02 billion) became the second and third largest models, respectively. 2018 was marked by considerable rapid growth of balance sheet models, though it is important to note that more than half of the FinTech firms operated according to the P2P lending model as well. This suggests that there is increasing emphasis on firms to take on origination risk, moving away from exclusively matching models.

Regional Variances

Regional volumes of crowdlending are summarized in Table 4.3. When we consider where crowdlending activities are geographically concentrated (while excluding China), the United States (cumulative lending

Table 4.3 Crowdlending models 2018 by model and region (in USD billion)

	P2P Consumer Lending	P2P Business Lending	P2P Property Lending	Balance Sheet Consumer Lending	Balance Sheet Business Lending	Balance Sheet Property Lending	Invoice Trading	Debt-based Securities
Africa	$0.11	$0.02	$0.00	$0.00	$0.05		$0.00	$0.01
APAC (excl. China)	$0.98	$1.77	$0.66	$0.88	$0.92	$0.02	$0.09	$0.00
Canada	$0.03	$0.05	$0.06	$0.12	$0.39	$0.01	$0.05	
Europe	$2.89	$1.00	$0.14	$0.10	$0.08	$1.38	$0.80	$0.17
LAC	$0.43	$0.13	$0.05	$0.14	$0.26	$0.01	$0.55	$0.13
Middle East	$0.10	$0.05	$0.56		$0.01		$0.04	
UK	$2.06	$2.54	$1.76	$0.64	$0.86	$0.07	$0.85	$0.53
US	$25.39	$2.03	$0.66	$7.52	$12.39	$9.53	$0.14	$0.01

$57.7 billion) ranks first, followed by the United Kingdom ($9.3 billion), the Asia-Pacific ($5.3 billion) and Europe ($6.6 billion). Moreover, if we look at the breakdown of lending activity by model type, we see that certain regions have greater emphasises on P2P lending activities versus balance-sheet lending activities. In Europe and the United Kingdom, for instance, there is a greater emphasis on P2P lending models, while in the United States and Canada, a greater emphasis is placed on balance sheet lending models.

As has been mentioned on a few occasions, the largest volume driving model is P2P Consumer Lending. However, it is worth mentioning that when we consider lending that was directed to business borrowers, nearly $28 billion dollars went to start-ups, SMEs and business entities. Interestingly, a large proportion of business borrowers came from P2P Consumer Lending platforms, receiving a consumer loan in order to support their business funding needs.

Businesses, particularly SMEs, are using various Digital Lending products to meet their working or expansion capital needs. To illustrate the importance of these channels for SME financing, we provide insights from the United Kingdom, which earned a reputation as a leader in P2P Business Lending, as well as an environment in which SME finance is recorded systematically.

Sources of UK SME Finance are presented in Fig. 4.4. The Bank of England estimates that £57.7 billion was lent to SMEs by national banks in 2018, which represents a slight increase compared to last year's figure of £57 billion (UK Finance 2018). By comparing the UK P2P Business Lending volume against that of the UK Finance annual estimate of new loans to SMEs, it has shown that business crowdlending has increased its share of total lending steadily from just 0.3% in 2012 to 14.55% in 2018.

Assuming that the vast majority of borrowers in peer-to-peer business lending are, in fact, small businesses with an annual turnover of less than £2 million, the chart below shows that the volume of P2P Business Lending in the United Kingdom is estimated to be equivalent to 34.8% of all bank lending to small businesses in 2018, almost 20% increase against the previous year. Therefore, P2P Business Lending is becoming an increasingly important contributor to overall SME financing in the United Kingdom in comparison to bank lending channels.

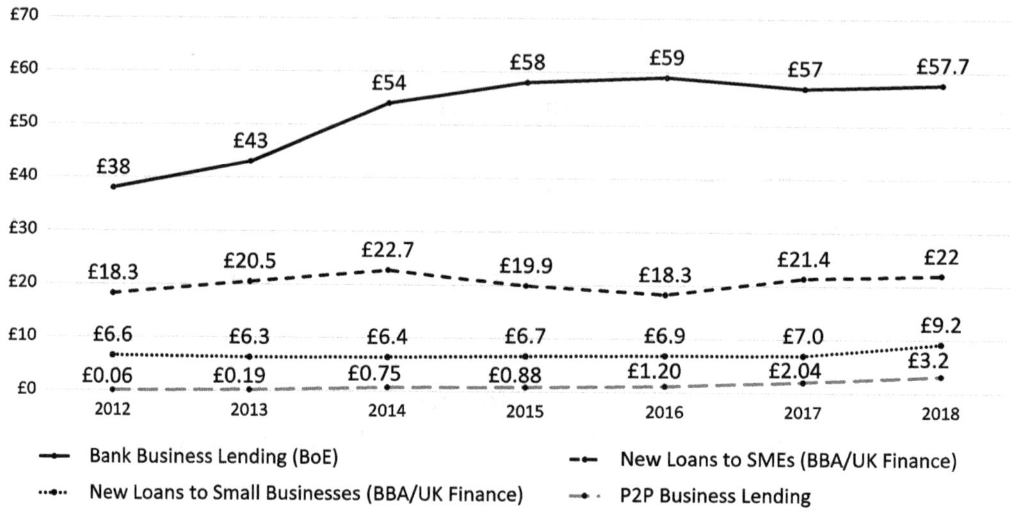

Fig. 4.4 Sources of UK SME finance 2012–2018 (in billion GBP)

Risk Assessment in Crowdlending

A fundamental problem underlying crowdlending is that of asymmetrical information (Leboeuf and Schwienbacher 2018), especially as it relates to mitigating potential risks presented when evaluating potential borrowers. Bachmann et al. (2011) refer to several key determinants that P2P Lending firms must evaluate in order to combat principal-agent problems and provide an overview of the financial characteristics of the borrower as the main indicator of creditworthiness.

Individuals seeking to lend via a P2P lending platform will not always have the requisite tools or skill set to comprehensively assess risk. Therefore, the platform often conducts an analysis of potential borrowers, assigning appropriate risk bands before offering credit. Whilst individual investors must still assess and determine the levels of risk they are willing to take, the risks associated with certain borrowers are often determined by the platform itself.

While in-house methodologies used by platforms for loan risk assessment are difficult to ascertain, as these are proprietary and disclosure is limited (Bank for International Settlements and Financial Stability Board 2017), they usually assess a borrower based on a number of set indicators.

Such indicators include the borrower's existing credit (using traditional credit scoring), any capital or collateral that may exist, the capacity to repay the loan (debt-to-income ratio), and the conditions which the borrower is willing to adhere to. In some cases, platforms may employ an alternative underwriting process using algorithmic-based approaches to credit scoring and non-traditional data, alongside more traditional methods, to determine if the loan is of an acceptable risk level.

When underwriting an *SME borrower*, the credit assessment requirements are usually more robust than in the case of individual borrowing. In such cases, a platform will typically restrict lending to firms with less than three years of credit history and will require recent filed company accounts and information on company management. In some cases, the platform may also restrict lending to firms with a certain level of annual turnover (for example—requiring more than USD $50,000 in annual turnover at minimum). Furthermore, in the case of underwriting a *property loan*, the platform should ideally assess the underlying asset, its location and sector, as well as procure independent valuations on the property and reassure itself that appropriate permission has been granted for any planned development. The platform should also assess the proposed exit strategy (sale, refinance etc.) for the property.

Alternative Credit Analytics

Crowdlending platforms may employ more varied and sophisticated credit assessment practices than traditional financiers. FinTech credit platforms may access a range of potential borrowers' data, which may not be typically sourced and analysed by banks. However, some 'mainstream' credit providers are also incorporating alternative credit analytics into the credit approval process. The types of data, include location-based information, social networking information, hardware data, online shopping and other online behaviour, but also more diffused data on educational attainment and performance, as well as labour market profile and performance (Hale 2019). The lender feeds available data into their algorithm to establish creditworthiness. As algorithms are generally proprietary, it is difficult to ascertain which data points are used and how they are weighted, when determining a credit rating. As a rule, however, there appears to be more evidence of previously excluded borrowers being accepted than of previously accepted borrowers being rejected based on alternative data (ibid.). In this context, machine learning can also be used to analyse data captured during the credit analysis phase. It can also be used to gather data on borrowers with a thin credit file.

While most platforms do not yet offer instantaneous, automated credit approval, some platforms can provide loan approval and disbursement within a few hours (for example, via mobile money). Others are working to bring approval times down to a few minutes. Alternative credit analytics reduces the need for case-by-case manual approval thus increasing the efficiency of the loan approval process.

Pricing

As crowdlending fundamentally occurs online, it reduces operating costs for credit intermediaries by removing the need for physical branches while allowing heavy (or full) automation of loan application, credit risk assessment and pricing processes (Bank for International Settlements and Financial Stability Board 2017). They are also not reliant on legacy infrastructure as banks may be and as a result, pricing will not be impacted by normal pricing considerations of traditional bank lenders. In addition, platforms may fall outside of certain licensing or other regimes, thus reducing regulatory or compliance costs. A study by Autonomous Research (2016) found that the ratio of operating expenses to total costs was less than 2% for Lending Club, a consumer and business P2P lending platform in the United States, and 6% for the largest traditional lenders.

For these reasons FinTech lending platforms may offer lower interest rates for borrowers and/or higher returns to investors (Bank for International Settlements and Financial Stability Board 2017). Research has shown varied outcomes, however, with some studies showing little difference in borrower interest rates and investor rate of return given a similar risk profile (De Roure et al. 2016). It is sometimes difficult to compare the two rates due to a lack of equivalent loans.

Ethical Considerations in Crowdlending

Taking into consideration recent experiences with irresponsible lending leading to high levels of personal lending via credit cards (Richards et al. 2008), which was further exacerbated by the subprime lending upheaval (Gilbert 2011), have all left their mark, and were part of the reasons for the emergence of alternative crowdlending channels. However, these problems were created by individuals who failed in their moral duties when making decisions that later led to significant harmful consequences from default and bankruptcy and all the way to suicide (Gilbert 2011; Richards et al. 2008).

Such moral pitfalls are also relevant for operators of crowdlending platforms, which must strike a delicate balance between business survival and growth and the intermediation of responsible lending. Furthermore, at a macro level, it remains to be seen to what extent does crowdlending reduces or increases long-term indebtedness of borrowers overall, as well as its relative burden on their economies. Research on these aspects of crowdlending are virtually absent and require further attention due to the importance of ethical practice for the well-being of all stakeholders involved.

Loan Defaults & Provision Funds

Some loan defaults are inevitable. Platforms therefore recommend that investors diversify their portfolio on-platform to offset some of the negative effects of default. For example—Funding Circle, a UK-based P2P business platform, recommends a minimum investment of £2000 split across at least 200 loans (McCorquodale 2018). Platforms can sometimes offer provision funds to protect investors from default—a small proportion of monthly loan repayments are placed into a segregated fund. In the event of a default, the provision fund may be utilised on a discretionary basis to ensure that investor repayment occurs as expected. The level of protection and the breadth of coverage depends upon the policy of the platform, as well as the characteristics of different loan cohorts.

While diversification across a large number of borrowers already provides lenders with substantial protection against default and loss (Milne and Parboteeah 2016), defaults do occur. In such cases, platforms attempt to extract as much of the value of the loans from the borrower as is possible within their responsible lending obligations. This involves a combination of soft interventions as well as legal ones carried out according to contract or to insolvency law. For example, the platform may, in acting for investors/creditors, appoint an administrator or receiver, and coordinate with other creditors. Or they might enforce against the security pledged by the borrower. In practice, recoveries are rarely a core competence of the platform operator and thus are often outsourced to debt collection agencies (Bank for International Settlements and Financial Stability Board 2017).

In this context, several academic studies have sought to identify key determinants of crowdlending defaults. Here, a study by Serrano-Cinca et al. (2015) analysing data from Lending Club, has showed that default was associated with borrowers with lower annual income, higher levels of indebtedness, shorter credit histories, and loan purpose where small business and education exhibiting highest likelihood of default. A different study by Lin et al. (2017) was conducted in the context of a Chinese crowdlending platform and showed that higher default rates were recorded among men vs. women, younger vs. older, divorced vs. married, low vs. highly educated individuals, short vs. long working experience, those working for small companies vs. those working for large companies, those who have high debt to income ration vs. those with low debt to income ratio, and those who have a delinquency history vs. those that don't have such history. Furthermore, the higher the amount of monthly repayments the higher likelihood of default. Overall, studies suggest that platforms capture many of the risks in their assessments, and the credit or risk ratings they present are good predictors of default likelihood (Serrano-Cinca et al. 2015; Emekter et al. 2015).

In addition, an interesting insight has been highlighted in a study by Ge et al. (2017), which tapped into the unique context of Chinese crowdlending, where social media is tightly intertwined with platform profiles. Their analysis found a significant decrease in loan default rate and increase in default repayment probability, when such information was shared by the platform on the borrower's social media accounts. This indicates that borrowers are deterred by potential social stigma, and that social information can be used both for credit scoring and default reduction and repayments.

Lender Characteristics

Both Individual or retail lenders/investors are non-professional individuals, that typically fall into one of three categories: (1) certified high net-worth or sophisticated investors; (2) ordinary investors who receive regulated advice (e.g. from a financial advisor); or (3) ordinary investors who self-certify and invest within a regulated prescribed cap (e.g. cap on the amount invested by an individual at a defined percentage of wealth or income, or a cap on the amount that can be invested in a single loan product).

Individual lenders may also be accredited or unaccredited, depending upon the jurisdiction. In many countries there are restrictions that allow only for accredited individuals to participate in digital lending. Accreditation permits individuals to purchase securities that are not registered with financial authorities or are public.

For example, the CCAF has produced an extensive investor-profiling for the UK FinTech credit market (Zhang et al. 2017). The results reveal that P2P Lending investors in the United Kingdom tend to be predominantly males aged over 55, with undergraduate degrees and earning above the average (~£26,500) per annum. They also tend to have some experience in investment or finance. Elsewhere in Europe, Oxera (2015) showed that awareness of P2P lending was associated with higher education and higher income.

The CCAF's research into the risk perceptions of United Kingdom alternative finance investors (Zhang et al. 2017) found that investors in P2P consumer loans see the asset class as similar to managed funds in terms of risk profile and should thus expect similar returns. P2P business loans, on the other hand, are seen as riskier, and of comparable risk level to listed equities. Property P2P is ranked somewhere in between the two.

Institutionalization of Investment in Crowdlending

Institutionalization refers to the proportion of volume which can be attributed to institutional investors, such as pension funds, mutual funds, asset management firms and banks in what is otherwise labelled as 'the crowd'. This excludes individual investors, such as accredited or unaccredited investors. However, the influx of institutional funding from traditional financial institutions, coupled with the increasing involvement of high net worth investors, is also blurring and pushing the boundaries of original conceptualization of the P2P Lending model.

To a certain degree, the involvement of institutional investors in crowd finance may be controversial. There is some evidence that they might have historically derived better returns on platforms than those platforms' individual investors (Mohammadi and Shafi 2017). Here, when institutions are able to self-select loan parts on a more granular basis than individuals, and if they get first pick of the loans on offer, then not only will they derive higher returns, but also make it very difficult for individual investors' portfolios to be optimised.

Figure 4.5 presents the share of institutional versus retail investors in crowdlending. Though retail investment remains the main driving force

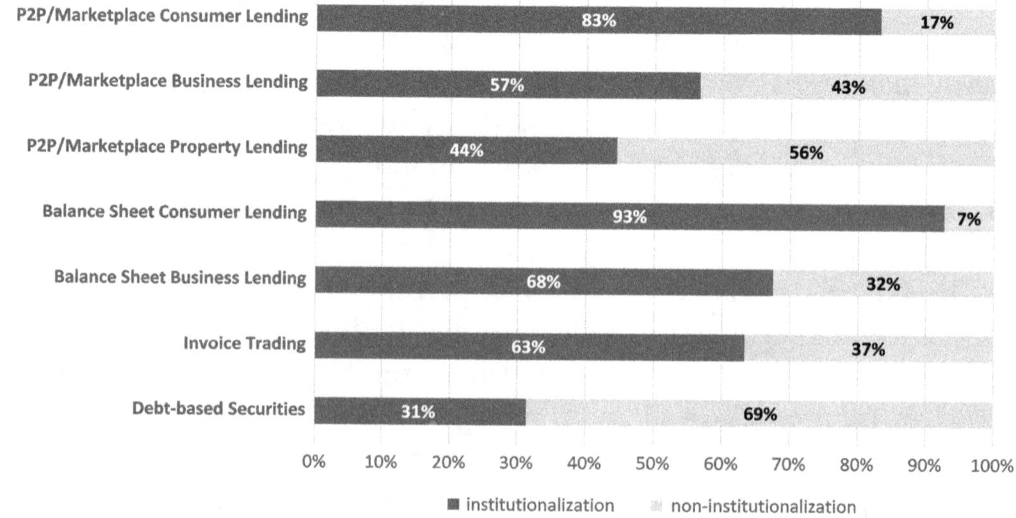

Fig. 4.5 Institutional vs. retail investors in crowdlending (globally) in 2018

of alternative finance volumes, institutional investors also contributed significant sums. The sources of institutional funding vary significantly between models, although P2P lending models tend to attract investment from traditional banks, pension funds, hedge funds and asset management firms. Public and governmental funders, such as local authorities, also actively lend through such channels. In the United Kingdom, during 2017 (Zhang et al. 2018), 40% (£815 million) of the P2P Business Lending volume came from institutional investors, a sharp increase from 28% in 2016. The corresponding figure for P2P Consumer Lending was 39% (£554 million) in 2017.

According to CCAF Global Report (2020), certain lending models lend themselves to greater institutionalization. In 2018, on a global basis, models of consumer lending are heavily influenced by institutional engagement, with balance sheet activities also having considerable influence from institutions. Regionally, the United States is heavily driven by institutional investors with 85% of funding originating from institutional investors. Africa and the Middle East, on the other hand represent regions with lowest proportion of institutional investments, with 17% and 12% respectively. In all other regions (Asia Pacific, Canada, Europe, Latin America, and the UK), institutional investors account for close to 50% of funding.

Matching

For crowdlending models to be successful, the platform must efficiently match compatible borrowers and lenders. This may be done manually or automatically, based on investor preferences. Retail investors may prefer to manually select the loans they invest in, whilst institutional investors may establish auto-investment criteria with the platform to reduce transaction time and costs. Platforms have an incentive to automate loan selection, to simplify the loan selection process and to reduce transaction costs.

Investors have numerous ways of participating in a digital lending platform. Early P2P Lending models allowed individuals to select the specific loans they wanted to participate in, and, on some platforms, bidding for loan parts in an auction at a price of their choice. However, what are commonly referred to as 'self-select' and 'auction' options are becoming increasingly rare. Instead, automated loan selection has become popular practice. In such process, lenders selecting 'investment criteria', which the platform uses to 'auto-invest' the lender's money in loans meeting that criteria.

The most common practice in automation is known as '*Automated Lender Diversification*'. Such approach implies that the lender is a passive investor, being matched against available loan parts/tranches that adhere to his or her predetermined preferences in terms of duration, risk appetite, amount, interest rate, etc. The platform will diversify exposure to new loans within the loan book that meet the investors pre-set selections. In this context, an approach growing in popularity, especially in the United States and the United Kingdom, is the '*Managed Portfolio Approach*'. In this case, lenders may select from two or three 'managed' lending options, where they are no longer selecting their desired duration or a specific interest rate. Rather, they will be joining a portfolio that offers a range of acceptable return, and the platform diversifies lender funds by exposing them across the loan book that fits the lender's 'managed option' (e.g. Zopa Cor & Zopa Plus). To ensure investors receive a consistent product, the platform will continuously move loans into and out of their portfolio so that the portfolio as a whole has the promised attributes.

Such automated assignment mechanisms are likely to attract increased scrutiny from regulators, as they could be construed as constituting investment advice, portfolio management, collective investment, or multilateral trading facilities. This may restrict platforms from offering the service or increase licensing requirements.

Success in Crowdlending

Success in crowdlending is associated with fulfilment of loans, indicating that target sums for a loan were successfully raised from prospective investors. A recent literature review by Shneor and Vik (2020) has identified nine persistent variables which were associated with successful loan fulfilment across multiple studies. First, with respect to borrowers, various signals of risk have been associated with success. Indeed, earlier studies show a positive association of credit scores and success (e.g. Kuwabara et al. 2017; Pope and Sydnor 2011), a negative association between debt to income ratio and success (e.g. Larrimore et al. 2011; Pope and Sydnor 2011), and positive association between previous successful loan raising and success in later loan raising (e.g. Barasinska and Schäfer 2014; Chen et al. 2017). In addition, studies suggest that female borrowers are more successful than men (e.g. Chen et al. 2017; Pope and Sydnor 2011), and this has sometimes been related to asking relatively smaller loans.

Second, certain loan terms were associated with greater success. Unsurprisingly, studies show that successful loans were associated with lower sums (e.g. Kuwabara et al. 2017; Yum et al. 2012), shorter time-horizons (e.g. Galak et al. 2011; Lee and Lee 2012), and higher interest rates (e.g. Feng et al. 2015; Larrimore et al. 2011). Furthermore, success was also positively associated with longer stated duration of campaigns (e.g. Larrimore et al. 2011; Lee and Lee 2012), and higher levels of on-site crowd interactions with borrowers via comments and Q&A (e.g. Lee and Lee 2012; Yum et al. 2012).

Conclusion

Crowdlending emerged as the leading model of crowdfunding in both scope and scale in every region. It is considered as both a challenge and supplement to traditional credit service providers by opening opportunities for investment and borrowing for wider groups of people. For lenders, it offers new investment opportunities, often involving better returns than some alternative investment channels, as well as opening to incorporate new small-scale investors that have not enjoyed such opportunities before. For borrowers, it offers new channels to access credit, often either offered at better terms or by including groups that have previously been marginalized and underserved by traditional credit service providers.

In the current chapter we present the brief history of crowdlending, its diversity of models, the current state or the industry, as well as the underlying mechanisms and principles guiding platform operations including risk assessment and the matching of borrowers and lenders. The discussion is supported by a review of related research, while highlighting trajectories of industry development trends.

Implications for Research

While receiving some attention, opportunities for research into crowdlending realities remain abundant. First, while most research focuses on P2P consumer lending, more research is needed into the particularities of business and property lending in the P2P model, as well as research examining alternative models to P2P including Balance Sheet lending, Invoice Trading, and Debt-based Securities. Here, with respect to all models, scholars are encouraged to examine the motivations for borrowers to use such channels vs. traditional ones, as well as the motivation of lenders to invest via such channels versus alternative investment channels. Furthermore, enhancing our knowledge about drivers of success in filling loans outside of the P2P consumer lending context may be valuable for would be borrowers and platforms that use such models. Alternatively, new research into success drivers in the P2P consumer lending space may also be conducted but should cover new national and cultural contexts beyond the United States and China, which represent most studies published thus far.

Second, of special importance are studies that may examine the impact of crowdlending in broad terms examining to which extent has it delivered on its promises. Here, studies should explore whether indeed access to credit has been improved in various contexts and social groups. Moreover, studies should examine whether crowdlending is used as a supplement or as an alternative to traditional credit services, and whether the conditions offered for such loans are indeed better than those offered elsewhere. Finally, in this context, future research may also examine the impact of crowdlending on indebtedness of individuals and organizations in different socio-economic contexts, studying whether debt burdens have increased, decreased, or remained unchanged following the use of crowdlending.

Implications for Practice

Practical implications are evident with respect to borrowers, lenders, platforms, and regulators. First, individuals and organizations interested in borrowing should examine and educate themselves about opportunities being provided by crowdlending platforms, while comparing them to other channels of credit. Once they decide to use such services, in order to improve their chances of receiving the loan, they should provide reliable information that may reduce the risk associated with their loan requests. At the same time, research suggested that they should aim for shorter term loans and be actively engaged with prospective lenders via social and platform communication tools.

Second, in terms of lenders, would be investors should educate themselves about the services offered by various crowdlending platforms, the different investment products available, and the risks associated with them. While research shows that platform risk assessments and ratings are good predictors of loan default, investors should examine a variety of risk indicators that can better inform their decision. Furthermore, in jurisdictions where automatic assignment of loans is allowed by law, investors should consider using such options for diversification and risk spreading across a portfolio of loans that match their preferences.

Third, platforms should engage in continuous learning about service developments in the industry with focus on process automation and streamlining, as well as the adoption of advanced machine learning in risk assessment and default prediction. This would enhance crowdlending FinTech platforms to fully tap into the cost efficiencies their mode of operations was set to achieve. Furthermore, despite temptation to onboard as many loans as possible, platforms should be wary of risky loans that may tarnish their reputation among prospective investors, as well as trigger regulatory crackdown that may limit industry development beyond the required risk management.

Finally, regulators should follow the industry and engage in active dialogue with its players towards developing regulatory frameworks that balance investor and borrower protection and industry growth, or support increase of access to credit while ensuring responsible use of it. Furthermore, public authorities should be concerned with informing the public about both the opportunities and risks associated with crowdlending engagements through encouraging and/or requiring training for individuals and organizations that use such services to a greater scale and frequency than others.

References

Armstrong, P. (2018). Here Are The U.K. Companies That Will Be Unicorns In 2019. Retrieved January 17, 2020, from https://www.forbes.com/sites/paularmstrongtech/2018/08/13/here-are-the-uk-companies-that-will-be-unicorns-in-2019/#308da7547c81.

Autonomous Research. (2016). Digital Lending: The 100 Billion Dollar Question. Retrieved January 19, 2020, from https://next.autonomous.com/digital-marketplace-lenders.

Bachmann, A., Becker, A., Buerckner, D., et al. (2011). Online Peer-to-Peer Lending – A Literature Review. *Journal of Internet Banking and Commerce, 16*(2), 1–18.

Bank for International Settlements & Financial Stability Board. (2017). Market Structure, Business Models and Financial Stability Implications Bank for International Settlements.

Barasinska, N., & Schäfer, D. (2014). Is Crowdfunding Different? Evidence on the Relation Between Gender and Funding Success from a German Peer-to-Peer Lending Platform. *German Economic Review, 15*(4), 436–452.

Barry, E. (2019). The History of US Peer-to-Peer Lending. Retrieved January 17, 2020, from https://www.finder.com/p2p-lending-usa.

Bruton, G., Khavul, S., Siegel, D., et al. (2015). New Financial Alternatives in Seeding Entrepreneurship: Microfinance, Crowdfunding, and Peer-to-Peer Innovations. *Entrepreneurship Theory and Practice, 39*(1), 9–26.

Chen, D., Li, X., & Lai, F. (2017). Gender Discrimination in Online Peer-to-Peer Credit Lending: Evidence from a Lending Platform in China. *Electronic Commerce Research, 17*(4), 553–583.

Chorzempa, M. (2018). Massive P2P Failures in China: Underground Banks Going Under. *China Economic Watch* [Online]. Retrieved from https://www.piie.com/blogs/china-economic-watch/massive-p2p-failures-china-underground-banks-going-under.

De Roure, C., Pelizzon, L., & Tasca, P. (2016). *How Does P2P Lending Fit into the Consumer Credit Market?* Deutsche Bundesbank Discussion Papers. Deutsche Bundesbank.

Dorfleitner, G., Rad, J., & Weber, M. (2017). Pricing in the Online Invoice Trading Market: First Empirical Evidence. *Economics Letters, 161*, 56–61.

Emekter, R., Tu, Y., Jirasakuldech, B., et al. (2015). Evaluating Credit Risk and Loan Performance in Online Peer-to-Peer (P2P) Lending. *Applied Economics, 47*(1), 54–70.

Feng, Y., Fan, X., & Yoon, Y. (2015). Lenders and Borrowers' Strategies in Online Peer-to-Peer Lending Market: An Empirical Analysis of ppdai.com. *Journal of Electronic Commerce Research, 16*(3), 242–260.

Galak, J., Small, D., & Stephen, A. T. (2011). Microfinance Decision Making: A Field Study of Prosocial Lending. *Journal of Marketing Research, 48*(SPL), S130–S137.

Ge, R., Feng, J., Gu, B., et al. (2017). Predicting and Deterring Default with Social Media Information in Peer-to-Peer Lending. *Journal of Management Information Systems, 34*(2), 401–424.

Gilbert, J. (2011). Moral Duties in Business and Their Societal Impacts: The Case of the Subprime Lending Mess. *Business and Society Review, 116*(1), 87–107.

Haddad, C., & Hornuf, L. (2019). The Emergence of the Global Fintech Market: Economic and Technological Determinants. *Small Business Economics, 53*(1), 81–105.

Hale, T. (2019). How Big Data Really Fits into Lending. Retrieved January 19, 2020, from https://ftalphaville.ft.com/2019/03/13/1552488421000/How-big-data-really-fits-into-lending/.

Hollas, J. (2013). Is Crowdfunding Now A Threat to Traditional Finance? *Corporate Finance Review, 18*(1), 27–31.

Kotarba, M. (2016). New Factors Including Changes in the Retail Banking Bustomer Relationship Management (CRM) and Their Exploration by the Fintech Industry. *Foundations of Management, 9*, 69–78.

Kuwabara, K., Anthony, D., & Horne, C. (2017). In the Shade of a Forest Status, Reputation, and Ambiguity in an Online Microcredit Market. *Social Science Research, 64*, 96–118.

Larrimore, L., Jiang, L., Larrimore, J., et al. (2011). Peer to Peer Lending: The Relationship Between Language Features, Trustworthiness, and Persuasion Success. *Journal of Applied Communication Research, 39*(1), 19–37.

Leboeuf, G., & Schwienbacher, A. (2018). Crowdfunding as a New Financing Tool. In D. Cumming & L. Hornuf (Eds.), *The Economics of Crowdfunding: Startups, Portals and Investor Behavior*. Cham: Springer International Publishing.

Lee, E., & Lee, B. (2012). Herding Behavior in Online P2P Lending: An Empirical Investigation. *Electronic Commerce Research and Applications, 11*(5), 495–503.

Lin, X., Li, X., & Zheng, Z. (2017). Evaluating Borrower's Default Risk in Peer-to-Peer Lending: Evidence from a Lending Platform in China. *Applied Economics, 49*(35), 3538–3545.

McCorquodale, R. (2018). How to Earn a More Stable Return with Diversification. Retrieved January 19, 2020, from https://www.fundingcircle.com/blog/2018/06/earn-stable-return-diversification/.

Milne, A., & Parboteeah, P. (2016). *The Business Models and Economics of Peer-to-Peer Lending*. Brussels: European Credit Research Institute.

Mohammadi, A., & Shafi, K. (2017, March). How Wise Are Crowd? A Comparative Study of Crowd and Institutions in Peer-to-Business Online Lending Markets. https://static.sys.kth.se/itm/wp/cesis/cesiswp450.pdf.

Nixon, G. (2020). Peer-to-Peer Trade Body Is Axed as Lenders such as Funding Circle, RateSetter and Zopa Join a Wider Fintech Group. Retrieved January 17, 2020, from https://www.thisismoney.co.uk/money/investing/article-7881555/Peer-peer-platforms-shut-independent-trade-body.html.

Oxera. (2015). Crowdfunding from an Investor Perspective. Retrieved January 19, 2020, from https://ec.europa.eu/info/sites/info/files/file_import/160503-study-crowdfunding-investor-perspective_en_0.pdf.

Pope, D. G., & Sydnor, J. R. (2011). What's in a Picture?: Evidence of Discrimination from Prosper.com. *Journal of Human Resources, 46*(1), 53–92.

Popescu, G. (2016). The Complete Guide to Regulation of Marketplace Lending. Retrieved January 17, 2020, from https://lending-times.com/2016/04/21/the-complete-guide-to-regulation-of-marketplace-lending/.

Richards, M., Palmer, P., & Bogdanova, M. (2008). Irresponsible Lending? A Case Study of a U.K. Credit Industry Reform Initiative. *Journal of Business Ethics, 81*(3), 499–512.

Serrano-Cinca, C., Gutiérrez-Nieto, B., & López-Palacios, L. (2015). Determinants of Default in P2P Lending. *PLOS ONE, 10*(10), e0139427.

Shneor, R., & Vik, A. A. (2020). Crowdfunding Success: A Systematic Literature Review 2010–2017. *Baltic Journal of Management, 5*(2), 149–182.

UK Finance. (2018). SME Finance in the UK: Past, Present and Future. Retrieved from https://www.ukfinance.org.uk/system/files/UK-Finance-SME-Finance-in-UK-AW-web.pdf.

Yum, H., Lee, B., & Chae, M. (2012). From the Wisdom of Crowds to My Own Judgment in Microfinance Through Online Peer-to-Peer Lending Platforms. *Electronic Commerce Research and Applications, 11*(5), 469–483.

Zhang, S., & Miller, M. (2017). China's New Illegal Fundraising Topped $36 billion Last Year. Retrieved April 30, 2019, from https://www.reuters.com/article/us-china-fraud-crackdown/chinas-new-illegal-fundraising-topped-36-billion-last-year-idUSKBN17R11X.

Zhang, B., Ziegler, T., Garvey, K., et al. (2017). *Entrenching Innovation: The 4th UK Alternative Finance Industry Report*. Cambridge, UK: Cambridge Centre for Alternative Finance.

Zhang, B., Ziegler, T., Mammadova, L., et al. (2018). *The 5th UK Alternative Finance Industry Report*. Cambridge, UK: Cambridge Centre for Alternative Finance.

Ziegler, T., Johanson, D., Zhang, B., et al. (2018). *The 3rd Asia Pacific Region Alternative Finance Industry Report*. Cambridge, UK: Cambridge Centre for Alternative Finance.

Ziegler, T., Shneor, R., Wenzlaff, K., et al. (2020). *The Global Alternative Finance Benchmarking Report*. Cambridge, UK: Cambridge Centre for Alternative Finance.

5

Equity Crowdfunding: Process, Investor Characteristics and Investor Motivations

Anna Lukkarinen

Introduction

Since the first online equity crowdfunding platform was established in France in 2008, equity crowdfunding has rapidly gained foothold across the world as an equity financing mechanism for early-stage entrepreneurial ventures. It allows ventures to gather funds for growth and expansion, and some ventures have indeed reached strong growth after their equity crowdfunding campaign, although many others have failed (Schwienbacher 2019). The investor base is composed of unaccredited as well as accredited investors, and increasingly also professional investors such as angel investors and venture capital funds (Wang et al. 2019).

The equity crowdfunding market grew strongly in the early 2010s across the world. From 2016 onwards, volumes in some regions have

---

Parts of the content of this chapter have been extracted from the overview chapter of the Aalto University Doctoral Dissertation referred to as — Lukkarinen (2019) and are provided here with the author's permission.

A. Lukkarinen (✉)
School of Science, Aalto University, Espoo, Finland
e-mail: anna.lukkarinen@aalto.fi

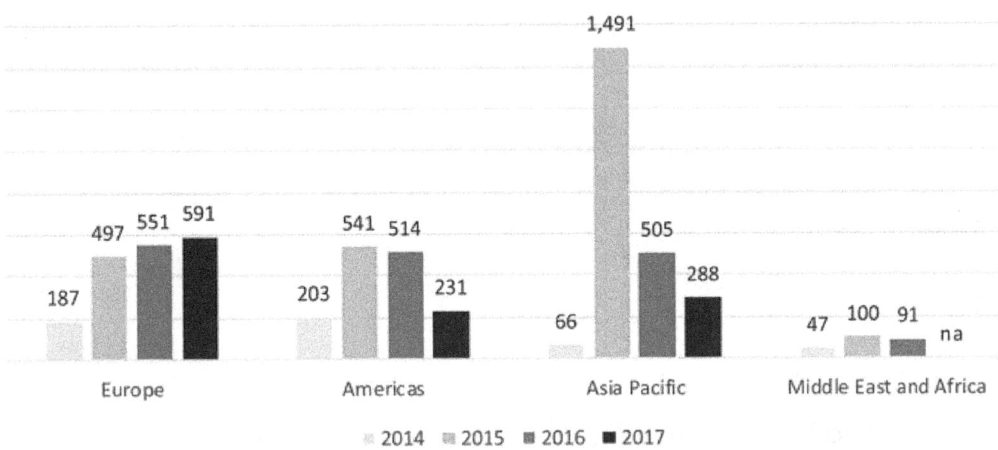

Fig. 5.1 Equity crowdfunding volumes (million EUR). (Source: Based on figures reported in Garvey et al. 2017; Zhang et al. 2018; Ziegler et al. 2018a, b, c, d, 2019)

experienced declines driven by regulatory uncertainty and constraints (Garvey et al. 2017; Ziegler et al. 2018a). The largest individual countries for equity crowdfunding are the United Kingdom (EUR 378 million in 2017) and the United States (EUR 209 million in 2017) (Ziegler et al. 2018a, 2019). Figure 5.1 presents yearly equity crowdfunding volumes by region.

Equity Crowdfunding Principles

While various different practices and conventions exist in equity crowdfunding across platforms and countries, certain principles have become widely established. Figure 5.2 presents a typical equity crowdfunding process.

The first contact between ventures and platforms is commonly inbound: interested ventures contact the platform. However, contact may also be established through outbound origination whereby the platform approaches attractive ventures, or through third-party referrals. Platforms vet and filter the ventures interested in conducting a campaign, with the extent of legal and financial due diligence varying by platform (Löher 2017; Schwienbacher 2019). If the outcome of the assessment is favourable, the venture proceeds to prepare and implement the

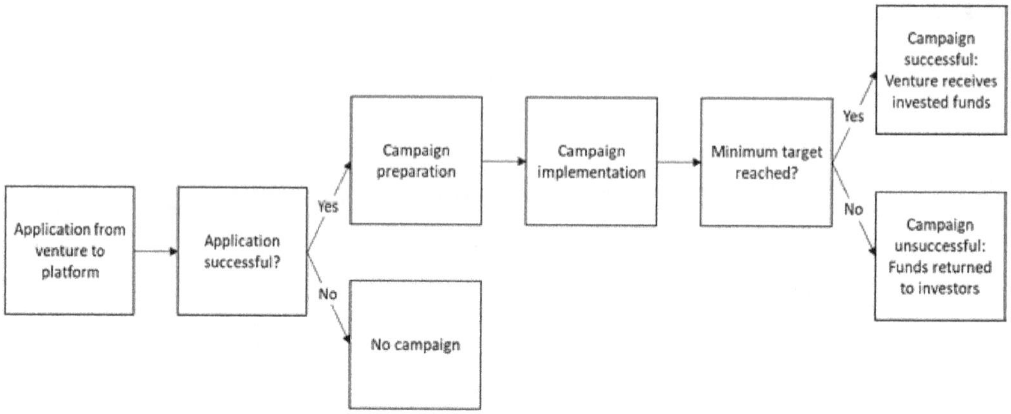

Fig. 5.2 Typical equity crowdfunding process under the all-or-nothing model. (Source: Modified from Lukkarinen et al. 2016)

crowdfunding campaign. The preselection funnel of platforms is often highly selective. In Europe, 6% of applicant ventures were deemed qualified by platforms and were thus onboarded to conduct a campaign in 2017 (Ziegler et al. 2019). Most equity crowdfunding platforms operate under the all-or-nothing model, in which the campaign must reach its pre-set minimum funding target in order to become successful and for the venture to receive the invested funds. If the minimum target is not reached, the funds are returned to investors (Tuomi and Harrison 2017).

The revenue model of platforms typically relies mostly on success fees or listing fees from fundraisers (Barbi and Mattioli 2019; Hornuf and Schwienbacher 2016; Shafi 2019). Compared with traditional forms of early-stage equity investing, the standardized online nature of the equity crowdfunding investment process allows for very low transaction costs. Indeed, low investor-side transaction costs, along with low minimum investment thresholds, are key factors enabling the participation of large crowds in equity crowdfunding (Kim and Viswanathan 2019). Accordingly, the bargaining power of individual crowd investors both pre- and post-investment is usually low. As fundraisers and platforms define the campaign details beforehand, prospective investors cannot influence transaction terms or covenants (Hornuf and Schmitt 2017). General shareholder rights vary by country and by platform. While some platforms call for the use of the same share class for equity crowdfunding investors as for other equity investors (Vismara 2018), others offer shareholders' agreements in which the shares offered via crowdfunding form a separate class with no voting rights (Frydrych et al. 2014; Hornuf and Neuenkirch 2017; Tuomi and Harrison 2017; Walthoff-Borm et al. 2018).

Investor Characteristics and Motivations

Investor Characteristics

Equity crowdfunding investors are a very diverse group of individuals with varying levels of professional and educational backgrounds (Lukkarinen et al. 2017) and investor professionalism (Guenther et al. 2018). Thus far, the majority of equity crowdfunding investments have been made by individuals who have no professional affiliation with investing. However, platforms are also attracting angel investors and venture capitalists who are seeking portfolio diversification and the convenience of standardized online investment processes (Bessière et al. 2019; Wang et al. 2019). For instance, in the Australia-based sample of Guenther et al. (2018), 10% of equity crowdfunding investors were accredited or professional investors.

Equity crowdfunding investors are predominantly male, although the share of female investors has been growing (Ziegler et al. 2018a, d, 2019). Investor age varies but averages at around 40, and investors' experience with other forms of investing ranges from none to extensive (Baeck et al. 2014; Guenther et al. 2014; Hornuf and Neuenkirch 2017; Lukkarinen et al. 2017; Mohammadi and Shafi 2018).

Heterogeneous Motivations

Investors' motivations for investing in equity crowdfunding are very heterogeneous, and they vary both between investors and between campaigns (Goethner et al. 2018; Lukkarinen et al. 2017). Accordingly, research has suggested that investments would be motivated mainly by an aim to earn financial returns (Baeck et al. 2014; Cholakova and Clarysse

2015; Kim and Viswanathan 2019), mainly by intrinsic reasons such as obtaining personal satisfaction (Schwienbacher and Larralde 2012), or by a combination of both (Collins and Pierrakis 2012; Daskalakis and Yue 2017). Survey results by Bretschneider and Leimeister (2017) indicate that equity crowdfunding investors are motivated by several factors, such as the ability to receive recognition, to influence campaign outcomes, to create an online image, and to receive returns or rewards, but not by altruistic motives. Vismara (2019), on the other hand, suggests that some equity crowdfunding investors may invest out of a wish to support sustainable development in the world. As such, no consensus exists as of yet about investor motivations in equity crowdfunding, perhaps due to their inherent heterogeneity and the rapid evolution of the industry.

Investors' Relationship with Fundraisers

While part of the investments in equity crowdfunding come from the family, friends, and other social connections of the entrepreneurs, the majority of investment activity is driven by the "true crowd" (Ahlers et al. 2015; Vismara 2018). According to a survey conducted by Guenther et al. (2014), 4% of equity crowdfunding investors are family members or friends of the fund seekers. Similarly, a survey by Lukkarinen et al. (2017) indicates that personal knowledge of the entrepreneur or the team was on average not considered an important decision criterion by equity crowdfunding investors. Furthermore, a dataset sourced from the database of an Australian equity crowdfunding platform indicates that 3% of equity crowdfunding investors are somehow connected to the venture (Guenther et al. 2018).

Thus, while some equity crowdfunding investments originate through the connections and marketing activities of fundraising ventures, platforms have a central role in attracting prospective investors to the campaign websites (Baeck et al. 2014). Consequently, rather than relying solely on their existing networks, entrepreneurs who conduct equity crowdfunding campaigns make an effort to build new ties and to expand their networks by attracting new investors via the platform (Brown et al. 2019).

Investing Behaviour

Investors' Limited Due Diligence

Although the equity crowdfunding market has been growing in size and relevance, with possibly significant implications for fundraising ventures (White and Dumay 2017), equity crowdfunding has limited centrality from the point of view of individual investors. It is usually a sporadic activity, with most investors having invested in only one or few equity crowdfunding campaigns on any focal platform (Baeck et al. 2014; Bapna 2019; Mohammadi and Shafi 2018), and with the median or average sums invested running relatively low, typically in the low thousands of euros (Bapna 2019; Block et al. 2018; Mahmood et al. 2019). Indeed, most investors describe the sums they invest via equity crowdfunding as "small" and as representing a small part of their overall investment portfolios (Estrin et al. 2018).

Accordingly, and in line with bounded rationality theory (Simon 1991), the investment target evaluation process of equity crowdfunding investors tends to be very limited. A survey of equity crowdfunding investors by Guenther et al. (2014) found that, on average, investors spend less than an hour to study the business plan, less than an hour on the campaign page, and less than an hour to study the venture's home page. Equity crowdfunding platforms, on the other hand, usually dedicate significant time and effort to evaluate each venture before deciding on its suitability for fundraising, thereby providing investors with a certain level of quality assurance for the campaigns that become available on platforms (Cumming et al. 2018; Guenther et al. 2018; Lukkarinen et al. 2016).

Investing time and effort in one-on-one communications between small-sum investors and fundraisers makes little economic sense in equity crowdfunding (Moritz et al. 2015). Accordingly, the majority of equity crowdfunding investors do not communicate directly with the entrepreneur (Guenther et al. 2014; Moritz et al. 2015). However, entrepreneurs and investors utilize digital pseudo-personal communications, such as videos, online investor relations channels, and social media, which enable investors to form a view of the venture and its management (Moritz et al. 2015).

Information asymmetries in the equity crowdfunding setting are high, as prospective investors possess considerably less knowledge about the fundraising venture than do the entrepreneurs (Piva and Rossi-Lamastra 2018). While investors do not usually conduct lengthy target evaluation processes or engage in personal communications to mitigate the hindering effect of information asymmetries, they do tend to take into account rapidly observable campaign features (Lukkarinen et al. 2016). These include the presence (Li et al. 2016) and length (Vismara et al. 2017) of videos, the minimum allowed investment (Hornuf and Schwienbacher 2018a; Lukkarinen et al. 2016), and visual cues such as logos (Mahmood et al. 2019). Investment decision criteria that equity crowdfunding investors have highlighted as important in investor surveys include the perceived informativeness of the campaign page and materials, clarity and uniqueness of the business idea and products, characteristics of the entrepreneur and the team, the explanation for the planned used of funds, perceived openness and trustworthiness, and the presence of a credible lead investor (Bapna 2019; Kang et al. 2016; Lukkarinen et al. 2017; Moritz et al. 2015; Ordanini et al. 2011).

Ventures can signal the attractiveness of the investment opportunity and the underlying venture quality to prospective investors in a variety of ways (Ahlers et al. 2015). The share of equity retained by the entrepreneurs in the equity offering signals the entrepreneurs' belief in the future prospects of the venture and influences investor interest (Ahlers et al. 2015; Vismara 2016). Entrepreneurs' human capital, as measured by business education and entrepreneurial experience, serves as a low-ambiguity signal of venture quality and thereby drives investments (Piva and Rossi-Lamastra 2018). A venture's intellectual capital can signal innovation capabilities, managerial skills, and overall venture quality (Ralcheva and Roosenboom 2016) while also creating entry barriers to competitors (Piva and Rossi-Lamastra 2018), although findings about the effect of the possession of intellectual property rights on campaign success remain mixed (Ahlers et al. 2015; Kleinert et al. 2020). As business failure can signal a lack of entrepreneurial skill, prospective equity crowdfunding investors discount entrepreneurs who have previously experienced a business failure, unless the investors receive evidence that the failure was due to bad luck rather than a lack of entrepreneurial skill (Zunino et al. 2017). Furthermore, investors prefer taking the high risks inherent in equity crowdfunding (Kleinert et al. 2020) when the entrepreneurs seek to reduce uncertainty by offering detailed financial information (Ahlers et al. 2015).

Updates posted by entrepreneurs on the campaign site during the campaign have a positive impact on fundraising performance, as they can convey messages about venture value to prospective investors in a trustworthy and easily observable manner (Hornuf and Schwienbacher 2018b; Li et al. 2016). Update content matters, with updates about developments that have taken place during the campaign considered most relevant by investors (Block et al. 2018).

Angel and venture capital investors typically conduct extensive, or at least moderate, due diligence on their investment targets (Fried and Hisrich 1994; Van Osnabrugge 2000). Ventures that have already secured Angel or venture capital investors are thus more likely to successfully raise funding in equity crowdfunding campaigns, as the presence of professional investors helps mitigate the adverse effect of information asymmetries (Kleinert et al. 2020; Mamonov and Malaga 2018).

Importance of Other Investors' Actions

Most equity crowdfunding platforms allow for digital visibility, with all prospective investors usually able to see in real-time the total amount already invested, the number of investors or investments already committed to a campaign, and investment-related comments written by other users (Ahlers et al. 2015; Hornuf and Schwienbacher 2018b; Kim and Viswanathan 2019; Lukkarinen et al. 2016). This contrasts the funding dynamics of initial public offerings, in which investors do not know the amount of money already invested by others at the time of subscription (Vismara 2016). Accordingly, when making investment decisions, equity crowdfunding investors consider not only the available venture information and predetermined campaign characteristics, but also the within-campaign funding dynamics, thereby at least partially relying on the behaviour of others.

In particular, later investors have the opportunity to take the behaviour of previous investors into account in their decision making (Vismara 2018). Campaigns with a larger number of early investors are more likely to become successful, possibly because early investments send a signal of trust and confidence to prospective later investors and because early investors may contribute to the word-of-mouth around a campaign (Lukkarinen et al. 2016; Vulkan et al. 2016). Experienced early investors, in particular, have a strong influence on the investment decisions of prospective later investors (Kim and Viswanathan 2019; Vismara 2018), and especially on the decisions of small crowdinvestors (Cumming et al. 2019).

Furthermore, the size of previous investments positively predicts subsequent investment activity at campaign level, as large investments may send a signal of the respective investor possessing knowledge that others do not have (Åstebro et al. 2018; Hornuf and Schwienbacher 2018b; Vulkan et al. 2016). Similarly, the amount of time that has passed since the most recent investment in a campaign has a negative effect on the likelihood and size of subsequent investments, as an absence of investments can be indicative of a lack of investors who would possess positive private signals of the campaign (Åstebro et al. 2018). Such herding behaviour can increase the likelihood of investors investing in low-quality ventures in which they might not invest without the cues observed from the crowd. Consequently, Stevenson et al. (2019) introduce the term *crowd bias* to refer to "an individual's tendency to follow the opinions of the crowd despite the presence of contrary objective quality indicators" (p. 348).

Most platforms host discussion boards on which users can pose questions to the entrepreneurs and discuss the investment opportunity with other users. Discussions tend to have a positive effect on investment activity, although the effect depends on the discussion topic (Kleinert and Volkmann 2019). Positive comments by previous investors, in particular, have a positive effect, as they may contain positive information about the attractiveness of the venture (Hornuf and Schwienbacher 2018b).

Local Bias

Much like investors in other forms of investing (e.g., Grinblatt and Keloharju 2001), equity crowdfunding investors are locally biased. Suggested reasons for equity crowdfunding investors' tendency to invest in ventures located geographically close to them include access to better and more tangible information and an ability to better monitor the venture (Guenther et al. 2018; Hornuf and Schmitt 2017). The local bias effect is weaker for financially more literate investors, perhaps because they are more likely to pursue risk reduction through portfolio diversification (Hornuf and Schmitt 2017).

A distinct aspect of local bias is investors' tendency to invest domestically. This preference stems from the benefits of geographic proximity, difficulties caused by differences in legal frameworks, and the burden and risks associated with foreign currency investments (Niemand et al. 2018). Interestingly, while investors are indeed sensitive to geographic distance when investing domestically, distance is not relevant in cross-border investments, perhaps because of the difficulty of leveraging local knowledge in any cross-border investment, regardless of distance (Guenther et al. 2018; Maula and Lukkarinen 2019).

The share of cross-border investments has been growing, however, along with platforms' increasing internationalization efforts. While the United States is still strongly domestically focused (Ziegler et al. 2018a), cross-border investments represented 9% of funding outflows and 16% of funding inflows among European platforms (Ziegler et al. 2019) and 31% and 22% of outflows and inflows, respectively, among Asia Pacific platforms (Ziegler et al. 2018d) in 2017.[1] The Australia-based sample of Guenther et al. (2018) portrayed a 9% share of cross-border investors, whereas the Finland-based sample of Maula and Lukkarinen (2019) and the Germany-based sample of Hornuf and Schmitt (2017) featured 8% and 9% cross-border investments, respectively. As cross-border investing opens up a large multiple of investment opportunities compared to domestic investing, the attention that cross-border investors pay to foreign campaigns becomes an important driver of investors' investment choices (Maula and Lukkarinen 2019).

Comparison of Early-Stage Equity Financing Forms

Equity crowdfunding addresses partly the same market as traditional forms of entrepreneurial finance, most notably angel investors, venture capitalists, and micro funders.[2] Partly, however, it serves to fund such ventures that might otherwise be left unfunded (Harrison and Mason 2019). Table 5.1 presents a comparative summary of different forms of early-stage equity financing. Salient similarities between neighbouring forms are highlighted in italic.

In several respects, equity crowdfunding investors bear resemblance to traditional micro funders. Both make relatively small high-risk investments using their own money, with the investing activity not being their main occupation. While some of their investments are motivated by returns, both can also invest out of a willingness to support the target venture. They both expend very limited effort to evaluate the target, although the decision making of equity crowdfunding investors may also partly rely on their knowledge of the platform having already pre-evaluated the target (Tuomi and Harrison 2017).

A key differentiator between equity crowdfunding and more traditional forms of early-stage equity financing is the digital nature of online crowdfunding, which renders it possible for ventures to gather investments from large numbers of people without personal entrepreneur-investor interactions and with a high degree of visibility towards investors (Horvát et al. 2018; Kim and Viswanathan 2019).

It is worth noting in this context that, from the viewpoint of an entrepreneurial venture, the different forms of financing need not be mutually exclusive, nor is their sequential order invariable. Entrepreneurial ventures can use different sources of funding at different lifecycle stages. Ventures that have successfully secured financing through equity crowdfunding have been shown to be more likely to attract investments from angel investors or venture capitalists in follow-up funding rounds (Hornuf et al. 2018), whereas ventures with unsuccessful equity crowdfunding campaigns may fail with no opportunities for follow-up funding (Walthoff-Borm et al. 2018). In addition, ventures can use several forms

Table 5.1 Comparison of different forms of early-stage equity financing

Features	Equity crowdfunding investors	Micro funders	Angel Investors	Venture capitalists
Funder characteristics				
Typical funder background	Often high education, many with no entrepreneurial background (Lukkarinen et al. 2017)	Often high education, many with entrepreneurial background (Avdeitchikova 2008)	High education, previous experience from entrepreneurship, consulting, and industry (Politis and Landström 2002)	Previous experience from finance, consulting, and industry (Wilson and Testoni 2014)
Heterogeneity of funder space	Very high: crowd composed of many different types of investors (Block et al. 2018; Moritz et al. 2015)	High: varying demographic backgrounds, investment amounts, and skills (Maula et al. 2005; Szerb et al. 2007)	Relatively high: diversity in competence, motivations, and investment activity (Sullivan and Miller 1996)	Low (although categories exist): firms unified by an aim to earn profits and efforts to hire suitable staff (MacMillan et al. 1985)
Source of funds	*Investor's own money* (Wilson and Testoni 2014)	*Investor's own money* (De Clercq et al. 2012)	*Investor's own* (Mason and Harrison 2008)	Others' money pooled into venture capital fund (Sahlman 1990)
Centrality of investing activity for funder	*Not central; limited contributions of time and money* (Estrin et al. 2018)	*Not central; limited contributions of time and money* (Szerb et al. 2007)	Often central (Mason and Harrison 2008; Politis and Landström 2002)	Very central; key purpose of venture capital firm (Tyebjee and Bruno 1984)
Venture characteristics				
Risk level	*Very high risk* (Signori and Vismara 2018; Walthoff-Borm et al. 2018)	*Very high risk* (De Clercq et al. 2012)	High risk (Avdeitchikova 2008; Landström 1993)	Rather high risk (De Clercq et al. 2012; Van Osnabrugge 2000)

Lifecycle stage	Very early-stage, early-stage, or advanced early-stage (Cumming and Vismara 2017; Rossi 2014)	Very early-stage; earlier than angel investors (Avdeitchikova 2008)	Early-stage; earlier than venture capital (Mason and Harrison 2008)	Advanced early-stage; later than angel investors (Mason and Harrison 2008)
Investment decision process				
Motivations for investing	*Various; including intrinsic and extrinsic* (Harrison and Mason 2019; Lukkarinen et al. 2017)	*Various; including intrinsic and extrinsic* (De Clercq et al. 2012; Maula et al. 2005)	Financial returns important, but also intrinsic motivations (Van Osnabrugge 2000)	Financial returns highly important (Sudek 2006; Wilson and Testoni 2014)
Extent of target evaluation	Limited (conducted by individual)/medium (conducted by platform) (Ahlers et al. 2015; Guenther et al. 2018)	Limited; conducted by individual (Maula et al. 2005)	Medium; conducted by individual, possibly with support from angel network (EBAN 2014; Wiltbank 2009)	Extensive; involves staff and often external advisors (Fried and Hisrich 1994; Wilson and Testoni 2014)
Key investment criteria	Rapid-to-observe venture and campaign features (Block et al. 2018; Lukkarinen et al. 2016)	Financial, social, and environmental venture and team features (De Clercq et al. 2012; Estapé-Dubreuil et al. 2016)	*Entrepreneur, team, product, market, business plan, exit opportunities* (Prowse 1998; Sudek 2006; Van Osnabrugge 2000)	*Product, market, entrepreneur, team, expected returns, exit opportunities* (MacMillan et al. 1985; Streletzki and Schulte 2013)
Funding mechanism characteristics				

(*continued*)

Table 5.1 (continued)

Features	Equity crowdfunding investors	Micro funders	Business angels	Venture capitalists
Role of digitalization	Central; all or most activity via online platform, allowing for high volumes and visibility (Horvát et al. 2018; Kim and Viswanathan 2019)	*Limited; in-person interactions via personal connections or organizations* (Estapé-Dubreuil et al. 2016; Maula et al. 2005)	*Limited but emerging; face-to-face contacts important, some are starting to use platforms* (Brown et al. 2019; Van Osnabrugge 2000)	*Limited; social networks, direct contacts and proactive outreach important* (Tyebjee and Bruno 1984)
Transaction costs	Very low due to standardized and automated processes and the online nature of communications (Hornuf and Schmitt 2017; Löher 2017)	Low; close pre-investment connections contribute to low screening and monitoring requirements (De Clercq et al. 2012)	Relatively low; administration costs are small (Landström 1993)	High; costs include advisory fees (Van Osnabrugge 2000)
Bargaining power of individual investors	Very low; deal terms pre-determined by venture (Hornuf and Schmitt 2017)	Medium; small investments but opportunity to make information requests (De Clercq et al. 2012)	Relatively high; personal negotiations before deal (Van Osnabrugge 2000)	Very high; formal contract formulation processes, high equity stakes, time devoted for negotiations (Tyebjee and Bruno 1984; Van Osnabrugge 2000)

Connections between funders and the venture				
Pre-investment relationship	Often no relationship (Guenther et al. 2018; Vismara 2018)	Rather often a pre-existing family or friendship relationship (De Clercq et al. 2012; Maula et al. 2005)	Often a relationship or prior knowledge of the entrepreneur (Avdeitchikova 2008)	Only occasionally prior knowledge of the entrepreneur (Fried and Hisrich 1994; Tyebjee and Bruno 1984)
Communication during investment process	Usually no personal communication (Guenther et al. 2014; Moritz et al. 2015)	Varying levels of social connection (De Clercq et al. 2012)	*Active, including face-to-face meetings* (Van Osnabrugge 2000)	*Very active, including many face-to-face meetings* (Fried and Hisrich 1994; Van Osnabrugge 2000)
Post-funding involvement of funders	Very limited, passive (Brown et al. 2019; Walthoff-Borm et al. 2018; Wilson and Testoni 2014)	Varied but often limited and light, sometimes passive (Avdeitchikova 2008; Estapé-Dubreuil et al. 2016)	*Often active via board position or advisory roles* (Mason and Harrison 2008)	*Active via board position or advisory roles; control* (Tyebjee and Bruno 1984; Van Osnabrugge 2000)

Source: Lukkarinen (2019)

simultaneously. Complementarities, such as a possibility of co-investing in deals, have been previously identified between venture capital funds and angel investors (Harrison and Mason 2000). Similarly, equity crowdfunding campaigns have begun attracting investments from angel investors and venture capital funds, with angel investors making use of the digital screening and investing opportunities offered by equity crowdfunding platforms, and with venture capitalists acting as lead investors in high-volume deals (Brown et al. 2019; Itenbert and Smith 2017).

Discussion

Since its inception in 2008, online equity crowdfunding has experienced strong market growth. Consequently, equity crowdfunding has gathered wide research interest, and it has come to justify its existence as a standalone research target.

The investor base in equity crowdfunding is diverse, with some investors originating from the close social networks of the entrepreneurs, but with much activity also being driven by the "true crowd". In addition, angel and venture capital investors are increasingly making use of the opportunities offered by equity crowdfunding platforms. While investors' motivations for investing are heterogeneous, a wish for financial returns is important. In accordance with the limited centrality of equity crowdfunding from the investor's point of view, crowdinvestors spend very limited time evaluating target ventures. They focus on rapidly observable campaign features, signals of venture quality, and the actions of other investors when making investment decisions. Equity crowdfunding complements the spectrum of traditional venture financing mechanisms. While it bears certain resemblance to other forms of early-stage equity financing, equity crowdfunding is clearly distinguishable by its special features stemming from its digital nature, in particular its high degree of investor-side visibility into campaign funding dynamics and the low contributions of time and money required for making an investment.

Implications for Research

Research on equity crowdfunding can anchor itself in the wider context of not only crowdsourcing or crowdfunding, but also that of early-stage equity investing or even public stock investing (Cummings et al. 2019). As findings can differ by investor type and by venture type, research on equity crowdfunding can benefit from taking into account the heterogeneity of investors' motivations, decision criteria, and characteristics, on the one hand, and the diversity of fundraisers, on the other hand. Furthermore, as investors and platforms are increasingly active across country borders, cross-country and cross-platform research identifying similarities and differences across country and platform contexts is increasingly needed. Finally, although research about campaign success factors and investor features in equity crowdfunding is already abundant (Mochkabadi and Volkmann 2020), it dates empirically back to the early stages of industry development. As industry characteristics and dynamics vary across lifecycle stages, further research on equity crowdfunding at platform, investor, and investment level becomes necessary as the industry matures. Furthermore, the maturing state of the industry makes it increasingly possible to assess post-campaign outcomes for investors and for fundraisers.

Implications for Practice

The present research findings on equity crowdfunding investors have also practical implications. An awareness of investors' limited due diligence and investors' reliance on non-traditional decision criteria when making equity crowdfunding investments can support policymakers in their pursuit of the optimal level of regulation. The heterogeneity of the funder space offers platforms opportunities to differentiate their services at platform level and at investor level. Platforms can accommodate the existence of different investor segments by focusing explicitly on certain segments and selecting fundraisers in accordance with segment preferences, or by targeting and serving different segments in different ways. As certain demographic segments, notably women, remain a minority, platforms and fundraisers may consider adopting approaches to increasingly attract such presently underserved segments. Platforms' increased targeting efforts can improve their ability to match investors and ventures and thus enhance ventures' ability to gather funding.

Conclusion

The key challenges presently faced by the equity crowdfunding industry relate to investor returns, share liquidity, and platform profitability (Schwienbacher 2019). Although the long-term term outcome of the industry is yet to be seen, equity crowdfunding carries potential to offer a positive impact on new venture financing and development (Brown et al. 2019; Mochkabadi and Volkmann 2020) and even on the wider society and environment (Testa et al. 2019; Vismara 2019). To entrepreneurial ventures, equity crowdfunding offers an alternative form of equity financing that they may turn to out of choice or out of necessity (Walthoff-Borm et al. 2018). To investors, it offers an opportunity to diversify their investment portfolios across company lifecycle stages, financial instruments, and, increasingly, across geographies.

Acknowledgement The author gratefully acknowledges that this work was supported by a grant from the Finnish Foundation for Share Promotion.

Notes

1. Funding inflows represent investments made into fundraisers located in the platform country by investors located outside that country. Funding outflows represent investments made into fundraisers located outside the platform country by investors located in the platform country (definitions as used in the survey by Ziegler et al. 2019).
2. Micro funders, or micro angels, can be defined as informal early-stage investors who contribute limited amounts of their personal financial and human capital resources to purchase equity in entrepreneurial ventures that are majority owned by others. They can include family, friends, as well as more distant "foolhardy" investors (Avdeitchikova 2008; De Clercq et al. 2012; Maula et al. 2005; Szerb et al. 2007). The concept dates back to the time before online crowdfunding.

References

Ahlers, G. K., Cumming, D., Günther, C., & Schweizer, D. (2015). Signaling in Equity Crowdfunding. *Entrepreneurship Theory and Practice, 39*(4), 955–980.

Åstebro, T., Fernández, M., Lovo, S., & Vulkan, N. (2018). Herding in Equity Crowdfunding. Retrieved May 26, 2019, from https://ssrn.com/abstract=3084140.

Avdeitchikova, S. (2008). On the Structure of the Informal Venture Capital Market in Sweden: Developing Investment Roles. *Venture Capital, 10*(1), 55–85.

Baeck, P., Collins, L., & Zhang, Z. (2014). *Understanding Alternative Finance: The UK Alternative Finance Industry Report.* Cambridge, UK: University of Cambridge.

Bapna, S. (2019). Complementarity of Signals in Early-stage Equity Investment Decisions: Evidence from a Randomized Field Experiment. *Management Science, 65*(2), 933–952.

Barbi, M., & Mattioli, S. (2019). Human Capital, Investor Trust, and Equity Crowdfunding. *Research in International Business and Finance, 49*, 1–12.

Bessière, V., Stéphany, E., & Wirtz, P. (2019). Crowdfunding, Business Angels, and Venture Capital: An Exploratory Study of the Concept of the Funding Trajectory. *Venture Capital,* forthcoming.

Block, J., Hornuf, L., & Moritz, A. (2018). Which Updates During an Equity Crowdfunding Campaign Increase Crowd Participation? *Small Business Economics, 50*(1), 3–27.

Bretschneider, U., & Leimeister, J. M. (2017). Not Just an Ego-trip: Exploring Backers' Motivation for Funding in Incentive-based Crowdfunding. *Journal of Strategic Information Systems, 26*(4), 246–260.

Brown, R., Mawson, S., & Rowe, A. (2019). Start-ups, Entrepreneurial Networks and Equity Crowdfunding: A Processual Perspective. *Industrial Marketing Management, 80*, 115–125.

Cholakova, M., & Clarysse, B. (2015). Does the Possibility to Make Equity Investments in Crowdfunding Projects Crowd Out Rewards-based Investments? *Entrepreneurship Theory and Practice, 39*(1), 145–172.

Collins, L., & Pierrakis, Y. (2012). *The Venture Crowd: Crowdfunding Equity Investment into Business.* London, UK: Nesta. Retrieved May 26, 2019, from http://www.nesta.org.uk/publications/venture-crowd.

Cumming, D. J., & Vismara, S. (2017). De-segmenting Research in Entrepreneurial Finance. *Venture Capital, 19*(1–2), 17–27.

Cumming, D., Hervé, F., Manthé, E., & Schwienbacher, A. (2018). Hypothetical Bias in Equity Crowdfunding. Retrieved May 26, 2019, from https://ssrn.com/abstract=3114526.

Cumming, D., Meoli, M., & Vismara, S. (2019). Investors' Choices Between Cash and Voting Rights: Evidence from Dual-class Equity Crowdfunding. *Research Policy, 48*(8), 103740.

Cummings, M. E., Rawhouser, H., Vismara, S., & Hamilton, E. L. (2019). An Equity Crowdfunding Research Agenda: Evidence from Stakeholder Participation in the Rulemaking Process. *Small Business Economics*, forthcoming.

Daskalakis, N., & Yue, W. (2017). User's Perceptions of Motivations and Risks in Crowdfunding with Financial Returns. Retrieved May 26, 2019, from https://ssrn.com/abstract=2968912.

De Clercq, D., Meuleman, M., & Wright, M. (2012). A Cross-country Investigation of Micro-angel Investment Activity: The Roles of New Business Opportunities and Institutions. *International Business Review, 21*(2), 117–129.

EBAN. (2014). Investment Principles and Guidelines. European Business Angel Network. Retrieved May 26, 2019, from http://www.eban.org/knowledge-center/.

Estapé-Dubreuil, G., Ashta, A., & Hédou, J.-P. (2016). Micro-equity for Sustainable Development: Selection, Monitoring and Exit Strategies of Micro-angels. *Ecological Economics, 130*, 117–129.

Estrin, S., Daniel Gozman, D., & Khavul, S. (2018). The Evolution and Adoption of Equity Crowdfunding: Entrepreneur and Investor Entry into a New Market. *Small Business Economics, 51*(2), 425–439.

Fried, V. H., & Hisrich, R. D. (1994). Toward a Model of Venture Capital Investment Decision Making. *Financial Management, 23*(3), 28–37.

Frydrych, D., Bock, A. J., Kinder, T., & Koeck, B. (2014). Exploring Entrepreneurial Legitimacy in Reward-based Crowdfunding. *Venture Capital, 16*(3), 247–269.

Garvey, K., Chen, H.-Y., Zhang, B., Buckingham, E., Ralston, D., Katiforis, Y., et al. (2017). *Cultivating Growth: The 2nd Asia Pacific Region Alternative Finance Industry Report*. Cambridge, UK: Cambridge Center for Alternative Finance.

Goethner, M., Luettig, S., & Regner, T. (2018). *Crowdinvesting in Entrepreneurial Projects: Disentangling Patterns of Investor Behavior*. Jena Economic Research Papers 2018-018. Friedrich-Schiller-University Jena.

Grinblatt, M., & Keloharju, M. (2001). How Distance, Language, and Culture Influence Stockholdings and Trades. *Journal of Finance, 56*(3), 1053–1073.

Guenther, C., Hienerth, C., & Riar, F. (2014). *The Due Diligence of Crowdinvestors: Thorough Evaluation or Gut Feeling Only?* Paper Presented at the 12th International Open and User Innovation Conference, Boston, Massachusetts, July 28–30.

Guenther, C., Johan, S., & Schweizer, D. (2018). Is the Crowd Sensitive to Distance? How Investment Decisions Differ by Investor Type. *Small Business Economics, 50*(2), 289–305.

Harrison, R. T., & Mason, C. M. (2000). Venture Capital Market Complementarities: The Links Between Business Angels and Venture Capital Funds in the United Kingdom. *Venture Capital, 2*(3), 223–242.

Harrison, R. T., & Mason, C. M. (2019). Venture Capital 20 Years On: Reflections on the Evolution of a Field. *Venture Capital, 21*(1), 1–34.

Hornuf, L., & Neuenkirch, M. (2017). Pricing Shares in Equity Crowdfunding. *Small Business Economics, 48*(4), 795–811.

Hornuf, L., & Schmitt, M. (2017). *Does a Local Bias Exist in Equity Crowdfunding?* Max Planck Institute for Innovation & Competition Research Paper No. 16-07. Retrieved May 26, 2019, from https://ssrn.com/abstract=2801170.

Hornuf, L., & Schwienbacher, A. (2016). Crowdinvesting: Angel Investing for the Masses? In H. Landström & C. Mason (Eds.), *Handbook of Research on Business Angels* (pp. 381–397). Cheltenham: Edward Elgar.

Hornuf, L., & Schwienbacher, A. (2018a). Internet-based Entrepreneurial Finance: Lessons from Germany. *California Management Review, 60*(2), 150–175.

Hornuf, L., & Schwienbacher, A. (2018b). Market Mechanisms and Funding Dynamics in Equity Crowdfunding. *Journal of Corporate Finance, 50*, 556–574.

Hornuf, L., Schmitt, M., & Stenzhorn, E. (2018). *Equity Crowdfunding in Germany and the UK: Follow-up Funding and Firm Failure*. Max Planck Institute for Innovation and Competition Research Paper No. 17–09.

Horvát, E.-Á., Wachs, J., Wang, R., & Hannák, A. (2018). *The Role of Novelty in Securing Investors for Equity Crowdfunding Campaigns*. Paper Presented at the 6th AAAI Conference on Human Computation and Crowdsourcing HCOMP 2018, Zurich, Switzerland, July 5–8.

Itenbert, O., & Smith, E. E. (2017). Syndicated Equity Crowdfunding: The Trade-off Between Deal Access and Conflicts of Interest. Retrieved May 26, 2019, from https://ssrn.com/abstract=2933822.

Kang, M., Gao, Y., Wang, T., & Zheng, H. (2016). Understanding the Determinants of Funders' Investment Intentions on Crowdfunding Platforms. *Industrial Management Data Systems, 116*(8), 1800–1819.

Kim, K., & Viswanathan, S. (2019). The Experts in the Crowd: The Role of Experienced Investors in a Crowdfunding Market. *MIS Quarterly, 43*(2), 347–372.

Kleinert, S., & Volkmann, C. (2019). Equity Crowdfunding and the Role of Investor Discussion Boards. *Venture Capital, 21*(4), 327–352.

Kleinert, S., Volkmann, C., & Grünhagen, M. (2020). Third-party Signals in Equity Crowdfunding: The Role of Prior Financing. *Small Business Economics, 54*(1), 341–365.

Landström, H. (1993). Informal Risk Capital in Sweden and Some International Comparisons. *Journal of Business Venturing, 8*(6), 525–540.

Li, X., Tang, Y., Yang, N., Ren, R., Zheng, H., & Zhou, H. (2016). The Value of Information Disclosure and Lead Investor in Equity-based Crowdfunding: An Exploratory Empirical Study. *Nankai Business Review International, 7*(3), 301–321.

Löher, J. (2017). The Interaction of Equity Crowdfunding Platforms and Ventures: An Analysis of the Preselection Process. *Venture Capital, 19*(1–2), 51–74.

Lukkarinen, A. (2019). *Drivers of Investment Activity in Equity Crowdfunding.* Doctoral dissertation, Aalto University School of Business. 190 pages. Aalto University publication series DOCTORAL DISSERTATIONS, 40/2019. ISBN 978-952-60-8444-2 (electronic). 978-952-60-8443-5 (printed) http://urn.fi/URN:ISBN:978-952-60-8444-2.

Lukkarinen, A., Teich, J. E., Wallenius, H., & Wallenius, J. (2016). Success Drivers of Online Equity Crowdfunding Campaigns. *Decision Support Systems, 87*, 26–38.

Lukkarinen, A., Seppälä, T., & Wallenius, J. (2017). Investor Motivations and Decision Criteria in Equity Crowdfunding. Retrieved May 26, 2019, from https://ssrn.com/abstract=3263434.

MacMillan, I. C., Siegel, R., & Narasimha, P. N. S. (1985). Criteria Used by Venture Capitalists to Evaluate New Venture Proposals. *Journal of Business Venturing, 1*(1), 119–128.

Mahmood, A., Luffarelli, J., & Mukesh, M. (2019). What's in a Logo? The Impact of Complex Visual Cues in Equity Crowdfunding. *Journal of Business Venturing, 34*(1), 41–62.

Mamonov, S., & Malaga, R. (2018). Success Factors in Title III Equity Crowdfunding in the United States. *Electronic Commerce and Research Applications, 27*, 65–73.

Mason, C. M., & Harrison, R. T. (2008). Measuring Business Angel Investment Activity in the United Kingdom: A Review of Potential Data Sources. *Venture Capital, 10*(4), 309–330.

Maula, M., & Lukkarinen, A. (2019). Attention Across Borders: Investor Attention as a Driver of Investment Choices in Cross-Border Equity Crowdfunding. Retrieved November 21, 2019, from https://papers.ssrn.com/sol3/papers.cfm?abstract_id=3487467.

Maula, M., Autio, E., & Arenius, P. (2005). What Drives Micro-angel Investments? *Small Business Economics, 25*(5), 459–475.

Mochkabadi, K., & Volkmann, C. K. (2020). Equity Crowdfunding: A Systematic Review of the Literature. *Small Business Economics, 54*(1), 75–118.

Mohammadi, A., & Shafi, K. (2018). Gender Differences in the Contribution Patterns of Equity-crowdfunding Investors. *Small Business Economics, 50*(2), 275–287.

Moritz, A., Block, J., & Lutz, E. (2015). Investor Communication in Equity-based Crowdfunding: A Qualitative-empirical Study. *Qualitative Research in Financial Markets, 7*(3), 309–342.

Niemand, T., Angerer, M., Thies, F., Kraus, S., & Hebenstreit, R. (2018). Equity Crowdfunding Across Borders: A Conjoint Experiment. *International Journal of Entrepreneurial Behavior and Research, 24*(4), 911–932.

Ordanini, A., Miceli, L., Pizzetti, M., & Parasuraman, A. (2011). Crowd-funding: Transforming Customers into Investors Through Innovative Service Platforms. *Journal of Service Management, 22*(4), 443–470.

Piva, E., & Rossi-Lamastra, C. (2018). Human Capital Signals and Entrepreneurs' Success in Equity Crowdfunding. *Small Business Economics, 51*(3), 667–686.

Politis, D., & Landström, H. (2002). Informal Investors as Entrepreneurs: The Development of an Entrepreneurial Career. *Venture Capital, 4*(2), 78–101.

Prowse, S. (1998). Angel Investors and the Market for Angel Investments. *Journal of Banking and Finance, 22*(6-8), 785–792.

Ralcheva, A., & Roosenboom, P. (2016). On the Road to Success in Equity Crowdfunding. Retrieved May 26, 2019, from https://ssrn.com/abstract=2727742.

Rossi, M. (2014). The New Ways to Raise Capital: An Exploratory Study of Crowdfunding. *International Journal of Financial Research, 5*(2), 8–18.

Sahlman, W. A. (1990). The Structure and Governance of Venture-capital Organizations. *Journal of Financial Economics, 27*(2), 473–521.

Schwienbacher, A. (2019). Equity Crowdfunding: Anything to Celebrate? *Venture Capital, 21*(1), 65–74.

Schwienbacher, A., & Larralde, B. (2012). Crowdfunding of Entrepreneurial Ventures. In D. Cumming (Ed.), *The Oxford Handbook of Entrepreneurial Finance* (pp. 369–391). Oxford, UK: Oxford University Press.

Shafi, K. (2019). Investors' Evaluation Criteria in Equity Crowdfunding. *Small Business Economics*, forthcoming.

Signori, A., & Vismara, S. (2018). Does Success Bring Success? The Post-offering Lives of Equity-Crowdfunded Firms. *Journal of Corporate Finance, 50*, 575–591.

Simon, H. A. (1991). Bounded Rationality and Organizational Learning. *Organization Science, 2*(1), 125–134.

Stevenson, R. M., Ciuchta, M. P., Letwin, C., Dinger, J. M., & Vancouver, J. B. (2019). Out of Control or Right on the Money? Funder Self-efficacy and Crowd Bias in Equity Crowdfunding. *Journal of Business Venturing, 34*(2), 348–367.

Streletzki, J.-G., & Schulte, R. (2013). Which Venture Capital Selection Criteria Distinguish High-flyer Investments? *Venture Capital, 15*(1), 29–52.

Sudek, R. (2006). Angel Investment Criteria. *Journal of Small Business Strategy, 17*(2), 89–103.

Sullivan, M. K., & Miller, A. (1996). Segmenting the Informal Venture Capital Market: Economic, Hedonistic, and Altruistic Investors. *Journal of Business Research, 36*(1), 25–35.

Szerb, L., Rappai, G., Makra, Z., & Terjesen, S. (2007). Informal Investment in Transition Economies: Individual Characteristics and Clusters. *Small Business Economics, 28*(2), 257–271.

Testa, S., Roed Nielsen, K., Bogers, M., & Cincotti, S. (2019). The Role of Crowdfunding in Moving Towards a Sustainable Society. *Technological Forecasting and Social Change, 141*, 66–73.

Tuomi, K., & Harrison, R. T. (2017). A Comparison of Equity Crowdfunding in Four Countries: Implications for Business Angels. *Strategic Change, 26*(6), 609–615.

Tyebjee, T. T., & Bruno, A. V. (1984). A Model of Venture Capitalist Investment Activity. *Management Science, 30*(9), 1051–1066.

Van Osnabrugge, M. (2000). A Comparison of Business Angel and Venture Capitalist Investment Procedures: An Agency Theory-based Analysis. *Venture Capital, 2*(2), 91–109.

Vismara, S. (2016). Equity Retention and Social Network Theory in Equity Crowdfunding. *Small Business Economics, 46*(4), 579–590.

Vismara, S. (2018). Information Cascades Among Investors in Equity Crowdfunding. *Entrepreneurship Theory and Practice, 42*(3), 467–497.

Vismara, S. (2019). Sustainability in Equity Crowdfunding. *Technological Forecasting and Social Change, 141*, 98–106.

Vismara, S., Benaroio, D., & Carne, F. (2017). Gender in Entrepreneurial Finance: Matching Investors and Entrepreneurs in Equity Crowdfunding. In A. N. Link (Ed.), *Gender and Entrepreneurial Activity* (pp. 271–288). Cheltenham: Edward Elgar.

Vulkan, N., Åstebro, T., & Sierra, M. F. (2016). Equity Crowdfunding: A New Phenomena. *Journal of Business Venturing Insights, 5*, 37–49.

Walthoff-Borm, X., Schwienbacher, A., & Vanacker, T. (2018). Equity Crowdfunding: First Resort or Last Resort? *Journal of Business Venturing, 33*(4), 513–533.

Wang, W., Mahmood, A., Sismeiro, C., & Vulkan, N. (2019). The Evolution of Equity Crowdfunding: Insights from Co-investments of Angels and the Crowd. *Research Policy, 48*(8), 103727.

White, B. A., & Dumay, J. (2017). Business Angels: A Research Review and New Agenda. *Venture Capital, 19*(3), 183–216.

Wilson, K. E., & Testoni, M. (2014). Improving the Role of Equity Crowdfunding in Europe's Capital Markets. Retrieved May 26, 2019, from http://ssrn.com/abstract=2502280.

Wiltbank, R. E. (2009). Siding with the Angels: Business Angel Investing – Promising Outcomes and Effective Strategies. London, UK: Nesta. Retrieved May 26, 2019, from https://www.effectuation.org/wp-content/uploads/2016/06/wiltbank-business-angel-investing-1.pdf.

Zhang, B., Ziegler, T., Mammadova, L., Johanson, D., Gray, M., & Yerolemou, N. (2018). *The 5th UK Alternative Finance Industry Report*. Cambridge, UK: Cambridge Center for Alternative Finance.

Ziegler, T., Johanson, D., King, M., Zhang, B., Mammadova, L., Ferri, F., et al. (2018a). *Reaching New Heights: The 3rd Americas Alternative Finance Industry Report*. Cambridge, UK: Cambridge Center for Alternative Finance.

Ziegler, T., Shneor, R., Garvey, K., Wenzlaff, K., Yerolemou, N., Hao, R., et al. (2018b). *Expanding Horizons: The 3rd European Alternative Finance Industry Report*. Cambridge, UK: Cambridge Center for Alternative Finance.

Ziegler, T., Suresh, K., Garvey, K., Rowan, P., Zhang, B., Obijiaku, A., et al.

(2018c). *The 2nd Annual Middle East & Africa Alternative Finance Industry Report*. Cambridge, UK: Cambridge Center for Alternative Finance.

Ziegler, T., Suresh, K., Johanson, D., Zhang, B., Shenglin, B., Luo, D., et al. (2018d). *The 3rd Asia Pacific Region Alternative Finance Industry Report*. Cambridge, UK: Cambridge Center for Alternative Finance.

Ziegler, T., Shneor, R., Wenzlaff, K., Odorović, A., Johanson, D., Hao, R., et al. (2019). *Shifting Paradigms: The 4th European Alternative Finance Benchmarking Report*. Cambridge, UK: Cambridge Center for Alternative Finance.

Zunino, D., van Praag, M., & Dushnitsky, G. (2017). *Badge of Honor or Scarlet Letter? Unpacking Investors' Judgment of Entrepreneurs' Past Failure*. Tinbergen Institute Discussion Paper; No. 2017-085/VII. Amsterdam, The Netherlands: Tinbergen Institute.

6

Exploring the Reward-Based Crowdfunding Model

Liang Zhao and Sunghan Ryu

Introduction

In the last decade, fundraising has dramatically changed by the emerging of crowdfunding (Mollick 2014). As an extension of crowdsourcing (Schwienbacher and Larralde 2012), crowdfunding is defined as "a collective effort by individuals who network and pool their money together, usually via the Internet, to invest in or support the efforts of others" (Ordanini et al. 2011). Via crowdfunding, individuals can contribute to different kinds of projects ranging from entrepreneurial to prosocial projects (Roma et al. 2017). Moreover, some have also suggested that as an

L. Zhao (✉)
School of Business and Law, University of Agder, Kristiansand, Norway
e-mail: liang.zhao@uia.no

S. Ryu
USC-SJTU Institute of Cultural and Creative Industry,
Shanghai Jiao Tong University, Shanghai, China
e-mail: shryu@sjtu.edu.cn

online fundraising method, in reward crowdfunding, the geographical barrier of traditional fundraising channels may be eliminated to a certain degree (Agrawal et al. 2015).

In this chapter, we focus on the reward-based crowdfunding model. Through reward-based crowdfunding supporters can provide funding to individuals, projects, or organizations in exchange for non-monetary rewards such as products or services, while accepting a certain degree of risk of non-delivery on campaign promises (Shneor and Munim 2019). Like other crowdfunding models, besides being a fundraising channel, reward-based crowdfunding can also work as a marketing tool (Brown et al. 2017) and a base of co-creation (Xu et al. 2016). Specifically, through the pre-ordering mechanism, entrepreneurs can boost their sales at the early stage market entry of new products. It can also be used to test the market potential of new products in order to diminish market uncertainty. Besides, entrepreneurs can improve products which may better match consumers' needs by engaging customers to take part in the developing process of new products (Messeni Petruzzelli et al. 2019).

The purpose of the current chapter is thus to review the fundamentals of reward-based crowdfunding, especially with respect to its potential influences on entrepreneurial financing and start-up incubation. Accordingly, we first discuss the definition, mechanisms, and unique aspects of reward-based crowdfunding. Next, the regional characteristics of reward-based crowdfunding development are presented. Then, through an extensive literature review, two main research streams of reward-based crowdfunding (success drivers and contributor behaviour) are summarized. Finally, this chapter highlights the implications for practice and research, as well as mentions potential contributions and limitations.

Definition, Mechanisms, and Unique Aspects

Reward-based crowdfunding can be considered as the most publicly familiar crowdfunding model, where backers contribute to projects without any monetary returns (Mollick 2014). Instead, they expect to receive material compensations (e.g. real products) as well as immaterial compensations (e.g. thank-you letter) in return of their contributions (Gerber et al. 2012).

The rewards commonly used in reward-based crowdfunding campaigns fall into three categories (Colombo et al. 2015; Thürridl and Kamleitner 2016): pre-orders, services, and recognition. Particularly, campaign creators offer their products in a pre-order mechanism through which backers have early access to the products. As part of the process, contributors also evaluate the products and may offer creators useful suggestion on how to make the products better at satisfying their needs. Recognition and services are examples of immaterial rewards. Recognition as a reward applies to the entry-level backers (backers contributing a small amount of money). Here, creators may write thank-you letters to such backers or display their names on the website in order to acknowledge their contribution. Creators may also provide special services, instead of physical products, as rewards for backers. Examples of these may include private performances and screenings, training and educational experiences, free usage of commercial services being developed, and so on.

Reward-based crowdfunding is a two-sided market (Tomczak and Brem 2013). Specifically, the supply side of the market consists of a group of backers who are willing to contribute to crowdfunding campaigns for achieving material or immaterial compensations. The demand side of the market consists of a group of campaign creators who design their campaigns in order to get projects they are developing funded. This two-sided market is in most cases operated through an online intermediary (crowdfunding platform) such as Kickstarter.

In this chapter, a framework (Fig. 6.1) is applied to explain the mechanism of reward-based crowdfunding. It consists of four essential elements (campaigns, creators, backers, and platforms) of the whole reward-based crowdfunding process (Ordanini et al. 2011). The three elements (creators, backers, and platforms) will be discussed separately at the different phases of the crowdfunding process namely—the preparation phase, the crowdfunding phase, and the outcome phase. Specifically, the preparation phase refers to the period before launching campaigns. The crowdfunding phase refers to the active fundraising period of campaigns, and

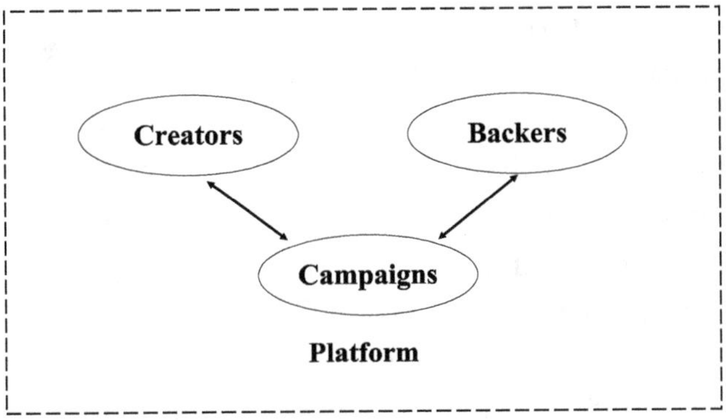

Fig. 6.1 The four-dimension framework of reward-based crowdfunding

the outcome phase refers to the consequences of crowdfunding campaigns, once they are closed and the fundraising period is over.

Campaigns

The process of decision-making and strategic thinking of the crowdfunding participants is mainly based on what is presented in the crowdfunding campaigns (Messeni Petruzzelli et al. 2019). Therefore, the campaign is the core of the framework. Here, project creators design their crowdfunding campaigns following guidelines of crowdfunding platforms and other sources of advice, often stressing the importance of information disclosure for crowdfunding success.

First, project creators need to set up the funding targets of their campaigns, as covering all related costs for fulfilling the projects' objectives. Here, funding "targets" mean the amount of money they aim to collect through the crowdfunding process. Next, in order to present their projects to the potential backers, project creators are required to describe their projects in comprehensive ways by providing adequate and truthful information in the forms of texts, images, and/or videos (Ahlers et al. 2015). The provided information relates to the project and its rewards, the background of the creator(s) and the perceived risks of surrounding the future project execution process. In addition, the rewards also play vital roles. Before launching their projects, project creators need to design their own reward schemes. In the reward schemes, creators are required to clarify the benefits to the backers based on the different levels of contributions. Usually, a reward scheme should include several reward tiers with different prices associated with each. These often come in the forms of different number of units of the products, different versions of same products, opportunities for creative collaborations of various kinds, creative experiences and creative mementoes depending on different contribution levels (Kuppuswamy and Bayus 2017).

As the campaigns are designed and officially launched online, backers should find out which campaigns are worth contributing to and how much to contribute based on the provided information. In the meanwhile, crowdfunding platforms provide the technical infrastructure for information presentation, payment facilitation, and interaction around campaigns in order to facilitate a smooth crowdfunding process.

Creators

Creators are individuals or organizations with a project that requires funding, are the source of information about the project, and are responsible for delivering on the campaign promises once the campaign is finished.

Preparation Phase: Before launching campaigns, creators should clearly define their business idea by answering the following questions: what the final product/service is, what the overall scope is, what the overall vision is, and what the final target is. Once all the answers to the above are known, creators can start to design their campaigns. Designing a crowdfunding campaign must follow according to the requirements of the crowdfunding platform and will often include multiple media elements and a textual description answering critical issues about the concept, the people behind it, and the project execution plan. Information related to legal issues, launch date, and duration should be taken into consideration when designing crowdfunding campaigns (Mollick 2014).

Crowdfunding Phase: Once the business idea is determined and the campaign is designed, the crowdfunding phase starts when a campaign is officially launched online. The campaign ends at the stated end date of the campaign's fundraising duration. From the creator's perspective, the crowdfunding phase is critical as it is closely related to the crowdfunding efforts' results. Therefore, creators should spend time and effort to establish and maintain the relationship with potential backers and niche groups in order to promote the awareness about their campaigns. In addition, to facilitate fundraising, creators should also provide extra information related to the campaigns through interaction with backers, social media promotional efforts, sharing of updates, and campaign improvements.

Outcome Phase: The outcome phase starts when the crowdfunding phase is finished. For platforms adopting the "all-or-nothing" mechanism, the entire amount of the fundraising will only be transferred to the creator if the campaign is successful (the final fundraising amount is equal or exceeds the fundraising target). A commission fee should be deducted from the total collected amount by the platform before funds are transferred to the creator. Alternatively, for platforms using the "keep-it-all" mechanism, the sum of contributions raised will be transferred to creators (after deducting the commission fee for platform services) irrespective of whether the campaigns' fundraising targets have been achieved or not. Regardless of fundraising model, creators have the responsibilities to execute the projects and deliver the promised rewards within the timeframe stated in the campaign, after they receive the funds raised.

Backers

Backers are individuals or organizations who provide financial contributions for the crowdfunding campaign in return for a promised reward.

Preparation Phase: Before contributing to crowdfunding campaigns, backers should be familiarized with the concept of reward-based crowdfunding and make sure they understand how it works, as week as its related risks and benefits.

Crowdfunding Phase: During the crowdfunding phase, backers should decide whether and how much to contribute to a campaign based on their evaluation of the provided campaign information and the perceived risk level of the campaign. In addition, backers may also be interested in acting as co-creators of the supported campaigns (Mollick 2014). They may interact with campaign creators by asking campaign-related questions on the crowdfunding platform or by writing comments concerning campaign updates in order to help the creators improve their products/services (Steigenberger 2017). In addition, with the embedding of social media, backers can easily spread campaign information and make their favourite campaigns go viral through their online social networking as social media exposure is positively associated with campaign success (Gerber et al. 2012). Indeed, research by Shneor and Munim (2019) has shown that both information-sharing intention and financial contribution intentions lead to actual financial contribution behaviour.

Outcome Phase: For campaigns run on platforms using the "all-or-nothing" mechanism, backers can only receive their rewards if a campaign is successful (the final fundraising amount equalizes or exceeds the fundraising target). However, if a campaign is failed, the contributions will be refunded to the backers. In terms of the "keep-it-all" platforms, backers will receive their rewards, regardless of the outcome of a campaign. Nevertheless, in most cases, backers don't receive rewards immediately but within pre-stated periods of time required for completing product development, manufacturing, and shipment.

Platforms

Paraphrasing Shneor and Flåten's (2015) definition of crowdfunding platforms into the reward crowdfunding context, a reward crowdfunding platform can be defined as an internet application bringing together project creators and their potential backers, as well as facilitating exchanges between them according to the reward crowdfunding conventions presented earlier.

Preparation Phase: In the preparation phase, as information intermediaries, platforms should host educational sessions about crowdfunding to the public in order to introduce crowdfunding to the general public. Such efforts are likely to help support the development of a crowdfunding community, which may consist of future backers and creators. In terms of backers, contributing to crowdfunding campaigns might be risky. As a novel fundraising channel, crowdfunding is tangled with market uncertainty and information asymmetry (Roma et al. 2017). To decrease perceived risks, crowdfunding platforms should set up an extensive campaign review process to verify whether a campaign has satisfied the basic requirements for launching online in terms of information disclosure and fundraiser identity verifications. In that way, platforms may ensure avoiding the publication of illegal and immoral campaigns, such as campaigns related to fraudulent activities, money laundering, criminal, and terrorist funding. For creators, platforms should give suggestions on defining, developing, and presenting creators' business ideas, as well as guide them in designing attractive crowdfunding campaigns. Besides, all fees related to the campaign process should also be disclosed to creators in advance for proper campaign budget planning.

Crowdfunding Phase: During the crowdfunding phase, crowdfunding platforms may help creators and backers to exchange information through different channels. For example, platforms are encouraged to integrate instant messaging tools, third-party social network websites and microblog links on campaigns' webpages to facilitate extensive interaction between creators and backers (Zheng et al. 2014). In addition, platforms can also support the promotion of campaigns through online marketing. Platforms may also selectively promote certain campaigns as part of "staff picks" recommendations, or in direct promotions to special interest groups among their users. Lastly, legal and ethical compliance should also be taken into consideration in the crowdfunding phase. Platforms should apply identity verification of backers to ensure ethical contributing practices.

Outcome Phase: In the final phase, depending on the different mechanisms ("all-or-nothing" or "keep-it-all"), platforms will transfer the total fundraising to the creators after deducting the commission fee for their services. Creators have the obligations to complete their projects and fulfil rewards once the money is received. However, given the uncertainty underlying the post-crowdfunding process, reward-based crowdfunding platforms may warn backers if they notice that some projects may not go as planned. For example, some campaigns may suffer from delivery delays or no delivery (Mollick 2014). However, platforms do not carry legal precautions about such problems as it is backers' responsibilities to understand the risks and their consumer rights by law before participating in crowdfunding activities. Nevertheless, a platform's long-term survival depends on the positive experience of users, and its engagement in follow-up on campaign promise delivery is linked to its own interest in long term success. In such cases, platforms may follow up on creators to ensure they meet their obligations. In addition, possible refunds or alternative options to complete the projects may also be offered to the backers. Finally, the platform should maintain relations with new users brought by with the campaign and continue informing them about future campaigns that they may find interesting, based on them opting to receive such information.

Regional Variances

Reward-based crowdfunding as a global phenomenon may not operate in the same way in different regions. Because some factors such as financial infrastructures, regulatory environments, and technological advancements may vary by region. Hence, consideration and discussion at the regional level is also warranted. In this section, we report the situation in different regions around the world in order to provide a better understanding of reward-based crowdfunding from a global perspective by taking regional features into consideration.

China

According to the 3rd Asia Pacific Region Alternative Finance Industry Report (Ziegler et al. 2018b), reward-based crowdfunding is a popular crowdfunding model in China in terms of the number of participants. Although reward-based crowdfunding works similar all over the world, there are still some special features in the Chinese reward-based crowdfunding market. Generally, reward-based crowdfunding market in China is still growing. However, the number of reward-based crowdfunding platforms in China is decreasing. It means the reward-based crowdfunding market in China is highly concentrated. For instance, the fundraising of several large reward-based platforms (e.g. JD, Taobao) account for approximately 90% of the total market fundraising volume. Almost all the reward-based crowdfunding platforms in China operate domestically. Most platforms do not have global websites and global brands. Reward-based crowdfunding platforms in China usually do not accept contributions out of China. Therefore, cross-border inflows and outflows in Chinese reward-based crowdfunding market are rare. Defaults, regulatory changes, and fraud are perceived as the main obstacles of reward-based crowdfunding development in China.

Asia-Pacific (APAC)

According to the same report (Ziegler et al. 2018b), the reward-based crowdfunding market is still growing in Asia-Pacific (APAC) areas (excluding China). Here, 96% of reward-based crowdfunding platforms place "media and promotion" as their key focus of R&D. Approximately 81% of all the reward-based crowdfunding platforms in APAC (excluding China) have been actively pursuing customer verification, payment processing, and e-learning. Around 69% of the reward-based crowdfunding platforms have pursued R&D into "community management". However, only 29% of the reward-based crowdfunding platforms in APAC refer gamification as their key R&D focus and for customer relationship management (CRM) the rate is 36%. With respect to female participation in the APAC region, 18% of all the reward-based crowdfunding fundraisers (e.g. campaign creators) are female, and female backers accounted for 27% of the total backers. Some 17% of the backers in APAC have supported campaigns abroad. Approximately 15% of reward-based platforms in the region are having both a global website and a global brand, but only 1% of the total fundraising of reward-based crowdfunding is contributed by backers out of APAC. Fraud and cybersecurity breach are perceived as the main risks of reward-based crowdfunding in the APAC area.

UK

According to the 5th UK Alternative Finance Industry Report (Zhang et al. 2018), reward-based crowdfunding is experiencing a decline in volume in the UK, which is likely related to the result of 63% of reward-based platforms reported slightly alternating their business model in 2017. Specifically, 14% of the operating costs of crowdfunding platforms account for the R&D mostly invested towards customer support tools for social media promotions. Moreover, approximately 75% of all the reward-based crowdfunding platforms in the UK choose to invest in e-learning, customer verification and payment processing as their R&D focuses. Half of the reward-based platforms in the UK have also pursued R&D into artificial intelligence, community management and performance enhancement features. In terms of female participation, in the UK, 56% of all the reward-based crowdfunding fundraisers are female and female backers accounted for 38% of total backers. Reward-based crowdfunding is the most international crowdfunding model in the UK with approximately 75% of platforms having both global websites and global brands and with approximately half of the inflow transactions made cross-border. In terms of risks, concerns about possible collapse of a platform due to malpractice is perceived as the main risk of reward-based crowdfunding industry in the UK.

Middle East and Africa

According to the 2nd Annual Middle East and Africa Alternative Finance Industry Report (Ziegler et al. 2018c), non-financial crowdfunding models (reward-based crowdfunding and donation-based crowdfunding) account for the majority proportion of the alternative finance market in the Middle East and Africa (MEA) region. It is the key feature distinguishing the alternative finance market in the MEA region from other alternative finance markets. Due to the low economic and infrastructural development level, all the reward-based crowdfunding activities in the Middle East and Africa areas remain domestic activities with no cross-border transactions, internationalization and R&D investment. In terms of female participation, 27% of the reward-based crowdfunding fundraisers are female and female backers account for 33% of the total backers. Reward-based crowdfunding development in the Middle East and Africa are exposed to various risks. For instance, fraud is perceived as the most serious risk in African reward-based crowdfunding market followed by collapse due to malpractice, defaults and changes to regulation. In the Middle East areas, defaults are placed as the greatest risk followed by changes to regulation, collapse due to malpractice and fraud.

Europe

According to the 4th Annual European Alternative Finance Report (Ziegler et al. 2019), 67% of reward-based crowdfunding platforms have placed community management as the key focus of R&D investment in European areas. This is closely followed by 66% of platforms that have pursued R&D into social media and promotional tools. Customer Relationship Management (CRM) is chosen by 48% of the reward-based platforms as their main R&D focus and process streamlining have been chosen as priority R&D focus by 37% of the European reward-based crowdfunding platforms. Referring to female participation, 49% of the reward-based crowdfunding fundraisers are female and female backers accounted for 54% of the total backers. About 27% of reward-based crowdfunding platforms in Europe only focus on the local markets with no global websites and brands. However, 58% of reward-based crowdfunding platforms have both global websites and global brands. About 6% of reward-based crowdfunding platforms in Europe choose to utilize a global brand name but localize the websites and contents for certain markets. Compared to other crowdfunding models in Europe, reward-based crowdfunding model has the lowest level of cross-border funding flows. Specifically, cross-border funding outflows account for 9% of the total market volume and 21% of the transactions are made by cross-border funding inflows. Finally, in terms of risks, cyber-security breach is perceived as the most significant risk factor followed by changes to regulation and campaign fraud in the European reward-based crowdfunding market.

The Americas

According to the 3rd Americas Alternative Finance Industry Report (Ziegler et al. 2018a), reward-based crowdfunding reported a decline in 2017 in the US and Canada. However, in Latin American and Caribbean (LAC) areas, reward-based crowdfunding has continued to grow with newly established alternative finance ecosystems. Regarding R&D, 88% of reward-based crowdfunding platforms in the Americas have emphasized customer support tools for social media promotion as their priority R&D focus. Some 63% of the platforms mention payment processing and e-learning as two important R&D focuses. Furthermore, half of the platforms have pursued R&D into community management features. In terms of internationalization, 80% of reward-based crowdfunding platforms in the US have both global websites and global brands. In the LAC areas, the rate is 87%. For cross-border inflow and outflow, 11% of transactions were associated with cross-border inflows, and 18% of transaction were associated with cross-border outflows in the US reward-based crowdfunding market in 2017. Regarding female participation, 50% of the reward-based crowdfunding fundraisers are female and female backers account for 32% of the total backers. Specifically, in the US, 47% and 53% of fundraisers and funders are female respectively. In the LAC area, 47% and 56% of fundraisers and funders are female respectively. In the reward-based crowdfunding market of the Americas, cybersecurity breach is perceived as the most significant risk factor followed by collapse due to malpractice and campaign fraud.

Literature Review

After presenting the stakeholders and the current status of reward-based crowdfunding globally, in the followings section we review the literature on reward crowdfunding in different disciplines, including management, entrepreneurship, and information systems. Based on database searches employing the terms "crowdfunding" and "reward-based" as the keywords, we collected and analysed 30 studies published in influential journals in each discipline. Based on the analysis, we identified two main research streams: (1) success drivers of crowdfunding campaigns and (2) factors affecting individual contributors' behaviour.

Success Drivers

A strand of literature on reward crowdfunding highlights factors critical for determining the success of a crowdfunding project. First, a stream of research found that effective dissemination of information regarding the project and creator via the crowdfunding platform is important to crowdfunding success (Mollick 2014). Information on project quality (e.g. a competition-winning business plan) and social information (e.g. other potential contributors' willingness to invest) serve as effective cues for potential contributors (Ciuchta et al. 2016). In relation to this, the characteristics of the creators play a significant role in attracting and retaining the attention of contributors and thereby in determining a campaign's success. For example, creators' social information and educational backgrounds have all been shown to affect the success of a campaign (Mollick 2014). Similarly, Boeuf et al. (2014) found that disclosure of personal information about project creators has positive influence on crowdfunding success because it helps obtain a higher level of trust from potential contributors. In the same vein, Frydrych et al. (2014) argue that information on the creator adds legitimacy to the project, attracting more contributors as a result. Ryu and Kim (2018) found that reward value and societal contribution of a campaign are influential campaign characteristics affecting crowdfunding success.

Second, information on project progress posted on the project page is another influential factor. Investor participation in early project stages is essential for signalling project quality and subsequently attracting more investors (Agrawal et al. 2015; Burtch et al. 2013; Colombo et al. 2015). The success of a campaign is fully mediated by the funds collected in the campaign's early days (Colombo et al. 2015). Kim and Viswanathan (2019) showed that information about early contributors with expertise has a distinct influence on later investors. Regarding communication between the creators and their contributors, Antonenko et al. (2014)

pointed out that intensive communication, such as reacting promptly to questions and providing frequent status updates, positively influences crowdfunding success.

Third, it has been found that different types of creator and contributor networks act as key influencers of crowdfunding success. For example, based on the social capital theory, Zheng et al. (2014) examined how project creators' social network ties, experience in funding other projects, and the shared meaning between creators and investors impact crowdfunding success. Particularly, internal social capital developed inside a crowdfunding community contributes significantly towards triggering "a self-reinforcing mechanism" of a crowdfunding project (Colombo et al. 2015). Social capital accumulated from the contributors' social networking site (SNS) is also positively associated with the success of the project (Kang et al. 2017).

Finally, campaign attributes are important. Belleflamme et al. (2014) find that the types of campaigns that are part of non-profit organizations are more successful than those of other organizational forms. Several design components, such as duration, goal, and inclusion of a video on a campaign site, are all associated with success (Mollick 2014). More specifically, Mollick (2014) argues that potential contributors are more likely to select realistic funding goals, as campaign goals that are too high or too low are not likely to lead to a successful campaign. Relatedly, Zhao and Vinig (2017) found that the application of lottery as a reward for a crowdfunding campaign has a positive influence on crowdfunding success. Linguistic styles and texts used in campaign descriptions also influence the success of crowdfunding campaigns (Parhankangas and Renko 2017; Allison et al. 2017). Linguistic styles that make a campaign more understandable and relatable to potential contributors enhance the success of social campaigns but hardly matter for commercial campaigns (Parhankangas and Renko 2017). Relatedly, based on the Elaboration Likelihood Model, Allison et al. (2017) found logically persuasive messages (cognitive) and emotionally persuasive cues (affective) influence crowdfunding campaign success.

Contributor Behaviour

A second stream of research on reward crowdfunding has documented various factors affecting contributors' behaviour. First, some studies show that different social influences drive the demand for crowdfunding. For example, Skirnevskiy et al. (2017) identified the significant role of peer effects in crowdfunding. The physical distance between creators and contributors are also found to have significant effects on contributor behaviours (Agrawal et al. 2015; Kang et al. 2017). Local contributors are more likely to pledge at the early stages of the funding period than distant contributors, and they are less sensitive to peer effects. They are also less sensitive to information about the cumulative amount of funding (Lin and Viswanathan 2015). In similar vein, contributors are more likely to contribute to "culturally similar and geographically proximate" creators' projects (Burtch et al. 2014). Relatedly, recognizing the importance of contributions at the early stages, a small set of studies has attempted to show why and who are more likely to make earlier contributions. For example, Kuppuswamy and Bayus (2017) showed the importance of goal proximity in explaining fund timing. Specifically, they found that people are more likely to contribute when a project approaches its funding goal, where they can make an impact on the ultimate success of fundraising, than when the funding goal has been reached. Also, research shows that contributors who are experts (Kim and Viswanathan 2019) or local (Kang et al. 2017; Agrawal et al. 2015; Giudici et al. 2018) tend to participate in crowdfunding earlier.

Second, beyond social influence, some research has investigated how the available information or format of crowdfunding affect funders' decisions. For example, Davis et al. (2017) found that contributors' decision to pledge is positively influenced by perceived product creativity and the influence of perceived product creativity is promoted when contributors perceive the creator as passionate. From the perspective of platform design, permission to control the disclosure of funding information was found to increase the number of contributions and simultaneously to decrease the amount of each contribution (Burtch et al. 2015).

Finally, an additional group of studies focused on psychosocial factors such as individual contributors' motivation. For example, Zheng et al. (2018) examined the positive effects of contributors' psychological ownership towards a campaign on their decision to contribute. Contributors also engage in crowdfunding campaigns with different intentions (Gerber et al. 2012). Contributors often seek rewards from the campaigns, in the form of tangible products or intangible rewards. Contributors would also support creators and their campaigns for upholding values. Some contributors may join crowdfunding to engage in a community where they are willing to be a part of. Shneor and Munim (2019) apply the "theory of planned behaviour" (TPB) for addressing the relationship between contribution intentions, behaviour, and their antecedents. They found that both financial contribution intentions and information-sharing intentions are positively related to actual contribution behaviour. Relatedly, Ryu and Kim (2016), with surveys and matched transaction data from platforms, identified four types of contributors based on their motivations to participate in crowdfunding. The four types of contributors are angelic backers, reward hunters, avid fans, and tasteful hermits. Angelic backers are similar in many aspects to charitable donors while reward hunters are similar to traditional investors. Avid fans are the most enthusiastic contributor group and similar to members of a brand community. Tasteful hermits fully support the crowdfunding campaigns but are less concerned with relational aspects of crowdfunding behaviour.

Implications

Implications for Research

Given the differences between reward-based crowdfunding and traditional funding channels, the drivers of crowdfunding campaign success, and the factors impacting individual contribution behaviour have both been extensively examined in the crowdfunding literature. The literature supports the view that reward-based crowdfunding possesses both common aspects as a funding channel and distinguished aspects as a new type of channel. That is, reward-based crowdfunding can be considered as a riskier form of online commerce, where people pre-order products before the products are fully developed and produced, while accepting a degree of risk of non-delivery or deviations from campaign promises. Reward-based crowdfunding is similar in some respects to the traditional funding sources in that potential contributors make a decision based on information they are exposed to and/or collect. This is important because creators in the reward-based crowdfunding context are still expected to present their resources and capabilities to potential contributors. The differences are that they may leverage different types of information. Social information and progress of a campaign may be more critical factors in the context of reward crowdfunding.

Although previous literature found some implicative mechanisms of reward-based crowdfunding, the current body of literature has several limitations, which indicate our future research directions. First of all, while the literature validated the factors influencing campaign success and individual contributors' behaviours, detailed theoretical mechanism of how a specific factor affects the campaign performance or contributor behaviour has not been well addressed. Future research can find more theoretical evidence for the findings so far, or develop new theories explaining the underlying dynamics in the specific context of reward-based crowdfunding.

Second, the main research streams on reward-based crowdfunding have focused on explicit factors related to creators and their projects as affecting the success of a crowdfunding campaign, but less attention has been paid to the motivation of players on both sides. Creators and contributors join crowdfunding for different motivations (Gerber et al. 2012; Ryu and Kim 2016, 2018). As discussed, a few pioneering studies dealt with motivations in the reward-based crowdfunding context, but the literature has not established how those motivations interact with other factors, such as campaign characteristics. To fill this gap, future research can delve deep into how different motivations interrelate with crowdfunding success and contributor behaviours. Specifically, because motivations are psychological factors, examining how motivations interact with other attributes such as demographics, campaign, or platform characteristics could be an important consideration.

Third, in consideration of the risks embedded in the context of reward-based crowdfunding, researchers are expected to deal with these risk factors. Reward-based crowdfunding is not free from drawbacks such as delays in fulfilment and potential fraud (Mollick 2014). Future research could identify that specific types of campaigns may be more prone to certain risks, compared to other campaigns. More importantly, examining the effectiveness of the current coping mechanisms of reward-based crowdfunding in mitigating such risks could be a promising research domain.

Finally, the extant literature on crowdfunding has myopically focused on the success of campaigns "inside" crowdfunding platforms. Recently, the perspective is expanding to post-campaign phenomena by examining the effects of crowdfunding success on follow-on performance of start-ups (Roma et al. 2017). Nevertheless, we still know little about how crowdfunding can influence entrepreneurial organizations' long-term performance and thus survival. Regarding this gap between the findings from previous literature and expected role of crowdfunding in longer term, future research can identify how crowdfunding affects subsequent performance.

Implications for Practice

The current body of literature on reward-based crowdfunding also provides practical implications, especially into the launch of crowdfunding campaigns and the management of platforms. For potential creators, the literature provides some guidance. Most of all, different aspects of information quality and effective communication of that information are critical for a reward-based crowdfunding campaign. A strand of research identified specific attribute or characteristics of campaigns and their creators that boost individual contributors' behaviour and thus crowdfunding success. Those results can provide practical aid in this regard. More importantly, in addition to polishing the campaign itself, understanding the social aspects of reward-based crowdfunding is critical to reaching the goal amount. Creators must understand the importance of earlier pledges and momentum throughout the campaign process. They are expected to develop a strategy to collect a group of earlier contributors according to the nature of the campaign. Strong social capital of a creator from inside and outside of the crowdfunding platform should help the creator initiate this momentum towards crowdfunding success.

For platform operators, the current literature provides implications related to building up a sustainable platform. Platform operators should not only try to expand their platforms but also understand the existence of different types of creators and contributors on their platforms. Based on this understanding, they can offer the most suitable benefits based on their distinct characteristics. For example, social campaigns and commercial campaigns may draw different types of (potential) contributors and thus need different formulas for crowdfunding success. If they can provide more customized guidance for novice creators, their platforms can enjoy higher rates of crowdfunding success and thus enhance their sustainability. Finally, in order to build up sustainable platforms, they are required to understand the combinative characteristics of reward-based crowdfunding, providing both commercial and communal values to both creators and contributors (Ryu and Kim 2018).

Conclusion

As an innovative entrepreneurial fundraising channel, crowdfunding has gained increasing popularity in the last few years (Mollick 2014). Specifically, reward-based crowdfunding, the best-known crowdfunding model, has attracted increasing attention from the public. It has offered feasible opportunities for entrepreneurs to test new business ideas, conduct market research, and access early-stage financing. Despite the growing popularity of reward-based crowdfunding research, as well as the increasing relevance of employing reward-based crowdfunding for entrepreneurial financing, relatively little literature has systematically investigated it as a unique phenomenon separated from other crowdfunding models.

To mitigate this gap, we have highlighted the reward-based crowdfunding model and the unique aspects of it. In this chapter, we have comprehensively discussed the reward-based crowdfunding phenomenon based on a four-dimension framework which includes the main players engaged in the crowdfunding process: the creators, the backers, the campaigns, and the platforms. In addition, an evidence-based introduction to the reward-based crowdfunding development across different regions is also provided. We have highlighted the regional variances by including the facts of developing trends, R&D priority, female participation, internationalization, cross-border transaction and risk in different reward-based crowdfunding markets. A literature review of the academic research on reward-based crowdfunding was also provided in this chapter by focusing on two main research aspects: success drivers and consumer behaviour. Based on the findings of the literature review, the practical and theoretical implications of what we know about reward-based crowdfunding were discussed.

References

Agrawal, A., Catalini, C., & Goldfarb, A. (2015). Crowdfunding: Geography, Social Networks, and the Timing of Investment Decisions. *Journal of Economics & Management Strategy, 24*(2), 253–274.

Ahlers, G. K. C., Cumming, D., Günther, C., & Schweizer, D. (2015). Signalling in Equity Crowdfunding. *Entrepreneurship Theory and Practice, 39*(4), 955–980.

Allison, T. H., Davis, B. C., Webb, J. W., & Short, J. C. (2017). Persuasion in Crowdfunding: An Elaboration Likelihood Model of Crowdfunding Performance. *Journal of Business Venturing, 39*(1), 53–73.

Antonenko, P. D., Lee, B. R., & Kleinheksel, A. J. (2014). Trends in the Crowdfunding of Educational Technology Startups. *TechTrends, 58*(6), 36–41.

Belleflamme, P., Lambert, T., & Schwienbacher, A. (2014). Crowdfunding: Tapping the Right Crowd. *Journal of Business Venturing, 29*(5), 585–609.

Boeuf, B., Darveau, J., & Legoux, R. (2014). Financing Creativity: Crowdfunding as a New Approach for Theatre Projects. *International Journal of Arts Management, 16*(3), 33–48.

Brown, T. E., Boon, E., & Pitt, L. F. (2017). Seeking Funding in Order to Sell: Crowdfunding as a Marketing Tool. *Business Horizons, 60(2), 189–195.*

Burtch, G., Ghose, A., & Wattal, S. (2013). An Empirical Examination of the Antecedents and Consequences of Contribution Patterns in Crowd-Funded Markets. *Information Systems Research, 24*(3), 499–519.

Burtch, G., Ghose, A., & Wattal, S. (2014). Cultural Differences and Geography as Determinants of Online Prosocial Lending. *MIS Quarterly, 38*(3), 773–794.

Burtch, G., Ghose, A., & Wattal, S. (2015). The Hidden Cost of Accommodating Crowdfunder Privacy Preferences: A Randomized Field Experiment. *Management Science, 61*(5), 949–962.

Ciuchta, M. P., Letwin, C., Stevenson, R. M., & McMahon, S. R. (2016). Regulatory Focus and Information Cues in a Crowdfunding Context. *Journal of Applied Psychology, 65*(3), 490–514.

Colombo, M. G., Franzoni, C., & Rossi-Lamastra, C. (2015). Internal Social Capital and the Attraction of Early Contributions in Crowdfunding. *Entrepreneurship Theory and Practice, 39*(1), 75–100.

Davis, B. C., Hmieleski, K. M., Webb, J. W., & Coombs, J. E. (2017). Funders' Positive Affective Reactions to Entrepreneurs' Crowdfunding Pitches: The Influence of Perceived Product Creativity and Entrepreneurial Passion. *Journal of Business Venturing, 32*(1), 90–106.

Frydrych, D., Bock, A. J., Kinder, T., & Koeck, B. (2014). Exploring Entrepreneurial Legitimacy in Reward-based Crowdfunding. *Venture Capital, 16*(3), 247–269.

Gerber, E. M., Hui, J. S., & Kuo, P. (2012). *Crowdfunding: Why People Are Motivated to Post and Fund Projects on Crowdfunding Platforms*. Paper presented at the International Workshop on Design, Influence, and Social Technologies: Techniques, Impacts and Ethics.

Giudici, G., Guerini, M., & Rossi-Lamastra, C. (2018). Reward-based Crowdfunding of Entrepreneurial Projects: The Effect of Local Altruism and Localized Social Capital on Proponents' Success. *Small Business Economics, 50*(2), 307–324.

Kang, L., Jiang, W., & Tan, C.-H. (2017). Remarkable Advocates: An Investigation of Geographic Distance and Social Capital for Crowdfunding. *Information & Management, 54*(3), 336–348.

Kim, K., & Viswanathan, S. (2019). The 'Experts' in the Crowd: The Role of Experienced Investors in a Crowdfunding Market. *MIS Quarterly, 43*(2), 347–372.

Kuppuswamy, V., & Bayus, B. L. (2017). Does My Contribution to Your Crowdfunding Project Matter? *Journal of Business Venturing, 32*(1), 72–89.

Lin, M., & Viswanathan, S. (2015). Home Bias in Online Investments: An Empirical Study of an Online Crowdfunding Market. *Management Science, 62*(5), 1393–1414.

Messeni Petruzzelli, A., Natalicchio, A., Panniello, U., & Roma, P. (2019). Understanding the Crowdfunding Phenomenon and Its Implications for Sustainability. *Technological Forecasting and Social Change, 141*, 138–148.

Mollick, E. (2014). The Dynamics of Crowdfunding: An Exploratory Study. *Journal of Business Venturing, 29*(1), 1–16.

Ordanini, A., Miceli, L., Pizzetti, M., & Parasuraman, A. (2011). Crowdfunding: Transforming Customers into Investors Through Innovative Service Platforms. *Journal of Service Management, 22*(4), 443–470.

Parhankangas, A., & Renko, M. (2017). Linguistic Style and Crowdfunding Success Among Social and Commercial Entrepreneurs. *Journal of Business Venturing, 32*(2), 215–236.

Roma, P., Petruzzelli, A. M., & Perrone, G. (2017). From the Crowd to the Market: The Role of Reward-based Crowdfunding Performance in Attracting Professional Investors. *Research Policy, 46*(9), 1606–1628.

Ryu, S., & Kim, Y.-G. (2016). A Typology of Crowdfunding Sponsors: Birds of a Feather Flock Together? *Electronic Commerce Research and Applications, 16*, 43–54.

Ryu, S., & Kim, Y.-G. (2018). Money Is Not Everything: A Typology of Crowdfunding Project Creators. *Journal of Strategic Information Systems, 27*(4), 350–368.

Schwienbacher, A., & Larralde, B. (2012). Alternative Types of Entrepreneurial Finance. In *The Oxford Handbook of Entrepreneurial Finance*. New York, NY: Oxford University Press.

Shneor, R., & Flåten, B.-T. (2015). Opportunities for Entrepreneurial Development and Growth through Online Communities, Collaboration, and Value Creating and Co-Creating Activities. In H. R. Kaufmann & S. M. R. Shams (Eds.), *Entrepreneurial Challenges in the 21st Century* (pp. 178–199). Basingstoke: Palgrave Macmillan.

Shneor, R., & Munim, Z. H. (2019). Reward Crowdfunding Contribution as Planned Behaviour: An Extended Framework. *Journal of Business Research, 103*, 56–70.

Skirnevskiy, V., Bendig, D., & Brettel, M. (2017). The Influence of Internal Social Capital on Serial Creators' Success in Crowdfunding. *Entrepreneurship Theory & Practice, 41*(2), 209–236.

Steigenberger, N. (2017). Why Supporters Contribute to Reward-Based Crowdfunding. *International Journal of Entrepreneurial Behaviour & Research, 23*(2), 336–353.

Thürridl, C., & Kamleitner, B. (2016). What Goes Around Comes Around? Rewards as Strategic Assets in Crowdfunding. *California Management Review, 58*(2), 88–110.

Tomczak, A., & Brem, A. (2013). A Conceptualized Investment Model of Crowdfunding. *Venture Capital, 15*(4), 335–359.

Xu, B., Zheng, H., Xu, Y., & Wang, T. (2016). Configurational Paths to Sponsor Satisfaction in Crowdfunding. *Journal of Business Research, 69(2), 915–927.*

Zhang, B., Ziegler, T., Mammadova, L., Johanson, D., Gray, M., & Yerolemou, N. (2018). *The 5th UK Alternative Finance Industry Report.* Cambridge: The Cambridge Centre for Alternative Finance.

Zhao, L., & Vinig, T. (2017). Hedonic Value and Crowdfunding Project Performance: A Propensity Score Matching-based Analysis. *Review of Behavioral Finance, 9*(2), 169–186.

Zheng, H., Li, D., Wu, J., & Xu, Y. (2014). The Role of Multidimensional Social Capital in Crowdfunding: A Comparative Study in China And US. *Information & Management, 51*(4), 488–496.

Zheng, H., Xu, B., Zhang, M., & Wang, T. (2018). Sponsor's Cocreation and Psychological Ownership in Reward-based Crowdfunding. *Information Systems Journal, 28*(6), 1213–1238.

Ziegler, T., Johanson, D., King, M., Zhang, B., Mammadova, L., Ferri, F., Trappe, R., et al. (2018a). *Reaching New Heights: The 3rd Americas Alternative Finance Industry Report.* Cambridge: The Cambridge Centre for Alternative Finance.

Ziegler, T., Johanson, D., Zhang, B., Ben, S., Wang, W., Mammadova, L., Hao, R., et al. (2018b). *The 3rd Asia Pacific Region Alternative Finance Industry Report.* Cambridge: The Cambridge Centre for Alternative Finance.

Ziegler, T., Suresh, K., Garvey, K., Rowan, P., Zhang, B., Obijiaku, A., Hao, R., & Alqahtani, F. (2018c). *The 2nd Annual Middle East and Africa Alternative Finance Industry Report.* Cambridge: The Cambridge Centre for Alternative Finance.

Ziegler, T., Shneor, R., Wenzlaff, K., Odorović, A., Johanson, D., Hao, R., & Ryll, L. (2019). *Shifting Paradigms: The 4th Annual European Alternative Finance Report.* Cambridge: The Cambridge Centre for Alternative Finance.

7

Donation-Based Crowdfunding: Core Features and Donor Behaviour

Liang Zhao and Rotem Shneor

Introduction

Crowdfunding, as an innovative fundraising channel, aims to exploit the power of the crowd for supporting various kinds of projects which may not easily get funded through traditional ways of fundraising (Lambert and Schwienbacher 2010). In the realm of donation funding, crowdfunding has simplified the process of fundraising for prosocial purposes by integrating information collection, donation transaction, and interactive communication into one standardized process (Belleflamme et al. 2013). This has led some to claim that donation-based crowdfunding has redefined the way of charitable giving is done, as it fuses traditional charitable giving and IT-enabled crowdfunding together (Gleasure and Feller 2016).

Compared with traditional charitable fundraising strategies, donation-based crowdfunding provides a way for potential donors to reach people/

L. Zhao (✉) • R. Shneor
School of Business and Law, University of Agder, Kristiansand, Norway
e-mail: liang.zhao@uia.no; rotem.shneor@uia.no

groups in need of help without the constraints of physical distance (Tanaka and Voida 2016). Furthermore, from a fundraiser perspective, donation crowdfunding allows for greater efficiencies in terms of geographical reach (Agrawal et al. 2015), reduced transaction and coordination costs (Choy and Schlagwein 2016), as well as richer and more frequent interactions with prospective donors. Accordingly, donation crowdfunding has been employed in a variety of contexts beyond pure charity causes (Gleasure and Feller 2016), and have been applied to support independent journalism (Jian and Shin 2015), indie documentary film productions (Sørensen 2012), cultural heritage projects (Oomen and Aroyo 2011), supporting educational work (Meer 2014), and scientific research (Wheat et al. 2013).

When compared to other crowdfunding models, donations represent one of the smallest models by volume in most regions. In 2017, donation crowdfunding volumes were estimated at, USD 290 million in the Americas (Ziegler et al. 2018a), USD 113 million in Europe including (EUR 53 million in mainland Europe and GBP 41 million in the UK) (Zhang et al. 2018; Ziegler et al. 2019), USD 63 million in the Middle East and Africa (Ziegler et al. 2018c), and USD 53 million in the Asia-Pacific region (Ziegler et al. 2018b). Except for the Middle East and Africa, where donations account for 17% of total the crowdfunding volume, in all other regions this model only represents 1% or less. Accordingly, the share of donation crowdfunding in the total global crowdfunding volume represents only 0.1%.

These more modest volumes may be associated with the fact that, unlike other crowdfunding models, donation-based crowdfunding does not include offering the backers material or monetary rewards for their contributions, hence implying different motivations driving related behaviour, as well as relations between fundraisers and backers. More specifically, supporters of donation-based crowdfunding campaigns are said to be motivated by altruism, peer recognition, respect, or esteem rather than by tangible and monetary rewards (Benkler 2011). Hence, to better understand donor behaviour in this context, as well as to boost success of donation campaigns, it is important to understand the working mechanisms of donation-based crowdfunding.

The purpose of this chapter is thus to review current knowledge about donation-based crowdfunding, while examining its core features, and factors driving donor behaviour in this context. Accordingly, we first discuss the current state and characteristics of donation-based crowdfunding, while highlighting its unique aspects. Next, the success factors of donation-based crowdfunding campaigns are summarized based on a review of earlier studies examining them. This is followed by a literature review and discussion concerning the factors impacting donor behaviour. Finally, we conclude by suggesting implications for practice and research.

Characteristics of Donation Crowdfunding

Donation-based crowdfunding has become a new channel to provide monetary support for non-profit, prosocial, and other "do good" initiatives. It is a type of philanthropy (Gerber and Hui 2013) reflecting an emerging and innovative online charity paradigm (Gerber et al. 2012). Similar to other crowdfunding models, the donation-based crowdfunding model is composed of three elements: the campaign initiators/fundraisers, the donors/backers, and the online platforms.

The donation-based crowdfunding platforms offer opportunities for fundraisers to launch campaigns as an open call over the internet for donations to charitable purposes within fixed time durations (Shneor and Munim 2019; Mollick 2014; Belleflamme et al. 2014; Gerber et al. 2012). Compared to the traditional charitable giving, with the help of information technology, donation-based crowdfunding is said to reduce the coordination and transaction costs associated with donation collections in a significant way (Choy and Schlagwein 2016). Besides, donation-based crowdfunding tends to collect small amounts from large crowds instead of seeking large amounts from a small group of affluent donors (Lu et al. 2014). With the involvement of the social network sites (SNS), donation-based crowdfunding initiators can easily broadcast their campaigns to a wider range of potential donors and establish social relationships with such crowds (Liang and Turban 2011).

While traditional charitable giving and donation crowdfunding share many commonalities, they may also differ to varying degrees with respect to several aspects. Here, internet-based crowdfunding platforms and social network sites (SNS), allow for greater real-time interaction (e.g. updates, comments, live streams, etc.) between donors and project initiators throughout the fundraising process (Kuppuswamy and Bayus 2017), as well as afterwards. Incorporating dedicated promotional efforts via SNS, help spread information to the public in new and effective ways (Lambert and Schwienbacher 2010), as in targeted advertising, which increase the probability of successful fundraising.

Other benefits reflect greater process efficiency. First, donation crowdfunding provides opportunities for wider geographical reach, where contributions may be collected from non-local donors with no previous connections to the fundraisers (Agrawal et al. 2015) in a manner that would have been a lot more expensive to achieve otherwise. Second, coordination and transaction costs associated with fundraising may be significantly reduced by the applications of advanced ICT tools (e.g. timely online interactions, digital and mobile payment systems, etc.) (Choy and Schlagwein 2016). And, third, donation crowdfunding also present opportunities to tap into more active donors who may be actively seeking opportunities to contribute to causes on crowdfunding platforms instead of passively waiting for opportunities (Gleasure and Feller 2016), as well as enabling a lower threshold for their involvement and activism, requiring supporters to simply share the campaign with their own networks often through a single-button click.

Success Factors of Donation Crowdfunding Campaigns

Since donation-based crowdfunding is a special type of charitable giving (Gerber and Hui 2013), some factors identified as influencing successful fundraising in traditional charitable giving may also be relevant in donation-based crowdfunding. Research on donor's willingness to donate in the context of traditional charitable giving is usually associated with altruistic orientation and tendencies (Choy and Schlagwein 2015). Donors are encouraged to donate by their sense of empathy towards specific charitable purposes (Gerber et al. 2012), while representing the emotional state of the individuals (Hoffman et al. 1999).

A recent literature review by Shneor and Vik (2020) has identified seven persistent variables which were found to impact successful donation crowdfunding across multiple studies. First, the target sum set for fundraising is positively associated with success, suggesting that the higher the target the greater the likelihood of success in donation crowdfunding. Second, inclusion of a video in the campaign materials is associated with greater success in comparison to donation campaigns that do not include a video. This finding was linked to lowering the cognitive efforts required for processing campaign information, which is effective at facilitating donations Third, donors react more positively to campaigns closer to them geographically or ideologically. Fourth, female campaign creators are associated with higher success than male campaign creators, which may be related to both more modest funding requirements and better social mobilization capacities of women as driven by empathy and relational focus. Fifth, availability of fundraisers' social capital as reflected by social network size, is also positively associated with success. Sixth, campaigns aiming at educational projects are more likely to receive donations for other purposes. And, finally, the level of maturity of the platform on which campaigns are published is also positively associated with success, suggesting that campaigning on more mature platforms is likely to enhance chances of funding success.

Nevertheless, these still represent slim pickings, as research of success drivers in donation crowdfunding remains limited and mostly explorative (Mollick 2014; Shneor and Vik 2020). Parallel to studies examining the impact of factors related to either the campaign, fundraiser, or platform, an additional line of inquiry into donor behaviour has gradually emerged. We review studies examining donor behaviour in the following sections.

Donor Behaviour in Donation Crowdfunding

Why individuals should contribute to donation-based crowdfunding campaigns has been identified as an interesting and important research question (Gerber and Hui 2013). It is interesting because contribution in the donation-based crowdfunding context may differ from that in other crowdfunding models. This is primarily because, while other crowdfunding models, offer individuals material or monetary rewards for their contribution (Zvilichovsky et al. 2015; Gerber and Hui 2013), donation crowdfunding does not offer such rewards (Gleasure and Feller 2016). Accordingly, the research into donor behaviour in the context of donation crowdfunding has referred to impure altruistic behaviour involving intangible rewards, which may satisfy both certain extrinsic and intrinsic motivations.

Altruism and Charitable Giving

Altruism is often used to explain individuals' charitable behaviour, and describes a situation where individuals try to help others, even if it comes at some personal cost (Khalil 2004). It is the motivation to increase another person's welfare, which is contrasted with egoism, the motivation to increase one's own welfare (Batson and Powell 2003). According, to Khalil (2004), altruism can be explained through two different dimensions: the interactional and the self-actional dimensions. On the one hand, the interactional dimension of altruism suggests that individuals' altruistic behaviour can be rationally explained. Such approach argues that altruistic behaviour tends to be triggered by delayed external rewards such as reciprocity (Cox 2004), vicarious enjoyment (Kahneman and Miller 1986), and natural-selection-based consequence (Haidt 2007). On the other hand, the self-actional dimension of altruism is normatively anchored. Hence, the self-actional dimension is not based on delayed external rewards but on the attributes of altruistic behaviour such as norms, mind structures, and culture (Khalil 2004).

When examining research conserving altruism in the context of donation crowdfunding, most references seem to rely on the self-actional dimension of altruistic behaviour. According to Andreoni (1990), the self-actional dimension of altruism includes pure altruism, warm glow, and impure altruism. Here, pure altruism describes the situation when individuals donate because it can improve the difficult situation of the recipients. External rewards such as hedonic benefits and warm-glow effects may not explain pure altruism donors' behaviour (Loewenstein and Small 2007; Andreoni 1990). Pure altruism donors are outcome-based and are primarily concerned with the extent to which a cause deserves support (Carpenter et al. 2008).

The warm-glow effect (Andreoni 1990) refers to the situation where individuals experience pleasure and satisfaction from helping others. Such senses of mental pleasure and satisfaction help to boost individuals' self-esteem (Fehr and Gächter 2000) and it also explains why individuals with the warm-glow mindset continue to conduct altruistic actions when they can otherwise "free-ride" and wait for others to help (Andreoni 1990). Warm glow is empathy-based. Donors are psychosocially connected with the receivers through the donor–receiver interaction (Park 2000), which is a process in which empathy tends to amplify the positive feelings from helping others or feelings of guilt when refusing to help (Andreoni et al. 2017). In such case, donors may feel compassion (Hoffman et al. 1999) towards certain causes, which may be described in donation crowdfunding campaigns while stimulating donation behaviour that enhance their sense of satisfaction and joy about supporting these causes (Gerber and Hui 2013; Gerber et al. 2012).

Though, the outcome-based pure altruism and empathy-dependent warm glow have provided valuable insights for understanding personal charitable behaviour, some argue that altruistic giving is always triggered by the impure altruism (Andreoni 1990). Impure altruism implies a situation where a combination of both pure altruism and warm glow will influence individuals' behaviour (Crumpler and Grossman 2008). And when examining the limited literature on donor motivation and behaviour specifically in the donation-based crowdfunding context, it appears that authors often explain donor behaviour by impure altruism (Gerber and Hui 2013; Burtch et al. 2013; Choy and Schlagwein 2015).

Motivation in Charitable Giving

Motivation directs and stimulates human behaviour (Murray 1964). It is viewed as the engine for satisfying physiological needs (Vallerand 1997) while capturing the degree to which a person is moved to perform a particular action (Deci et al. 1991). According to theory, motivations may be classified as either intrinsic or extrinsic (Deci et al. 1991), as well as either individually driven or socially driven (Alam and Campbell 2012; Kaufmann et al. 2011).

One of the prominent motivation theories is the "self-determination theory" (SDT), which explores the individual's self-motivated or self-determined behaviour (Ryan and Deci 2000). As such, it offers a detailed framework to differentiate between intrinsic and extrinsic motivations, while acknowledging that their mutually reinforcing nature also affects individuals' behavioural intentions (ibid.). Intrinsic motivation is derived from individual's inherent enjoyment of doing something, and extrinsic motivation stems from the separable outcome of doing something (ibid.). Thanks to its wide appeal and acceptance, this classification has also been employed in earlier crowdfunding literature (e.g. Gerber and Hui 2013; Wang et al. 2019; Zhang and Chen 2019).

Some studies have suggested that charitable giving can be caused by extrinsic motivations such as the satisfaction of personal heroism (Piliavin and Charng 1990) and personal atonement of sins (Schwartz 1973). However, evidence with respect to donation-based crowdfunding, mainly suggests that intrinsic motivations dominate such behaviour (Zhao and Sun 2020; Gleasure and Feller 2016; Bretschneider et al. 2014; Gerber and Hui 2013).

Specifically, individuals were found to contribute to donation-based crowdfunding in order to help others, support causes, or be part of a community (Gerber and Hui 2013). These may be triggered by a sense of empathy, sympathy, nostalgia, reciprocity, or commemoration (Andreoni 1990; Eisenberg and Miller 1987; Sargeant 1999), which may enhance positive feelings with contribution behaviour. Such positive feelings may represent intangible rewards in the form of a sense of enjoyment, competence, and autonomy (Deci and Ryan 1985; Oliver 1980). Such intrinsic motivations may explain donor behaviour, which does not involve material compensation. Furthermore, an earlier study by Zhao and Sun (2020) has shown that providing extrinsic rewards in prosocial campaigns will diminish donors' intrinsic motivations to donate in the donation-based crowdfunding context.

An alternative approach to the differentiation between intrinsic and extrinsic motivations, as suggested by the SDT (Ryan and Deci 2000), emphasizes that motivation is more than a personal concept and has social attributes (Akerlof 2006). Accordingly, classifying motivations as either individually driven or socially driven may also provide valuable insights to investigations of contribution behaviour in the crowd economy in general (Alam and Campbell 2012; Kaufmann et al. 2011), and donation crowdfunding in particular.

Individual motivation is generated by the desire of individuals regardless of the existence of a social group (Cohen et al. 2005). In contrast, social motivation stems from the presence of a social group and individual actions are triggered by the social group (Akerlof 2006). Furthermore, when combining the intrinsic vs. extrinsic dimensions (Deci et al. 1991) with the individual vs. social dimensions of motivation, four subcategories emerge: individual-extrinsic motivation, individual-intrinsic motivation, social-extrinsic motivation, and social-intrinsic motivation (Choy and Schlagwein 2015). At the individual level, the extrinsic motivation refers to the desire to achieve a specific result by doing something and the intrinsic motivation relates to the individual's personal satisfaction of doing something. At the social level, an individuals' social-extrinsic motivation related to signalling compliance with group expectations in terms of action beyond words, and social-intrinsic motivation relates to achieving a sense of belonging to a collective of like-minded people.

In terms of donation-based crowdfunding, donors' motivations such as helping others and supporting causes are typically individual (Gerber and Hui 2013). For example, individuals may donate to donation-based campaigns because they feel passionate about the campaigns (Choy and Schlagwein 2015). In addition, some donors are socially motived (Akerlof 2006). They donate to achieve social belonging and peer recognition (Alam and Campbell 2012; Bretschneider et al. 2014; Kaufmann et al. 2011). Here, donors donate because they want to be parts of the charity crowdfunding community and they enjoy engaging and collaborating with the community (Gerber et al. 2012).

Conclusion

Despite representing a small share of global crowdfunding volumes, donation crowdfunding is a unique model for supporting a wide range of prosocial and charitable causes, while allowing fundraisers to leverage benefits afforded by ICT solutions for more effective and efficient fund-raising efforts than traditional methods and channels. This chapter has taken stock of the knowledge emerging from the limited research available in the donation crowdfunding context. We have highlighted the motivations of contributors to donate funding to such campaigns as driven by impure altruism, while acknowledging that most work has stressed intrinsic motivations both at the individual and at the social level. Furthermore, the success drivers of donation crowdfunding campaigns have been presented with respect to factors at the fundraiser, campaign, and platform levels. Nevertheless, donation crowdfunding remains an understudied context with much room for further exploration. Some ideas in this direction are presented below.

Implications for Research

While preliminary insights on factors impacting donation crowdfunding success factors are available, they tend to follow recipes adopted from studies conducted in commercial and investment-oriented models. Hence, it is recommended that future studies should devote more attention to examining factors unique to the donation context. Here, research should embark on capturing what successfully triggers aspects associated with donor behaviour, and how do campaign features support the necessary emotive reactions of joy, satisfaction, warm glow, as well as a sense of group belonging and compliance with social expectations. Such approach would require a departure from reliance on platform data, and a shift towards primary data collection through surveying and/interviewing of users. This would help bridge the gap between campaign success and donor behaviour and provide valuable insights how the two hang-together in a theoretically sound manner.

An additional venue for future research may include comparative studies of donation crowdfunding versus traditional donation fundraising practices, crowdfunding dynamics across models, as well as across social, cultural, and sectoral groups. First, studies that will compare crowdfunding versus traditional donation collection channels, may provide evidence and insights about the added value or costs associated with the practice of each, and will be go beyond the speculative suggestions that have been outlined in research thus far. Second, a comparative study across crowdfunding models, can better clarify what are the common drivers and aspects of crowdfunding in general, while highlighting the unique aspects associated with donation crowdfunding beyond the clear differentiation between tangible and intangible rewards and benefits. Finally, studies comparing donation crowdfunding across differing contexts, may help identify sectors, social and cultural groups that may be more receptive to donation crowdfunding than others, as well as different strategies employed in different contexts to encourage donor engagements and contributions.

Implications for Practice

Insights from our review of the current state of donation crowdfunding research and practice may inform platforms in designing their products and services, as well as inform fundraisers interested in running a donation crowdfunding campaign. In this context, platforms should develop features that may enhance donors' sense of satisfaction and joy from giving. Such features may include interactive visualizations of impact such as progression bars, number of people affected, improved conditions (e.g. gas emission reductions, quantity of water cleansed, etc.), number of equipment units provided to needy, and so on. In addition, platforms may invest in community management features that will allow members to join certain interest groups, while receiving symbolic acknowledgement for their contributions to these groups (e.g. virtual badges, status levels, and public endorsements).

From the fundraiser perspective, fundraisers need to invest in creating a sense of ideological proximity with their prospective donors, employing emotional cues to trigger empathy in their messaging, as well as proactively engage with targeted groups via social media. In addition, since donors do not receive material rewards for their contributions, fundraisers should ensure smooth and ongoing communication with donors about project progress, execution, and impact during and after the campaign. This is both to enable a sense of satisfaction about donation at different points in time and to strategically establish long-term relations with fans, who are prospective future donors as well.

References

Agrawal, A., Catalini, C., & Goldfarb, A. (2015). Crowdfunding: Geography, Social Networks, and the Timing of Investment Decisions. *Journal of Economics & Management Strategy, 24*(2), 253–274.

Akerlof, R. J. (2006). A Theory of Social Motivation. Unpublished manuscript, Cambridge, MA.

Alam, S. L., & Campbell, J. (2012). *Crowdsourcing Motivations in a Not-for-Profit GLAM Context: The Australian Newspapers Digitisation Program.* Australasian Conference on Information Systems.

Andreoni, J. (1990). Impure Altruism and Donations to Public Goods: A Theory of Warm-Glow Giving. *The Economic Journal, 100*(401), 464–477.

Andreoni, J., Rao, J. M., & Trachtman, H. (2017). Avoiding the Ask: A Field Experiment on Altruism, Empathy, and Charitable Giving. *Journal of Political Economy, 125*(3), 625–653.

Batson, C. D., & Powell, A. A. (2003). Altruism and Prosocial Behavior. In I. B. Weiner (Ed.), *Handbook of Psychology* (pp. 463–484). John Wiley & Sons, Inc.

Belleflamme, P., Lambert, T., & Schwienbacher, A. (2013). Individual Crowdfunding Practices. *Venture Capital, 15*(4), 313–333.

Belleflamme, P., Lambert, T., & Schwienbacher, A. (2014). Crowdfunding: Tapping the Right Crowd. *Journal of Business Venturing, 29*(5), 585–609.

Benkler, Y. (2011). The Unselfish Gene. *Harvard Business Review, 89*(7–8), 76–85.

Bretschneider, U., Knaub, K., & Wieck, E. (2014). *Motivations for Crowdfunding: What Drives the Crowd to Invest in Start-ups?* European Conference on Information Systems, Tel Aviv, Association for Information Systems.

Burtch, G., Ghose, A., & Wattal, S. (2013). An Empirical Examination of the Antecedents and Consequences of Contribution Patterns in Crowd-Funded Markets. *Information Systems Research, 24*(3), 499–519.

Carpenter, J., Connolly, C., & Myers, C. K. (2008). Altruistic Behavior in a Representative Dictator Experiment. *Experimental Economics, 11*(3), 282–298.

Choy, K., & Schlagwein, D. (2015, May). *IT Affordances and Donor Motivations in Charitable Crowdfunding: The "Earthship Kapita" Case.* ECIS.

Choy, K., & Schlagwein, D. (2016). Crowdsourcing for a Better World: On the Relation Between IT Affordances and Donor Motivations in Charitable Crowdfunding. *Information Technology & People, 29*(1), 221–247.

Cohen, A. B., Hall, D. E., Koenig, H. G., & Meador, K. G. (2005). Social Versus Individual Motivation: Implications for Normative Definitions of Religious Orientation. *Personality and Social Psychology Review, 9*(1), 48–61.

Cox, J. C. (2004). How to Identify Trust and Reciprocity. *Games and Economic Behavior, 46*(2), 260–281.

Crumpler, H., & Grossman, P. J. (2008). An Experimental Test of Warm Glow Giving. *Journal of Public Economics, 92*(5–6), 1011–1021.

Deci, E. L., & Ryan, R. M. (1985). The General Causality Orientations Scale: Self-Determination in Personality. *Journal of Research in Personality, 19*(2), 109–134.

Deci, E. L., Vallerand, R. J., Pelletier, L. G., & Ryan, R. M. (1991). Motivation and Education: The Self-Determination Perspective. *Educational Psychologist, 26*(3–4), 325–346.

Eisenberg, N., & Miller, P. A. (1987). The Relation of Empathy to Prosocial and Related Behaviors. *Psychological Bulletin, 101*(1), 91.

Fehr, E., & Gächter, S. (2000). Cooperation and Punishment in Public Goods Experiments. *American Economic Review, 90*(4), 980–994.

Gerber, E. M., & Hui, J. (2013). Crowdfunding: Motivations and Deterrents for Participation. *ACM Transactions on Computer-Human Interaction (TOCHI), 20*(6), 34.

Gerber, E. M., Hui, J. S., & Kuo, P. Y. (2012, February). Crowdfunding: Why People Are Motivated to Post and Fund Projects on Crowdfunding Platforms. In *Proceedings of the International Workshop on Design, Influence, and Social Technologies: Techniques, Impacts and Ethics* (Vol. 2, No. 11, p. 10). Evanston, IL: Northwestern University.

Gleasure, R., & Feller, J. (2016). Does Heart or Head Rule Donor Behaviors in Charitable Crowdfunding Markets? *International Journal of Electronic Commerce, 20*(4), 499–524.

Haidt, J. (2007). The New Synthesis in Moral Psychology. *Science, 316*(5827), 998–1002.

Hoffman, D. L., Novak, T. P., & Peralta, M. (1999). Building Consumer Trust Online. *Communications of the ACM, 42*(4), 80–85.

Jian, L., & Shin, J. (2015). Motivations Behind Donors' Contributions to Crowdfunded Journalism. *Mass Communication and Society, 18*(2), 165–185.

Kahneman, D., & Miller, D. T. (1986). Norm theory: Comparing reality to its alternatives. *Psychological review, 93*(2), 136.

Kaufmann, N., Schulze, T., & Veit, D. (2011, August). More than Fun and Money. Worker Motivation in Crowdsourcing-A Study on Mechanical Turk. *AMCIS, 11*(2011), 1–11.

Khalil, E. L. (2004). What Is Altruism? *Journal of Economic Psychology, 25*(1), 97–123.

Kuppuswamy, V., & Bayus, B. L. (2017). Crowdfunding Creative Ideas: The Dynamics of Project Backers in Kickstarter. A Shorter Version of This Paper Is In "*The Economics of Crowdfunding: Startups, Portals, and Investor Behavior*", L. Hornuf & D. Cumming (eds.).

Lambert, T., & Schwienbacher, A. (2010). An Empirical Analysis of Crowdfunding. *Social Science Research Network, 1578175*, 1–23.

Liang, T. P., & Turban, E. (2011). Introduction to the Special Issue Social Commerce: A Research Framework for Social Commerce. *International Journal of Electronic Commerce, 16*(2), 5–14.

Loewenstein, G., & Small, D. A. (2007). The Scarecrow and the Tin Man: The Vicissitudes of Human Sympathy and Caring. *Review of General Psychology, 11*(2), 112–126.

Lu, C. T., Xie, S., Kong, X., & Yu, P. S. (2014, February). Inferring the Impacts of Social Media on Crowdfunding. In *Proceedings of the 7th ACM International Conference on Web Search and Data Mining* (pp. 573–582). ACM.

Meer, J. (2014). Effects of the Price of Charitable Giving: Evidence from an Online Crowdfunding Platform. *Journal of Economic Behavior & Organization, 103*, 113–124.

Mollick, E. (2014). The Dynamics of Crowdfunding: An Exploratory Study. *Journal of Business Venturing, 29*(1), 1–16.

Murray, E. J. (1964). *Motivation and Emotion*. Prentice-Hall.

Oliver, R. L. (1980). A Cognitive Model of the Antecedents and Consequences of Satisfaction Decisions. *Journal of Marketing Research, 17*(4), 460–469.

Oomen, J., & Aroyo, L. (2011, June). Crowdsourcing in the Cultural Heritage Domain: Opportunities and Challenges. In *Proceedings of the 5th International Conference on Communities and Technologies* (pp. 138–149). ACM.

Park, E. S. (2000). Warm-Glow Versus Cold-Prickle: A Further Experimental Study of Framing Effects on Free-Riding. *Journal of Economic Behavior & Organization, 43*(4), 405–421.

Piliavin, J. A., & Charng, H. W. (1990). Altruism: A Review of Recent Theory and Research. *Annual Review of Sociology, 16*(1), 27–65.

Ryan, R. M., & Deci, E. L. (2000). Intrinsic and Extrinsic Motivations: Classic Definitions and New Directions. *Contemporary Educational Psychology, 25*(1), 54–67.

Sargeant, A. (1999). Charitable Giving: Towards a Model of Donor Behaviour. *Journal of Marketing Management, 15*(4), 215–238.

Schwartz, S. H. (1973). Normative Explanations of Helping Behavior: A Critique, Proposal, and Empirical Test. *Journal of Experimental Social Psychology, 9*(4), 349–364.

Shneor, R., & Munim, Z. H. (2019). Reward Crowdfunding Contribution as Planned Behaviour: An Extended Framework. *Journal of Business Research, 103*, 56–70.

Shneor, R., & Vik, A. A. (2020). Crowdfunding Success: A Systematic Literature Review 2010–2017. *Baltic Journal of Management, 15*(2), 149–182.

Sørensen, I. E. (2012). Crowdsourcing and Outsourcing: The Impact of Online Funding and Distribution on the Documentary Film Industry in the UK. *Media, Culture & Society, 34*(6), 726–743.

Tanaka, K. G., & Voida, A. (2016, May). Legitimacy Work: Invisible Work in Philanthropic Crowdfunding. In *Proceedings of the 2016 CHI Conference on Human Factors in Computing Systems* (pp. 4550–4561). ACM.

Vallerand, R. J. (1997). Toward a Hierarchical Model of Intrinsic and Extrinsic Motivation. In *Advances in Experimental Social Psychology* (Vol. 29, pp. 271–360). Academic Press.

Wang, T., et al. (2019). Exploring Individuals' Behavioral Intentions Toward Donation Crowdfunding: Evidence from China. *Industrial Management & Data Systems, 119*(7), 1515–1534.

Wheat, R. E., Wang, Y., Byrnes, J. E., & Ranganathan, J. (2013). Raising Money for Scientific Research Through Crowdfunding. *Trends in Ecology & Evolution, 28*(2), 71–72.

Zhang, H., & Chen, W. (2019). Backer Motivation in Crowdfunding New Product Ideas: Is It about You or Is It about Me? *Journal of Product Innovation Management, 36*(2), 241–262.

Zhang, B., Ziegler, T., Mammadova, L., et al. (2018). *The 5th UK Alternative Finance Industry Report*. Cambridge, UK: Cambridge Centre for Alternative Finance.

Zhao, L., & Sun, Z. (2020). Pure Donation or Hybrid Donation Crowdfunding. *Baltic Journal of Management, 15*(2).

Ziegler, T., Johanson, D., King, M., et al. (2018a). *Reaching New Heights: The 3rd Americas Alternative Finance Industry Report*. Cambridge, UK: Cambridge Centre for Alternative Finance.

Ziegler, T., Johanson, D., Zhang, B., et al. (2018b). *The 3rd Asia Pacific Region Alternative Finance Industry Report*. Cambridge, UK: Cambridge Centre for Alternative Finance.

Ziegler, T., Suresh, K., Garvey, K., et al. (2018c). *The 2nd Annual Middle East & Africa Alternative Finance Industry Report*. Cambridge, UK: Cambridge Center for Alternative Finance.

Ziegler, T., Shneor, R., Wenzlaff, K., et al. (2019). *Shifting Paradigms – The 4th European Alternative Finance Benchmarking Report*. Cambridge, UK: Cambridge Centre for Alternative Finance.

Zvilichovsky, D., Inbar, Y., & Barzilay, O. (2015). *Playing Both Sides of the Market: Success and Reciprocity on Crowdfunding Platforms*. Available at SSRN 2304101.

8

Crowdfunding Practice and its Ethics

Rotem Shneor and Stina Torjesen

Introduction

Parallel to the impressive growth of crowdfunding in recent years, we are also witnessing a growing concern with ethical aspects of crowdfunding practice. Here, while not representing mainstream developments, stories about platforms and campaigns suspected of fraud have attracted both public and media attention. For example, at the platform-level, investigation into misappropriation of funds, as in the case of Sweden-based crowdlending platform TrustBuddy, ended up with it filing for bankruptcy in 2015 with substantial losses for its lenders (Palmer 2016). In China, the Ezubao crowdlending platform, succumbed to government crackdown on illegal fundraising, revealing its operations as a 'Ponzy scheme' (Zhang and Miller 2017). Moreover, at the campaign level, and within the reward-crowdfunding context, an independent study (Mollick 2015) showed that 9% of campaigns failed to deliver on promised

R. Shneor (✉) • S. Torjesen
School of Business and Law, University of Agder, Kristiansand, Norway
e-mail: rotem.shneor@uia.no; stina.torjesen@uia.no

rewards, 8% of dollars pledged went to failed projects, and 7% of backers failed to receive their chosen reward. Such cases include non-delivery on commercial concepts like iBackPack, which raised USD 720K on Indiegogo for its urban backpack concept, and Central Standard Timing, which raised more than USD 1 million on Kickstarter for the 'world's thinnest watch', to name just two (Carpenter 2017). Other cases are more sinister, including the GoFundMe donation campaigns by US citizen Jennifer Flynn Cataldo, requesting help in paying medical bills associated with cancer she did not have, raising more than USD 38K, before being convicted of fraud (ibid.).

The above examples can serve as triggers for a discussion of ethical issues in crowdfunding practice, which, surprisingly, has largely been absent in earlier research. An exception here has been a short communication by Snyder et al. (2016), who called for ethics-focused research on medical crowdfunding in particular, as it raises concerns with exposure to fraudulent campaigns, loss of privacy, and fairness in how medical crowdfunding funds are distributed. Other related studies have taken a legalistic rather than ethical perspective, while addressing legal anchoring of investor protection in crowdfunding (e.g. Heminway 2014; Pierce-Wright 2016). Indeed, ethical aspects in finance have been obscured by the preoccupation with legalization, under the incorrect assumption that what is legal is also ethical, versus how ethics serve as the foundation for regulation (Boatright 2010).

The current study will address this gap by mapping and classifying ethical considerations in crowdfunding practice, while relating them to the different stakeholders who are parties to the development of the crowdfunding activities, including—fundraisers (entities that raise capital for a project), platforms (web applications facilitating the fundraising), funders (actual and potential funding providers to crowdfunding campaigns), and regulators (public authorities overseeing the law-making related to crowdfunding practice). Furthermore, crowdfunding can be viewed as a phenomenon at the intersection between the disciplines of finance, entrepreneurship, marketing, e-commerce, and social networking. Hence, since, to the best knowledge of the authors, no earlier study has addressed ethical considerations specifically in the context of crowdfunding, we draw on principles discussed in studies of ethics in finance

(Boatright 2010), entrepreneurial finance (Fassin and Drover 2017), entrepreneurship (Bucar and Hisrich 2001), marketing (Dunfee et al. 1999), e-commerce (Roman 2007), and online social networking (Light and McGrath 2010).

In the following sections, we first address classical approaches to business ethics, and we then delve deeper into the context of crowdfunding, while exploring related dilemmas from a multiple stakeholder perspective. We then suggest a framework outlining potential ethical pitfalls in crowdfunding practice, as well as some mechanism for addressing them. Finally, we conclude by highlighting the contributions, limitations, and implications of the current study.

Classical Approaches to Ethical Decision Making in Business

Simply put, business ethics deals with what people in business *ought* to do. In business ethics neither do we merely describe business practices, nor do we attempt to predict what will happen on, say, the stock market, or with company sales following a distinct type of marketing campaign (Sandbu 2011; DesJardins 2009). Instead we ask, in a given business situation, what is the *right* thing to do (Sandbu 2011). More specifically we identify moral reasons for or against different courses of action and weight them against each other (ibid., p. 12). These reasons may often correspond to our moral instincts, or gut feelings of what is right or wrong, but they are not derived from our intuition. Instead, in business ethics we search for moral claims, or underlying principles of what may, from a given perspective, constitute good behaviour and we attempt to logically and consistently apply these when we make decisions.

There are several 'schools' in business ethics and these offer different sets of ethical reasons or principles that can guide decision making. The three main schools are 'Kantian deontology', utilitarianism, and virtue ethics.

'Kantian deontology' derives from the works of the philosopher Immanuel Kant (1785/1991). In Kantian approaches business managers are advised to search for a general principle that can offer guidance when faced with a specific ethical challenge. A key test to whether a principle can be seen as morally robust is to ask if the manager could get all other mangers to follow the same principle in all similar situations (Kant's categorical imperative in Donaldson and Dunfee 1994). In crowdfunding this 'do unto other as you would have them do unto you' approach would manifest itself if a fundraiser was tempted to over-exaggerate the benefits of a product being developed. Would it be rational for the funder to operate in a market where all suppliers, competitors, and customers over-exaggerated their products' performance or customers over-exaggerated their willingness to pay? The likely answer here is no. In Kantian business ethics this means the fundraiser must reason that he or she has a duty not to over-exaggerate and that suppliers, competitors, and customers have a right to be given truthful information by the manager.

In Kantian business ethics we deliberate the reasons for why an action is the right thing and we seek to fulfil our duties and uphold the rights of others as best we can. Utilitarianism (Mill 2016), by contrast, is less concerned with prior reasoning and individual rights, but focus instead on the overall consequences of our actions. When faced with alternative courses of action a manager should choose the action that will maximize the future welfare, wellbeing or happiness of the most people (Donaldson and Dunfee 1994; Mill 2016). In this context, and in line with Veenhoven (1991), happiness can be considered as incorporating both a sense of contentment when comparing life-as-it-is to perceptions about how-life-should-be, and how one feels affectively in terms of gratification of basic bio-psychological needs.

Accordingly, crowdfunding fits the spirit of utilitarianism well. Many products and initiatives either leave well-being at the same level or increase it for a large number of people. Few initiatives would, when all consequences are calculated, produce a total sum of happiness that is lower than when the campaign commenced. Utilitarian ethics encourages fundraisers to develop campaigns, products, or initiatives where the positive consequences for the largest number of people is maximized. This resonates well with campaigns where social entrepreneurship is at the core, but commercial and profit-seeking campaigns may also fit the utilitarian logic.

In both utilitarianism and Kantian business ethics we have dictums which we can attempt to logically and consistently apply, that is, 'greatest sum of happiness to the greatest number of people' and 'do unto others as you would have them do unto you'. In the third school 'virtue ethics' it is harder to distil unified principles. Instead, when searching for guidance on actions and decision making, we are prompted to ask ourselves, 'What would a virtuous person do?' Aristoteles and his book *Nicomachean Ethics* serves as a centre piece in virtue ethics. Aristoteles advices us to develop our moral wisdom through a combination of knowledge and life experience (practical wisdom). We are on a journey of personal development where we increasingly come to understand and experience what virtue is. A virtue often resides on the 'golden mean' between two excesses. For example, if we develop the virtue temperance, we are increasingly avoiding greed as well as unnecessary abstinence. Similarly, as many initiators of crowdfunding platforms or fundraiser will likely develop a keen understanding of, when launching a campaign, you can neither be cowardly nor foolhardy, but must demonstrate the virtue courage (DesJardins 2009).

Donaldson and Dunfee (1994) note that while these three ethical schools of thought provide useful overall guidance to decision making, they fail to reflect and assist with often complex and very context specific challenges facing business managers. In crowdfunding we also have the added problem that platforms and campaigns may attract interest and support from across countries and even continents. Donaldson and Dunfee's "integrative social contract theory" addresses these challenges by laying out some general ('macrocontract') principles, and then, within the confines of these principles, encourages business managers to elucidate the informal ('microcontract') 'rules of the game' in the transactions they engage in. The latter includes the understanding and adhering to local expectations for ethical behaviour. Some of the general principles that can and should constrain managers regardless of location can be 'core human rights, including those to personal freedom, physical security and well-being, political participation, informed consent, the ownership of property, the right to subsistence, and the obligation to respect the dignity of each human person (ibid., p. 267).

Finally, it bears stressing that the way business ethics is studied and taught has been challenged in recent years by Mary Gentile and the movement 'Giving Voice to Values' (GVV) (Gentile 2010). Gentile argues that teachers and scholars of business ethics spend too much time debating abstract questions of right and wrong, when the real struggles of employees and managers is not to understand that practices they may be observing or form part of are wrong, but rather to find the strength to voice their concerns. 'Giving Voice to Value' urges business schools to alter teachings from primarily debating moral philosophical problems and prioritize building confidence and the ability to raise concerns. The implications for crowdfunding are that platforms and fundraisers should strive to create a culture where employees and managers are deliberately empowered and encouraged to speak up if they encounter dubious business practices.

Crowdfunding: An Ethical Solution or Problem?

Crowdfunding can be considered both as an ethical solution to old problems and as a source for new ethical challenges to be addressed. The very concept of crowdfunding, at its core, represents a solution to traditional barriers of access to finance, which resonates well with the utilitarian ethos of reform and social improvement. Similarly, crowdfunding presents an answer to growing scepticism towards, and disillusionment with, traditional financial institutions, which have triggered and overseen cycles of economic booms and busts in recent decades. In this view, anyone with access to internet can potentially raise funds for a project of their choice from anyone else with access to internet. This implies greater democratization in the use and allocation of financial resources, as well as greater say of the public in its choices of future consumption, provisioning of public goods, and the free promotion of ideas.

First, building on the principles of the democratization of finance (Erturk et al. 2007), crowdfunding practice implies that: (1) the exclusive (if not monopolistic) control of traditional financial institutions and their criteria for allocating financial resources to individuals, organizations, or projects is weakened through competitive offerings from the crowd; (2) more individuals, organizations, and projects can be financed overall, and especially those from environments where discrimination based on gender, sexuality, ethnicity, and religiosity are rampant; (3) more individuals and organizations can influence product and service development efforts towards fulfilling needs of their future consumption, while somewhat weakening the power of manufacturers, wholesalers, and retailers in making such choices for them; (4) individuals and organizations can have more opportunities for investment in general, and for high- and medium-risk investments in particular; and (5) through greater access to finance and investment opportunities, inequalities in society can be minimized in the longer term.

Second, in terms of provisioning of public goods, crowdfunding may be especially relevant where existing institutions fail to provide them. Such projects can include the financing of health care services and equipment for needy individuals (e.g. Berliner and Kenworthy 2017), education services and equipment for needy individuals (e.g. Meer 2014), research work and equipment (e.g. Byrnes et al. 2014), communal purchases of renewable energy solutions for electricity consumption (e.g. Lam and Law 2016), funding of communal cultural activities and institutions, as well as their restoration/renovation and maintenance (e.g. Josefy et al. 2017), etc.

And, third, crowdfunding can serve as a platform for free and democratic distribution and exchange of ideas through financially supporting social, political, religious, and environmental activism. Here, funds can be raised for financing civic and social initiatives, political parties, public legal actions, production and distribution of ideologically infused media (i.e. books, magazines, videos, etc.), and so forth.

Overall, these ethical advantages, seem to relate closely to notions of what has been referred to as the 'collective level of consumer empowerment', where alternative modes of social organization around consumption are constructed and emerge from collaboration with others (Papaoikonomou and Alarcón 2015). Here, traditional information asymmetries are destabilized and may be remedied via alternative and more democratic fundraising channels, which may also serve as social aggregation platforms around causes of interest that may go beyond consumption.

On the other hand, some also view crowdfunding as a source of new ethical problems. Such view challenges the assumption that the 'wisdom of the crowd' is coming up with optimal solutions. Here some critics warn about the 'madness of the crowd', the 'tyranny of the majority', and unintentional legitimization of institutional failures. First, the concerns with the madness of the crowd, involve situations where groups of people can be collectively misguided and even illogical and delusional (Mackay 2006). Such situations are exacerbated by herding behaviours and information cascades, where later decision making is based on inferences from earlier decision making by others (Shiller 2015). Hence, when a critical mass of individuals makes a decision based on incomplete information or outright misinformation, risk assessment based on others' behaviour can be heavily misguided. Such situations represent a far cry from Kantian business ethics suggesting that managers should continuously consider their rights and duties in relation to others, including vulnerable individuals. Here, while these concerns are mostly associated with investor protection and related disclosure requirements (Heminway 2014), they are also relevant for non-investment campaigning in terms of consumer and donor protection.

Second, concerns with the tyranny of the majority (Guinier 1995), as adopted from political science, relates to situations where decisions made by a majority groups do not account for the needs of minorities, or comes at the expense and even directly hurting minority groups. The very definition of crowdfunding is based on public funding of small sums from a large group of people, but what about small groups of people who are unable to raise large sums from the crowd, or when a large group raises funding for an initiative that implies an oppression of a minority.

And, third, by replacing failing public institutions in funding of public goods (i.e. health care, education, environmental protection, etc.), the crowd indirectly legitimizes these institutional shortcomings. Here, while some failure to finance public goods is a result of objective lack of funding, some of it may also be a result of mismanagement of public funds and even corruption in certain cases (Dorotinsky and Pradhan 2007). Hence, funding of public goods via crowdfunding reduces the pressure on, and responsibility of, public institutions and may indirectly legitimize cases of their mismanagement. While this may lead to considerable improvement in well-being in the short-term, utilitarian principles of achieving greatest happiness for the greatest number of people may be violated in the long-term.

In the following section we delve deeper and outline potential ethical pitfalls for the stakeholders involved in crowdfunding practice, as well as some mechanisms for addressing such challenges and dilemmas.

Mapping Ethical Considerations in Crowdfunding

Since crowdfunding practice involves multiple stakeholders, the current section will outline ethical dilemmas and pitfalls with respect to each of the four key stakeholders involved, including—platform, fundraiser, funder, and regulator. This review will follow the approach of Waters and Bird (1989), highlighting that unethical practice can be both 'against' the firm (e.g. false costs reporting for personal gain) and 'for' the firm (e.g. paying bribes for closing deals or getting licences). Accordingly, we address ethical considerations that relate to actions both for and against the relevant stakeholder. Now, while all stakeholders may be subjected to ethical dilemmas common to practice outside the context of crowdfunding, our review will focus on the dilemmas most relevant specifically to the context of crowdfunding.

Crowdfunding Platforms

A crowdfunding platform is 'an internet application bringing together project owners and their potential backers, as well as facilitating exchanges between them, according to a variety of business models' (Shneor and Flåten 2015, p. 188). Platforms operate in accordance with crowdfunding models that include both investment (i.e. peer-to-peer lending, equity CF, revenue sharing, etc.) and non-investment models (i.e. reward and donation CF). Due to the young nature of the industry, most platforms represent relatively young start-ups with limited resources and a survivalist modus operandi. As such, they are subjected to pressures and

Table 8.1 Ethical pitfalls for platforms

Ethical pitfalls		Options for addressing
For platform success	Against platform success	
• Misappropriation of crowd funds for covering platform expenses • Misuse of user data and privacy violation • Hidden and unclearly specified pricing • Misrepresentation of campaign results and dynamics • Approve publication of unethical/untrustworthy campaigns • Cutting corners in quality and security • Operating outside existing legal frames	• Ideological biases in campaign approval • Provide ill advice to fundraisers (not experts in everything)	• State regulation of platform operations and published content • Self-regulation by industry organizations • Self-regulation by industry and users • Accounting reviews • Periodic external audits on ethical practices • Platform-level ethical concern reporting and communication lines • Ethics training of employees

dilemmas common to other entrepreneurial ventures (Hannafey 2003; Harris et al. 2009), primarily including the liability of newness and decision making under conditions of resource scarcity.

Table 8.1 outlines key ethical pitfalls platforms may fall into when attempting to deal with the pressures of liability of newness and resource scarcity. Such pitfalls include intentional and non-intentional instances of abuse of power, compromise on quality and security, as well as misinformation. All of which may be characterized as violations of ethical intent, means, or ends captured in the third basic perspective of ethical marketing (Laczniak and Murphy 2006). Abuse of power can come in the forms of misappropriating crowd funds for covering platform expenses (in jurisdictions where platforms can manage crowd funds), the misuse of user data while violating privacy or harvesting commercial value from such data without consent and/or knowledge of the users. Alternatively, abuse of power may also be evident in unfair exclusion of otherwise ethical campaigns based on ideological biases of platform managers, and the provision of ill advice on areas outside the specialization of platform employees. A different challenge relates to compromise on quality that may be manifested in approving publication of ethically questionable projects, as well as cutting corners in quality checks of campaigns, quality of service, and data security. In addition, instances of misinformation may include hidden and unclearly specified pricing, and the misrepresentation of campaign results and dynamics all to attract more fundraisers and funders to the platform.

In addition, since generally innovation comes before regulation, some crowdfunding platforms may be faced with dilemmas of operating in national jurisdictions completely lacking relevant regulations, or where existing regulation results in less ethical solutions for the public. In the former, platforms operating without clear regulatory guidelines and under heavy resource constraints, may be tempted to adopt more relaxed interpretations of user validation procedures, campaign quality filtering needs, investor and customer protection requirements, as well as limitations on the use of funders' monetary contributions. In such cases, self-regulation via platform management, industry associations, as well as via critic media and public opinion may replace national regulation in the short term, but stakeholders should engage authorities towards establishing relevant legal frameworks in the long run.

Alternatively, examples of the latter cases can be related to excessive costs associated with entry barriers and compliance requirements for loan facilitators, which enshrine monopolies of large credit providers offering loans with higher interest rates and under worse conditions than those offered via crowd lending platforms; limitation of platforms abilities to manage portfolio investments for funders resulting in higher rather than lower risks for users; limitations on distribution of equity campaign information in the age of social media networking and free information flows online; as well as long and expensive permit procedures for donation fundraising projects, to name a few. In such situations, while regulatory amendment can be encouraged via public debates and lobbying, platforms are faced with the options of either exiting the market until regulatory changes are implemented or walking the fine lines of civil disobedience (Falkenberg and Falkenberg 2009) with tight legal support and often under special permission and under supervision of financial authorities.

Some of the mechanisms that may help ensure the ethical practice of crowdfunding platforms include adherence to and work on advancing crowdfunding-related state regulations. In addition to state regulation, which may require long political negotiation cycles, self-regulation through industry associations' codes of conduct, as well as self-regulation by users in flagging out ethically questionable campaigns and practices can also prove useful. Hence, ethical platforms need to ensure that both they and the fundraisers using them achieve a behavioural standard in excess of obligations specified in existing laws, a requirement corresponding with Laczniak and Murphy's (2006) second basic perspective of ethical marketing.

Furthermore, and regardless of formal legal requirements, platforms can be required to engage in periodic financial auditing, as well as ethical auditing (Laczniak and Murphy 2006), possibly by third-party organizations. Finally, other mechanisms for ensuring ethical practices at the platform level, may include ethical training to employees (ibid.), as well as establishment of communication and reporting procedures for ethical concerns of both employees and the public. The latter providing the crowd with an opportunity to exercise its own responsibility in demanding ethical campaigns and campaigning.

Fundraisers

A fundraiser, in the context of crowdfunding, can be defined as an individual or organization actively raising funds from the crowd for a specified purpose outlined in a fully or partially publicly available campaign or loan request. In earlier research, and often pending on the crowdfunding model involved, fundraisers are also referred to as 'campaign creators' or 'creators' in most models of crowdfunding, 'loan takers' or 'borrower' specifically in the peer-to-peer lending, and 'donation collectors' in context of donation crowdfunding. Here, it is important to stress that our understanding of fundraising goes well beyond charitable gift giving with which the concept has been most frequently associated earlier (e.g. Anderson 1996). Hence, fundraising in crowdfunding can be associated with sales and investment, as well as donation. And accordingly, ethical

Table 8.2 Ethical pitfalls for fundraisers

Ethical pitfalls		Options for addressing
For fundraiser success	Against fundraiser success	
• Overselling and provision of misleading info • Share personal sensitive information • Fundraising for projects with unethical objectives • Fundraising for projects with unethical outcomes • Misrepresentation of campaign results and dynamics	• Misuse of funds raised (from bad choices to criminal use) • Delivering substandard products and services to funders • No or misinformation after campaign end in case of delays or failure	• Quality checks and verifications by platform • Regulating eligibility to run campaigns + rights and obligations • Guidelines for ethical fundraising • Require supportive materials for critical fundraiser claims • Ethical concern reporting and communication lines

considerations for salespeople (i.e. Valentine and Barnett 2002), entrepreneurs (i.e. Hannafey 2003; Harris et al. 2009), and charity collectors (i.e. Anderson 1996) may apply.

Table 8.2 outlines key ethical pitfalls fundraisers may fall into when attempting to deal with the pressures to perform, succeed, and avoid failure. Here, paraphrasing Laczniak and Murphy's (2006) first basic perspective of ethical marketing, fundraisers should never view funders (and other supporters) as merely a means to a profitable end, but should place people first and ensure that their projects achieve real social benefit beyond satisfying a narrow customer segment need.

Relevant pitfalls here include intentional and non-intentional instances of abuse of power, compromise on quality, misinformation, as well as directly or indirectly hurting humans, animals, or the environment. Cases of abuse of power may be manifested in failing to deliver on campaign promises by misusing of funds raised for other purposes than the ones stated in campaign. A different situation can also involve in using personal information of investors without their consent or knowledge. Instances of compromise on quality may be in the delivery of substandard products and services, or those produced under ethically questionable conditions for saving costs, while deviating from specifications and promises outlined in campaign. Cases of misinformation can include situations in which fundraisers engage in 'overselling' while providing misleading and partial information, misrepresenting campaign results and dynamics as the campaign develops, or misinforming, or even failing to inform funders in case of delivery delays or project failure once campaign is finished. Finally, fundraisers may engage in projects with unethical objectives and/or outcomes that can hurt humans (i.e. actions against minority groups, fraudulent activities, criminal activities, etc.), animals (i.e. involving animal cruelty and abuse, etc.), or the environment (i.e. production and/or consumption damaging environment, etc.).

Various mechanisms may help ensure the ethical practice of fundraisers in crowdfunding which include adherence to crowdfunding-related state regulations. In addition to requirements specified in law, platforms can issue ethical guidelines for fundraisers with a checklist fundraises can go through before submitting campaigns. Other actions by platforms can include systematic quality checks and verifications activities both as specified by law and as not specified by law but required for ethical practice. More specifically, requirements for proper disclosure of information about critical aspects of the campaign, risks involved in fulfilment of its promises, as well as the identity of the fundraisers should be closely observed and enforced by platforms. Finally, platforms may provide a dedicated communication line for flagging concerns about unethical practice by fundraisers, and when needed leading to the freezing of a running campaign until ethical concerns are removed. Such option provides an outlet for the crowd to exercise its own responsibility to demand ethical campaigns and campaigning.

Funders

A Funder, in the context of crowdfunding, can be defined as an individual or organization providing financial resources in response to a concrete call for funding in the form of a crowdfunding campaign or peer-to-peer loan application/request, and based on pre-specified conditions stated in such calls. Funders have also been referred to as 'backers', 'contributors', and

Table 8.3 Ethical pitfalls for funders

Ethical pitfalls		Options for addressing
For funder success	Against funder success	
• Bully/Pressure others into support • Funding projects with unethical objectives • Funding projects with unethical outcomes • Learning about opportunity on platform but closing deals without platforms	• Public harassment or shaming of fundraisers, causes, or other funders • Public misinformation about campaigners, causes, or other funders	• Platform sanctions against funders and campaigners • Guidelines for ethical CF support • Ethical concern reporting and communication lines • Regulating funder rights and obligations

'supporters' in all crowdfunding models; 'investors' in the various investment models of crowdfunding; 'loan givers' or 'lenders' specifically in peer-to-peer lending; and 'donors' in donation crowdfunding. Accordingly, ethical considerations of funders in the context of crowdfunding may relate to those relevant to investors (Drover et al. 2014), lenders (e.g.—in case of institutional lenders—Cowton 2002), customers, and donors (e.g. as in ethics as value sought by consumers—Smith 1996).

Table 8.3 outlines key ethical pitfalls funders may fall into when being concerned with the success of crowdfunding campaigns they have or have not supported, as well as considering the ethical value proposition of such campaigns. Relevant pitfalls here include intentional and non-intentional instances of abuse of power, misinformation, as well as directly or indirectly hurting humans, animals, or the environment. Abuse of power may be evident in instances of bullying and unfair pressure of others to financially support campaigns through actual or implied harassment and/or public shaming on social media. Alternatively, wealthy supporters may force fundraisers to close deals they have learned about on platforms outside the platform and without its involvement, at the expense of platform income and public profit. In terms of misinformation, here situations may involve the public spreading and sharing misleading and/or inaccurate information (not originating from the fundraiser) about campaigns and the fundraisers behind them for enhancing either the success or the failure of a campaign. And, in terms of potentially hurting humans, animals, and the environment, funders may fail to assess negative ethical implications of projects with clear or hidden unethical objectives and/or outcomes.

Here, again, some mechanisms may help ensure the ethical practice of funders in crowdfunding which include adherence to crowdfunding-related state regulations. In addition to requirements specified in law, platforms can issue ethical guidelines for funders about engagement with other prospective funders about campaigns. Other actions by platforms may include a dedicated communication line for flagging concerns about unethical practice by funders, and when needed leading to the freezing of relevant accounts until ethical concerns are removed, and even informing users about false information being shared about the relevant campaign and/or fundraiser. And, finally, platforms can also include an incentive or sanctions scheme for funders based on the extent to which they behave ethically.

Regulators

A regulator, for the purpose of our discussion, refers to the governmental authority/body responsible for formulation, amendment, and entry of laws into the national law books that control practices related to crowdfunding. Such authorities include national legislators/parliaments, which rely on input provided by institutions including (but not limited to) ministries of finance and economy, financial regulatory authorities, national consumer protection agencies, and so on. Indeed, earlier theorizing effort building on institutional theory, has highlighted the importance of regulators for crowdfunding success (Kshetri 2015) and investor protection (Heminway 2014). Others have reported a significant association between perceived adequacy of crowdfunding regulation (by platforms) and its volumes per capita in European countries (Ziegler et al. 2019), as well as globally (Ziegler et al. 2020).

Accordingly, the very process in which the regulator defines boundaries for the crowdfunding industry may also include ethical considerations of its own, primarily addressing ethical objectives of regulation, ethical regulation process, and ethical outcomes of regulation. Table 8.4 presents

Table 8.4 Ethical pitfall for regulators

Ethical pitfalls		Options for addressing
For public protection	Against public protection	
• Enforce new laws that are excessive and reduce ethical outcomes (lower access to finance with worse conditions) • Enforce new laws that are too permissive reducing ethical outcomes (encouraging irresponsible and risky behaviour)	• Avoid amendments to law while enforcing existing laws that provide less ethical outcomes (lower access to finance with worse conditions) • Protection of traditional financial monopolies • Not providing opportunities for public hearings on ethical implications of laws	• Parliamentary hearings about ethical implications of existing regulation • Sandbox regulatory processes for involving stakeholders in regulation review • Setting national ethical concern reporting and communication lines • Commission expert assessments of ethical aspects in current regulation

potential ethical pitfalls in this context. First, in terms of ethical objectives of regulation, regulators must avoid reluctance to review ethical implications of existing regulation under changing technological and social conditions. Such situations may include intentional and non-intentional bureaucratic avoidance of law amendments that may enhance ethical objectives. Second, regulation processes should follow ethical procedures, as when not providing opportunities for public hearings on the ethical implications of existing laws, or avoidance of sandbox processes where both industry players and regulators interact in formulating laws that fit new technological and social conditions. And third, failing to address negative ethical implications of existing or proposed laws. In case of existing laws, regulators should consider whether they provide unnecessary protection for monopolistic powers reducing overall public welfare. And in the case of new proposed laws, regulators should strike a balance between over- and under-regulation, which may result in excessive or too permissive laws that will lead to differing ethically questionable outcomes.

Certain actions and practices may help ensure the ethical outcomes of regulatory work in the context of crowdfunding. First, regulators may commission expert assessments as well as hold parliamentary hearings on the ethical implications of current regulation in face of new technological and social conditions. Second, regulators can closely engage with industry players in a sandbox process for both mapping potential ethical pitfalls in crowdfunding practice and developing legal remedies for them. And, third, regulators can establish a formal unit or function where members of the public can report and flag unethical practices that can serve as input for future regulation, or as basis for suspending operations of relevant actors when relevant.

Conclusion

The current discussion is one of the first to address ethical considerations in crowdfunding practice. It does so from the perspectives of multiple stakeholders including platforms, fundraisers, funders and the regulator, and outlines concrete potential ethical pitfalls and mechanisms for addressing them. Overall, we suggest that while crowdfunding practice can serve as a solution to earlier ethical challenges in the financial sector, it also presents some new ethical challenges that need to be addressed by stakeholders with relevant policy and action.

From a practical perspective, our mapping of ethical pitfalls and mechanisms for addressing them can serve as prescriptive guidelines for the various stakeholders in their efforts to ensure, enhance, and improve ethical practice in crowdfunding. Here, crowdfunding platforms can formulate ethical guidelines for fundraisers and funders, introduce incentive and sanction schemes for ethical practice by both, train its employees, and develop codes of conduct for them to follow. In addition, regulators can engage in activities that enable evaluation of the ethical implications of existing regulation under new technological and social conditions of the internet economy and social media age, as well as engage in ethical procedures of regulatory amendments towards better ethical outcomes of new laws.

Finally, in terms of research, due to the absence of earlier research on ethics in the context of crowdfunding, opportunities for relevant discoveries are abundant. Accordingly, we hereby outline several such opportunities. First, future studies may identify and analyse the implications and effects of ethical practices of platforms in various crowdfunding models, as well as national, sectoral, and segment contexts. Second, researchers may examine the role played by ethical considerations in the decision of funders to financially support campaigns, as well as share information about them. Third, researchers can assess the impact of ethical cues in campaign content and materials on the success of such campaigns. And, fourth, other studies may attempt to assess the ethical implications of existing regulatory frameworks in different countries, while examining whether they correlate with better market results overall, and ethical outcomes in particular.

References

Anderson, A. (1996). *Ethics for Fundraisers*. Bloomington, IN: Indiana University Press.

Berliner, L. S., & Kenworthy, N. J. (2017). Producing a Worthy Illness: Personal Crowdfunding Amidst Financial Crisis. *Social Science and Medicine, 187*, 233–242.

Boatright, J. R. (2010). Ethics in Finance. In J. R. Boatright (Ed.), *Finance Ethics: Critical Issues in Theory and Practice*. Hoboken, NJ: John Wiley & Sons Inc..

Bucar, B., & Hisrich, R. D. (2001). Ethics of Business Managers vs. Entrepreneurs. *Journal of Developmental Entrepreneurship, 6*(1), 59–82.

Byrnes, J. E. K., Ranganathan, J., Walker, B. L. E., et al. (2014). To Crowdfund Research, Scientists Must Build an Audience for Their Work. *PLoS One, 9*(12), 1–29.

Carpenter, N. (2017). The 5 Biggest Crowdfunding Failures of All Time. Retrieved April 30, 2019, from https://www.digitaltrends.com/cool-tech/biggest-kickstarter-and-indiegogo-scams/.

Cowton, C. J. (2002). Integrity, Responsibility and Affinity: Three Aspects of Ethics in Banking. *Business Ethics: A European Review, 11*(4), 393–400.

DesJardins, J. R. (2009). *An Introduction to Business Ethics*. New York, NY: McGraw-Hill Higher Education.

Donaldson, T., & Dunfee, T. W. (1994). Toward a Unified Conception of Business Ethics: Integrative Social Contracts Theory. *Academy of Management Review, 19*(2), 252–284.

Dorotinsky, W., & Pradhan, S. (2007). Exploring Corruption in Public Financial Management. In E. J. Campos & S. Pradhan (Eds.), *The Many Faces of Corruption: Tracking Vulnerabilities at the Sector Level*. Washington, DC: The World Bank.

Drover, W., Wood, M. S., & Fassin, Y. (2014). Take the Money or Run? Investors' Ethical Reputation and Entrepreneurs' Willingness to Partner. *Journal of Business Venturing, 29*(6), 723–740.

Dunfee, T. W., Smith, N. C., & Ross, W. T. (1999). Social Contracts and Marketing Ethics. *Journal of Marketing, 63*(3), 14–32.

Erturk, I., Froud, J., Johal, S., et al. (2007). The Democratization of Finance? Promises, Outcomes and Conditions. *Review of International Political Economy, 14*(4), 553–575.

Falkenberg, A. W., & Falkenberg, J. (2009). Ethics in International Value Chain Networks: The Case of Telenor in Bangladesh. *Journal of Business Ethics, 90*(3), 355–369.

Fassin, Y., & Drover, W. (2017). Ethics in Entrepreneurial Finance: Exploring Problems in Venture Partner Entry and Exit. *Journal of Business Ethics, 140*(4), 649–672.

Gentile, M. C. (2010). *Giving Voice to Values: How to Speak Your Mind When You Know What's Right*. New Haven: Yale University Press.

Guinier, L. (1995). *Tyranny of the Majority: Fundamental Fairness in Representative Democracy*. New York, NY: The Free Press.

Hannafey, F. T. (2003). Entrepreneurship and Ethics: A Literature Review. *Journal of Business Ethics, 46*(2), 99–110.

Harris, J. D., Sapienza, H. J., & Bowie, N. E. (2009). Ethics and Entrepreneurship. *Journal of Business Venturing, 24*(5), 407–418.

Heminway, J. M. (2014). Investor and Market Protection in the Crowdfunding Era: Disclosing to and for the 'Crowd'. *Vermont Law Review, 38*, 827–847.

Josefy, M., Dean, T. J., Albert, L. S., et al. (2017). The Role of Community in Crowdfunding Success: Evidence on Cultural Attributes in Funding Campaigns to 'Save the Local Theater'. *Entrepreneurship Theory and Practice, 41*(2), 161–182.

Kant, I. (1785/1991). *'Perpetual Peace: A Philosophical Sketch'. Kant: Political Writings*. Cambridge: Cambridge University Press.

Kshetri, N. (2015). Success of Crowd-Based Online Technology in Fundraising: An Institutional Perspective. *Journal of International Management, 21*(2), 100–116.

Laczniak, G. R., & Murphy, P. E. (2006). Normative Perspectives for Ethical and Socially Responsible Marketing. *Journal of Macromarketing, 26*(2), 154–177.

Lam, P. T. I., & Law, A. O. K. (2016). Crowdfunding for Renewable and Sustainable Energy Projects: An Exploratory Case Study Approach. *Renewable and Sustainable Energy Reviews, 60*, 11–20.

Light, B., & McGrath, K. (2010). Ethics and Social Networking Sites: A Disclosive Analysis of Facebook. *Information Technology & People, 23*(4), 290–311.

Mackay, C. (2006). *Extraordinary Popular Delusions and the Madness of Crowds*. Petersfield, Hampshire: Harriman House.

Meer, J. (2014). Effects of the Price of Charitable Giving: Evidence from an Online Crowdfunding Platform. *Journal of Economic Behavior & Organization, 103*, 113–124.

Mill, J. S. (2016). Utilitarianism. In S. M. Cahn (Ed.), *Seven Masterpieces of Philosophy*. New York, NY: Routledge.

Mollick, E. (2015). *The Kickstarter Fulfillment Report* [Online]. Kickstarter.com. Retrieved April 30, 2019, from https://www.kickstarter.com/fulfillment.

Palmer, K. (2016). Peer-to-Peer Firm Tells Lenders They Will Lose a Quarter of Their Cash. Retrieved April 30, 2019, from https://www.telegraph.co.uk/finance/newsbysector/banksandfinance/12109898/Peer-to-peer-firm-tells-lenders-they-will-lose-a-quarter-of-their-cash.html.

Papaoikonomou, E., & Alarcón, A. (2015). Revisiting Consumer Empowerment: An Exploration of Ethical Consumption Communities. *Journal of Macromarketing, 37*(1), 40–56.

Pierce-Wright, C. H. (2016). State Equity Crowdfunding and Investor Protection. *Washington Law Review, 91*(2), 847–886.

Roman, S. (2007). The Ethics of Online Retailing: A Scale Development and Validation from the Consumers' Perspective. *Journal of Business Ethics, 72*(2), 131–148.

Sandbu, M. E. (2011). *Just Business: Arguments in Business Ethics*. Upper Saddle River, NJ: Prentice Hall.

Shiller, R. J. (2015). *Irrational Exuberance: Revised and Expanded* (3rd ed.). Princeton, NJ: Princeton University Press.

Shneor, R., & Flåten, B.-T. (2015). Opportunities for Entrepreneurial Development and Growth Through Online Communities, Collaboration, and Value Creating and Co-creating Activities. In H. R. Kaufmann & S. M. R. Shams (Eds.), *Entrepreneurial Challenges in the 21st Century*. Basingstoke: Palgrave Macmillan.

Smith, C. N. (1996). Ethics and the Typology of Customer Value. In K. P. Corfman & J. G. J. Lynch (Eds.), *Advances in Consumer Research*. Provo, UT: Association for Consumer Research.

Snyder, J., Mathers, A., & Crooks, V. A. (2016). Fund My Treatment!: A Call for Ethics-Focused Social Science Research into the Use of Crowdfunding for Medical Care. *Social Science & Medicine, 169*, 27–30.

Valentine, S., & Barnett, T. (2002). Ethics Codes and Sales Professionals' Perceptions of Their Organizations' Ethical Values. *Journal of Business Ethics, 40*(3), 191–200.

Veenhoven, R. (1991). Is Happiness Relative? *Social Indicators Research, 24*(1), 1–34.

Waters, J. A., & Bird, F. (1989). Attending to Ethics in Management. *Journal of Business Ethics, 8*(6), 493–497.

Zhang, S., & Miller, M. (2017). China's New Illegal Fundraising Topped $36 Billion Last Year. Retrieved April 30, 2019, from https://www.reuters.com/article/us-china-fraud-crackdown/chinas-new-illegal-fundraising-topped-36-billion-last-year-idUSKBN17R11X.

Ziegler, T., Shneor, R., Wenzlaff, K., et al. (2019). *Shifting Paradigms – The 4th European Alternative Finance Benchmarking Report*. Cambridge, UK: Cambridge Centre for Alternative Finance.

Ziegler, T., Shneor, R., Wenzlaff, K., et al. (2020). *The Global Alternative Finance Market Benchmarking Report*. Cambridge, UK: Cambridge Centre for Alternative Finance.

9

Crowdfunding Campaigns: Role of Legal Institutions and Social Capital

Wanxiang Cai, Friedemann Polzin, and Erik Stam

Introduction

The recent emergence of financial investment crowdfunding (i.e., equity and lending crowdfunding) has attracted substantial attention from policy makers and academic researchers alike. Crowdfunding exhibits tremendous potential to support entrepreneurial activities. The market size of equity crowdfunding is expected to reach $36 billion by 2020, exceeding the size of the venture capital market at that time (Cumming et al. Forthcoming). Financial investment crowdfunding (hereafter 'financial crowdfunding') involves a range of risks from an investor's point of view (Kirby and Worner 2014). The great number of 'unsophisticated investors' (defined according to level of income and wealth) in financial crowdfunding makes governance problems more pronounced (Cumming et al. Forthcoming) and thus requires more attention.

Institutions, defined as 'the rules of the game in a society' (North 1991), can mitigate the risks in financial crowdfunding to some extent.

W. Cai (✉) • F. Polzin • E. Stam
Utrecht University School of Economics, Utrecht, Netherlands
e-mail: w.cai@uu.nl; f.h.j.polzin@uu.nl; e.stam@uu.nl

Research on venture capital has shown that legal institutions, measured by government effectiveness, quality of regulatory policies, control of corruption, rule of law, political stability, and voice and accountability, have a positive effect on the development of the venture capital market (Li and Zahra 2012). Social capital can to some degree substitute legal institutions in financial markets when legal institutions are deficient (Peng and Heath 1996). Social capital (e.g., trust, reciprocity, and social norms) punishes individuals whose behaviours deviate from social norms (Bowles and Gintis 2002). For instance, in group lending, social capital enhances an individual's willingness to borrow money via monitoring the loans and punishing defaults in a group liability arrangement (Karlan 2007). Especially in a virtual context, in which members temporarily work together to complete a joint task through digital technologies, trust involves establishing and monitoring standards to improve team performance (Crisp and Jarvenpaa 2013). Thus, in crowdfunding contexts, we expect that social capital will contribute to the group outcome (i.e., campaign success).

Previous research on the relationship between social capital and financial crowdfunding has focused mainly on the micro level, that is, how entrepreneurs' social capital affects the success of crowdfunding campaigns and backers' involvement (Vismara 2016; Colombo et al. 2015; Eiteneyer et al. 2019). Little crowdfunding research has investigated the role of legal institutions and social capital at the macro level. To the best of our knowledge, only one paper has empirically demonstrated that both legal institutions and social capital have a positive effect on national crowdfunding volume (Rau 2017). On the one hand, a standard macro-to-macro research cannot explicitly identify *how* legal institutions and social capital affect the development of crowdfunding markets. On the other hand, it is difficult for research at the micro level to take institutional variation into account. Thus, cross-level research may clarify the role of legal institutions and social capital at the macro level in financial crowdfunding governance. For instance, trust in strangers (relational social capital at the macro level) increases investors' propensity to invest in equity crowdfunding (crowdfunding outcomes at the micro level) (Kshetri 2018), and legal institutions can protect investors' benefits, thereby affecting their funding intentions.

Previous research has suggested that legal institutions at the macro level may not fully explain the heterogeneity in entrepreneurial activities across countries and that the meso level should thus be involved to bridge the research on macro and micro levels (Kim et al. 2016). The effect of legal institutions on financial markets depends not only on the degree to which laws protect investor rights but also on the degree to which those laws are enforced (La Porta et al. 2006).

Crowdfunding involves three main actors: Fundraisers post their project online, crowds observe these projects and decide whether to invest, and platforms function as a bridge to connect fundraisers and investors. A recent study suggested that in crowdfunding campaigns, platforms play the active role of providing due diligence (Cumming and Zhang 2018). To some extent, the due diligence provided by platforms reflects the degree to which platforms enforce legal regulations on crowdfunding, because most regulators require platforms to check the validity of documents provided by issuers before posting their project online. Thus, the protection of investors also relies on platforms' enforcement of regulations on financial crowdfunding. Moreover, social capital embedded in platforms affects the formation of fundraisers' social capital at the micro level. From a micro-to-macro perspective, the number of successful campaigns on platforms and the number of platforms also affect the aggregation of crowdfunding outcomes at the macro level. Thus, we introduce a platform-level analysis that provides a deeper understanding of the relationship among legal institutions, social capital, and crowdfunding performance.

The rest of the chapter is organized as follows: the 'Conceptual Background' section briefly introduces the concepts of legal institutions and social capital, as well as their effect on general financial crowdfunding. 'Crowdfunding and Institutions at Macro and Micro Levels' section clarifies the traditional macro-micro-level model to explain how legal institutions and social capital at both macro and micro levels affect individual crowdfunding campaigns and the development of financial crowdfunding markets. 'Towards a Multilevel Analysis of Financial Crowdfunding and Institutions' section introduces the meso-level analysis. 'Conclusion' section summarizes how legal institutions and social capital affect financial crowdfunding with a three-level model.

Conceptual Background

In this section, we introduce the main conceptual building blocks of our study. Two streams of literature have investigated how risks in financial crowdfunding, and entrepreneurial finance more generally, can be mitigated.

Legal Institutions

Legal institutions play an important role in the governance of financial markets. North (1991) originally highlighted the role of secure property and contractual rights in discouraging investments and specialization. Later research demonstrated that legal institutions are essential in the development of financial markets and entrepreneurial activities. La Porta et al. (1997, 1998) explored the effect of legal protections of investors on financial development. They suggested that countries with legal systems which protect the right of investors, enforce private property rights, and support private contractual arrangements have more flourishing financial markets.

More recent research has also demonstrated a relationship between different legal institutions and the development of entrepreneurial finance. For example, legal institutions (aggregated by government effectiveness, rule of law, political stability, voice and accountability, and quality of regulatory policies, etc.) are positively associated with the volume of venture capital in a country (Li and Zahra 2012). Grilli et al. (2016) created a framework to explain how both formal and informal institutions affect venture capital activities. They divided legal institutions into fiscal policy and other legal regulations: tax rate on capital gains, fiscal regulations on investee companies, and corporate income tax are conducive to the development of venture capital activities; other legal regulations, including the legal system, labour regulations, investor protection regulations, and regulations on protection of property rights, affect venture activities as well.

As a novel channel of entrepreneurial finance, financial crowdfunding has some similarities with venture capital; thus, we expect that legal institutions will also influence the development of the financial crowdfunding market. A second stream of literature has extensively discussed social capital, as a type of informal institution, in relation to crowdfunding (Cai et al. 2019).

Social Capital

Social capital is an informal institution that disciplines individuals' behaviours. Adler and Kwon (2002, p. 23) defined social capital as 'the goodwill available to individuals or groups. Its source lies in the structure and content of the actor's social relations. Its effects flow from the information, influence, and solidarity'. In the field of business and economics, especially in relation to finance, social capital has been discussed mainly at micro and macro levels.

At the micro level, Nahapiet and Ghoshal (2000) divided social capital into three dimensions: structural, relational, and cognitive social capital. Regarding entrepreneurial finance, entrepreneurs' structural social capital is normally measured by their social networks, their relational social capital can be measured by investors' trust in them, and their cognitive social capital comprises the shared values, culture, and goals of fundraisers and investors. The authors developed a framework to elaborate on how different dimensions of social capital create intellectual capital through the exchange and combination of knowledge. Later research demonstrated a positive relationship between different dimensions of social capital and access to different forms of entrepreneurial finance. For example, entrepreneurs rely on their social networks to gain access to venture capital (Batjargal and Liu 2004; Shane and Cable 2002). Business angels make use of their structural, relational, and cognitive social capital to identify and evaluate investment opportunities (Sørheim 2003). In banking, network complementarity can enhance a firm's access to bank loans and reduce the cost of capital (Uzzi 1999). Moreover, the shared culture of borrowers and lenders reduces the default rate in group lending (Karlan 2007).

At the macro level, social capital is viewed as a type of soft territorial capital which contributes to regional development (Camagni 2017; Westlund and Bolton 2003). The interplay of different types of social relationships leads to dense combinations of such relationships, which are dependent on geographic proximity and thus lay the foundation of regional social capital (Malecki 2012). Westlund and Bolton (2003, p. 79) defined regional social capital as 'spatially-defined norms, values, knowledge, preferences, and other social attributes or qualities that are reflected in human relationship. In regional studies, social capital functions as both "glue" and "lubricant"', maintaining cooperation and facilitating the interaction and flows within organizations (Malecki 2012). Social capital has a positive effect on macroeconomic growth (Knack and Keefer 1997), regional innovation, and entrepreneurship (Akçomak and Ter Weel 2009; Feldman and Zoller 2012). Regional social capital also affects the development of financial markets. A previous study suggested that social capital contributes to the development of stock markets in Italy (Guiso et al. 2004). A cross-country study demonstrated a positive relationship between social capital and both financial depth and efficiency (Calderón et al. 2002).

Crowdfunding and Institutions at Macro and Micro Levels

In this section, we analyse previous research and, based on its results, build a two-level model to elaborate on how legal institutions and social capital affect financial crowdfunding at macro and micro levels.

In line with previous studies (Martínez-Climent et al. 2018; Rau 2017), we focus only on the two types of financial return models (lending and equity). Investors in financial crowdfunding are driven mainly by financial returns, and the motivation to support others ranks among the least important factors (Vismara 2018). Financial crowdfunding is closer to other forms of financial investment, such as microlending, business angels, and venture capital, making it more applicable to economic approaches like signalling theory (Ahlers et al. 2015; Bapna 2017; Vismara 2016). Financial crowdfunding involves higher risks compared to nonfinancial crowdfunding. Among the main risks faced by investors are default or nonpayment, fraud, illiquidity by fundraisers, lack of transparency in operations, closing or failure of the platform, and cyber-attacks (Kirby and Worner 2014). This is supported by interviews with fundraisers and investors, who indicate that they regard equity crowdfunding investing as high risk and high return (Estrin et al. 2018). Moreover, most investors in financial crowdfunding are less experienced and face large information asymmetries when evaluating the quality of projects (Ahlers et al. 2015; Bapna 2017).

Macro-Level Dynamics

Some features of financial crowdfunding resemble those of entrepreneurial finance, such as business angels and venture capital (Lukkarinen et al. 2016). For example, in both financial crowdfunding and investment by business angels, investors driven by financial return invest their own funds in projects. In the United Kingdom, angel investors are normally found in equity crowdfunding platforms. In China, on the other hand, most equity crowdfunding platforms adopt the leader–follower model, in which both business angels and venture capitalists do the due diligence for and endorse the projects, thereby attracting subsequent investors. Some research has indicated that equity crowdfunding is more likely to be the complement of business angels (e.g., Hornuf and Schwienbacher 2016). Therefore, we expect that the influence of both legal institutions and social capital on financial crowdfunding will be similar to that on other entrepreneurial financial sources, such as business angels and venture capital.

Rau (2017) investigated the correlation between legal institutions and crowdfunding volume. He focused on the effect of overall legal regimes (the regulations on financial crowdfunding are excluded). He found that overall legal regimes (including control of corruption and the overall financial market development) and social capital (measured by trust in strangers) have a positive effect on national financial crowdfunding volume. Because legal regimes and regulations on financial crowdfunding may have different effects on crowdfunding volume, we discuss them separately.

Regulations on financial crowdfunding protect investors by setting requirements for the minimum income or net assets to enter the market (Hornuf and Schwienbacher 2017). The effect of regulations on crowdfunding might play out differently: On the one hand, the protections of investors encourage them to invest in financial crowdfunding. For example, a recent report found a positive relationship between the platform owners' perceived adequacy of regulation and national crowdfunding volume (Ziegler et al. 2019). On the other hand, excessively strong protections of investors reduce the number of qualified investors and harm the motivation of fundraisers. Hence, regulators need to strike a balance between crowdfunding market promotion and the protection of retail investors.

As for social capital, Rau (2017) quantitatively demonstrated that trust in strangers has a positive effect on national financial crowdfunding volume. Therefore, we suggest that social capital at the macro level may have a positive impact on the development of financial crowdfunding markets.

Micro-Level Dynamics

At the micro level, we discuss only the role of social capital. Previous research on crowdfunding has examined the determinants of crowdfunding success mainly at the micro level and has demonstrated that structural, relational, and cognitive dimensions of social capital affect the success of crowdfunding campaigns at the micro level (Cai et al. 2019).

Previous research on structural social capital in financial crowdfunding has suggested that entrepreneurs can make use of their private social networks (i.e., family and friends) to raise money (Lukkarinen et al. 2016). The size of entrepreneurs' social networks is perceived as reflecting the quality of the project and thereby attracts more investors to support the campaign (Vismara 2016). Such investor networks can trigger herding, which increases the chance of campaign success (Liu et al. 2015).

Regarding relational social capital, investors' trust in fundraisers plays an important role in their decision-making. In lending crowdfunding, lenders' economic status, including credit grades, verified bank accounts, and debt-to-income ratio, reflects their ability to pay the interest on time, thereby exerting a positive influence on crowdfunding success (Greiner and Wang 2010). Previous successful campaigns are also positively associated with fundraisers' trustworthiness (Yum et al. 2012). Other measurements of trust in fundraisers include third-party endorsements (Greiner and Wang 2010; Chen et al. 2016), entrepreneur–sponsor interactions (Xu and Chau 2018), and the disclosure of personal information (Ge et al. 2017). All of these studies demonstrated that investors' trust in fundraisers encourages them to invest in the projects.

Cognitive social capital has received less attention in financial crowdfunding research. Only one paper has investigated lending crowdfunding. Burtch et al. (2014) found that the cultural distance between borrowers and lenders has a negative influence on lending actions.

Interactions Between Financial Crowdfunding and Institutions at Macro and Micro Levels

Above, we show that both legal institutions and social capital at the macro level affect individual behaviours at the micro level, thereby affecting the performance of individual crowdfunding campaigns (*macro-micro mechanism*). This mechanism is depicted in Fig. 9.1.

Legal institutions at the macro level affect individual crowdfunding campaigns directly and through the mediation effect of social capital. First, mandatory information disclosure requires firms to post certain information on the platform, which can send signals reflecting the quality of the projects to potential investors (Ahlers et al. 2015). Such signals can reduce the information asymmetry between investors and entrepreneurs, helping them evaluate the true value of the projects. Moreover, legal protections of investors encourage them to invest in the project without worrying about potential defaults in crowdfunding.

Legal institutions are positively associated with trust (Berggren and Jordahl 2006). The enormous risks associated with financial crowdfunding discourage investors to support campaigns. Stronger legal protections of investors can increase their trust in both the project and fundraisers: First, comprehensive registration requirements allow only high-quality projects to be listed on the platform (Cumming and Zhang 2018),

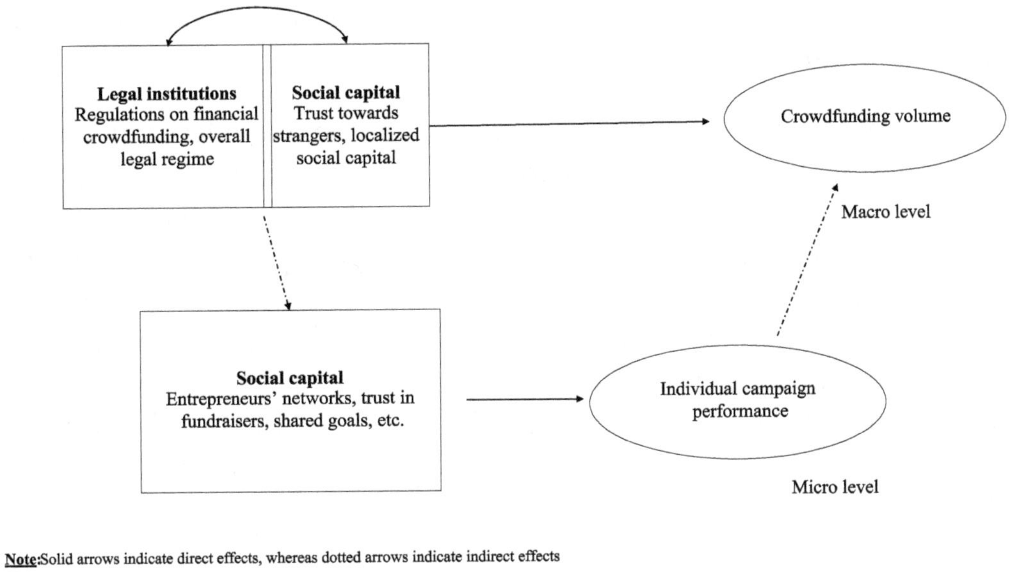

Fig. 9.1 Interactions between financial crowdfunding and institutions at macro and micro levels

increasing investors' trust in the campaign. Stricter legal regulations prevent fundraisers from intentionally deceiving investors, thereby enhancing investors' trust that fundraisers are listing projects in good faith. Thus, the legal institutions affect individual crowdfunding campaigns by increasing investors' trust in the projects. Based on these arguments, we put forward our first proposition:

Proposition 1 Social capital at the micro level can mediate the effect of legal institutions on the success of individual crowdfunding campaigns.

Social capital at the macro level also has an impact on individual crowdfunding campaigns. Giudici et al. (2018) measured localized relational social capital by the number of nonprofit organizations, recycling, voter turnout, and satisfaction with relationships with friends. They found that social capital at the macro level affects the performance of reward-based crowdfunding campaigns by enhancing the effect of local altruism on the contributions from local investors. In a qualitative study of equity crowdfunding, Kshetri (2018) argued that investors' trust in strangers increases their tendency to invest in the projects. Therefore, social capital at the macro level has a positive effect on the performance of crowdfunding campaigns.

The aggregation of crowdfunding success at the micro level affects the crowdfunding volume at the macro level. In line with prior findings that excessively strong legal protection of crowdfunders may reduce the number of crowdfunding campaigns in a country, stronger legal institutions may not lead to higher regional crowdfunding volume. Thus, higher individual crowdfunding performance does not entail higher regional crowdfunding volume. In fact, before 2015, the United States allowed only sophisticated investors to enter crowdfunding markets, but the country subsequently lowered the requirement in an effort to attract more funding from small investors.

Entrepreneurship research has suggested that social capital plays a more important role when legal institutions are weaker. For instance, in emerging economies, venture capitalists rely on social relationships and their networks to screen potential investment opportunities and monitor investees (Ahlstrom and Bruton 2006). Moreover, the effect of trust on financial development is less important when the legal system is more efficient (Guiso et al. 2004). A comparative study indicated that the effect of fundraisers' social capital on campaign success in China is higher than that in the United States (Zheng et al. 2014). Although the authors attributed this finding to cultural differences between the two countries, it still indicates that in a developing market, investors rely on social sanctions to protect their benefits. Therefore, we believe that entrepreneurs' social capital, as well as social capital at the macro level, can replace legal institutions in financial crowdfunding; that is, when the legal institutions are weaker, fundraisers' social capital has a stronger effect on crowdfunding success. Thus, we arrive at our second proposition:

Proposition 2 Legal institutions moderate the relationship between social capital (at both macro and micro levels) and individual crowdfunding success.

Towards a Multilevel Analysis of Financial Crowdfunding and Institutions

The Role of Platforms in Crowdfunding

Crowdfunding platforms are an active intermediary between entrepreneurs and investors. First, they enforce the regulations on financial crowdfunding to supervise transactions between investors and fundraisers. Second, they establish specific rules to reduce potential risks in crowdfunding. Finally, they provide some value-added services for projects.

On financial crowdfunding platforms, inexperienced investors face abundant risks. Regulators require fundraisers to publish a prospectus and platforms to ensure the validity of information disclosed by fundraisers. Therefore, platforms conduct due diligence for fundraisers to mitigate the information asymmetry between fundraisers and investors. They aim at sorting out both lower-quality projects and lower-quality investors. The degree of due diligence varies across platforms. Fierce competition among platforms may result in allowing unsecured fundraisers to enter the market (Yoon et al. 2019). In fact, some regulators (e.g., the Financial Conduct Authority in the United Kingdom) did not establish specific requirements for information disclosure, allowing crowdfunding platforms to follow their own standards for due diligence. Further, to attract more funding, some platforms did not check the qualifications of investors. A popular article attributed the increasing default rates of Chinese P2P lending projects partly to platforms' practice of pooling funds illegally from investors (Liu 2018). Moreover, UK platforms are obligated to educate investors about the risks involved in financial crowdfunding. Apparently, the degree to which investors are educated varies: Some platforms list only the potential risks for investors, whereas others require investors to pass a test during the registration process.

Second, platforms create their own rules for running campaigns, which affect the behaviours of both entrepreneurs and crowdfunders. There are two main types of business models for crowdfunding: 'all-or-nothing' and 'keep-it-all'. In the all-or-nothing model, only successful campaigns can collect money from investors, making entrepreneurs more likely to disclose information about the projects to ensure the success of the crowdfunding project (Cumming and Zhang 2018). Platforms also establish different rules for investors' decision-making. For instance, in some platforms, all investors have to make decisions together (e.g., investors in AngelList have to join a syndicate and follow a leader to invest in certain projects), whereas in most other platforms, investors can make decisions independently. In some P2P lending platforms, borrowers must disclose their economic status (e.g., debt-to-income ratio, credit grades, verified bank accounts), which reflect their ability to the money (Greiner and Wang 2010). Recently, some platforms (e.g., Zopa and Lending Club) have adopted artificial intelligence to create credit scores for borrowers. In Chinese P2P lending markets, platforms have adopted various methods of reducing potential risks involved in investing, including risk reserves funding, third-party endorsements, and fund custodian mechanisms (Yoon et al. 2019). The fee structure also influences platform-specific rules. Platforms which charge fees only for successful projects are more willing to conduct due diligence, whereas those that receive fees from all projects may devote less effort to due diligence (Cumming and Zhang 2018).

Overall, platforms provide a series of additional services for fundraisers to pursue crowdfunding success and even future funding successes, including promotion services, business planning, financial analysis, strategic guidance, exist assistance, and advisory services for future funding (Cumming and Zhang 2018; Rossi and Vismara 2018). Both theoretical and empirical research have investigated how these services affect individual crowdfunding success. For instance, Wu et al. (2018) built a theoretical model to examine how the quality and matching services provided by platforms affect their performance. They suggested that excluding low-quality projects is profitable if investors' preference for project quality is substantial enough. Rossi and Vismara (2018) tested the relationship between platform services and the number of successful campaigns. They found that only post campaign services offered by platforms (e.g., exit assistance, second market, advisory services for future funding, etc.) positively affect the number of successful campaigns.

Platforms as the Meso Level

As discussed above, a simple macro-micro-level research design may face two analytical shortcomings: the ecological fallacy and disaggregation bias (Kim et al. 2016). In our case, the ecological fallacy means that the inferences of macro-to-micro research may be misleading if they are attributed to a lower level of analysis. Thus, it might be arbitrary to attribute the negative effect of excessively strong protection of investors on crowdfunding volume to the damage of entrepreneurial initiatives. Disaggregation bias describes situations in which the results of micro-level research may not be transferable to the macro level. Therefore, we cannot simply conclude that the results at the micro level can be replicated at the macro level or vice versa. A recent study suggested that the factors that contribute to crowdfunding success vary across platforms (Dushnitsky and Fitza 2018), which indicates that crowdfunding research should take into consideration the nature of the platform.

For two reasons, we follow Kim et al. (2016) by introducing the platform as a meso-level factor in the multilevel analysis of institutions and financial crowdfunding. First, both social capital and legal institutions exist at the meso level. Through interactions among participants, trust, networks and shared goals can be developed on crowdfunding platforms (Cai et al. 2019), while platforms create their own rules and business models, which to some extent can be seen as regulations at the meso level (e.g., establishing specific information-disclosure requirements, designing mechanisms to reduce potential risks, educating investors, and using specific fee structures).

Second, platforms are essential in creating social capital and enforcing legal institutions in crowdfunding activities. The term 'crowdfunding community' has been used widely in crowdfunding research (e.g., Belleflamme et al. 2014; Agrawal et al. 2014). Even in financial crowdfunding, investors can also benefit from 'community benefits', such as investment experience (Belleflamme et al. 2014). Thus, investors rely to some extent on interactions with others to alleviate information asymmetry in financial crowdfunding (Liu et al. 2015; Wang et al. 2019). In addition, platforms conduct due diligence as well as put forward platform policies, which not only enforce the legal institutions at the macro level but also strengthen trust among investors. This forms the basis for our third proposition:

Proposition 3 Crowdfunding platforms at the meso level mediate the effect of legal institutions and social capital on crowdfunding success.

Social capital and legal institutions are associated with social capital and legal institutions at other levels. For example, trust can penetrate to other levels; that is, the higher the trust towards strangers (macro level), the higher the trust towards platforms and fundraisers will be. In addition, legal institutions at the macro level affect crowdfunding campaigns through the enforcement of regulations. Furthermore, legal institutions also affect trust at different levels (this phenomenon is discussed further in the next section). Thus, we suggest that platforms constitute the meso level in a multilevel model, which can mitigate both the ecological fallacy and the disaggregation bias.

Although social capital is a multidimensional concept, we focus only on trust—the most frequently discussed dimension in social-capital-based research on financial crowdfunding—in our three-level model. This approach can clearly explain how social capital and legal institutions across different levels jointly affect financial crowdfunding.

Three-Level Model of Institutions and Financial Crowdfunding

Legal institutions and social capital at the macro level can directly and indirectly (via social capital) affect crowdfunding campaigns. The direct effect can be seen in the two-level model proposed above. The meso level plays an important role in the indirect effect. The degree to which legal institutions protect investors also depends on the enforcement of regulations by crowdfunding platforms. Only strong enforcement of regulations on financial crowdfunding by platforms enhances the protection of investors, affecting their decision-making. Moreover, platforms may follow their own standards in information disclosure, which can affect the number and the content of signals sent by projects' information, which can in turn mitigate the information asymmetry between investors and fundraisers. Second, platforms must educate and select investors. If platforms allow only qualified investors to enter the markets and inform them of potential risks, investors have a greater chance of identifying high-quality campaigns.

Legal institutions also affect social capital on both meso and micro levels. Regulations on financial crowdfunding affect the quality of platforms, because they can operate only after being approved by the financial authority. Only high-quality platforms are allowed to operate, which enhances investors' trust that platforms are a reliable venue on which to invest and can protect their interests. Second, regulations on financial crowdfunding may clarify platforms' responsibility for conducting due diligence. For instance, in the United Kingdom, platforms must ensure that the information disclosure of the project is fair, clear, and not misleading (FCA n.d.). Thus, platforms which conduct adequate due diligence receive higher trust from investors, because such due diligence enables investors to screen low-quality projects (Cumming and Zhang 2018).

Trust at macro and meso levels increases the trust in fundraisers, thereby enhancing their funding intentions. Trust at the macro level (trust in strangers) reflects people's willingness to be vulnerable to others' actions (Mayer et al. 1995). In financial crowdfunding, investors risk losing their money. Higher trust at the macro level may increase investors' trust in platforms and fundraisers, because they are more willing to take the risks involved in crowdfunding investments. Moreover, investors' trust at the meso level increases their trust in fundraisers, because platforms enforce rules for the listed projects. Empirical research has demonstrated that trust in platforms (meso level) is positively associated with trust in fundraisers (micro level) (Chen et al. 2014).

We suggest that the relationship between crowdfunding outcomes at micro and macro levels requires further elaboration, especially regarding the role of platforms. First, legal institutions affect the creation of platforms. For instance, Dushnitsky et al. (2016) found that the strength of legal rights in a country's credit market has a positive effect on the creation of lending crowdfunding platforms and a negative influence on

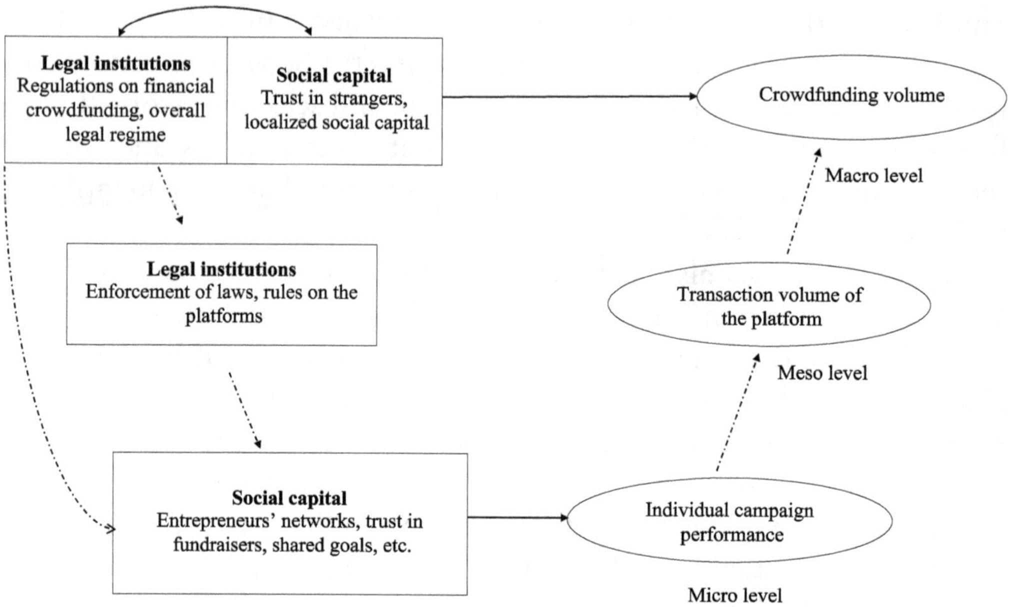

Fig. 9.2 Interactions between financial crowdfunding and institutions at macro, meso, and micro levels

equity crowdfunding platforms. Second, the services of platforms also affect the number of successful campaigns conducted on them. For instance, post campaign services increase the number of successful campaigns on a platform (Rossi and Vismara 2018). Therefore, taking platforms into account may provide a deep understanding of how the aggregation of successful crowdfunding campaigns affects regional crowdfunding volume. Figure 9.2 illustrates the overall framework of the three-level model.

Conclusion

Using a two-level model, this chapter explains how legal institutions and social capital at macro and micro levels affect crowdfunding performance across micro and macro levels. We suggest that legal institutions and social capital (at both macro and micro levels) affect crowdfunding campaigns and that the role of social capital may replace that of legal institutions in financial investment crowdfunding.

To enhance the explanatory power of the two-level model, we introduce crowdfunding platforms as a meso level. We explain the role of platforms in the crowdfunding market and then elaborate on the mechanism by which the meso level bridges macro- and micro-level analyses. Platforms moderate the effect of regulations on financial crowdfunding and increase investors' trust in fundraisers by due diligence. The number of successful campaigns of platforms and the total number of platforms in turn affects the aggregation of crowdfunding outcomes at the macro level. These mechanisms improve our understanding of the role of platforms in the development of financial crowdfunding markets.

This chapter suggests directions for future crowdfunding research. Compared to micro-level research, macro- and meso-level crowdfunding studies are rare. To determine whether the empirical results of micro-level research can be replicated at meso and macro levels, more empirical evidence is required. Furthermore, the interactions between legal institutions and social capital across different levels require more exploration. This chapter provides a framework for conducting such research (e.g., analysing the moderation of due diligence on the relationship between legal institutions at the macro level and individual crowdfunding campaigns).

This chapter also has practical implications for both policy makers and platform owners. On the one hand, policy makers should consider the enforcement of regulations by crowdfunding platforms. Although most regulators demand that platforms ensure the validity of information disclosed by fundraisers, supervision of platforms is lacking. Only if platforms follow relevant regulations on crowdfunding can these regulations effectively regulate the crowdfunding market. On the other hand, platform owners should recognize the role of platform rules in platform performance. By adopting suitable rules and a suitable business model, owners can improve their business performance.

References

Adler, P. S., & Kwon, S.-W. (2002). Social Capital: Prospects for a New Concept. *Academy of Management Review, 27*(1), 17–40.

Agrawal, A., Catalini, C., & Goldfarb, A. (2014). Some Simple Economics of Crowdfunding. *Innovation Policy and the Economy, 14*(1), 63–97.

Ahlers, G. K. C., Cumming, D., Günther, C., & Schweizer, D. (2015). Signaling in Equity Crowdfunding. *Entrepreneurship Theory and Practice, 39*(4), 955–980.

Ahlstrom, D., & Bruton, G. D. (2006). Venture Capital in Emerging Economies: Networks and Institutional Change. *Entrepreneurship Theory and Practice, 30*(2), 299–320.

Akçomak, İ. S., & ter Weel, B. (2009). Social Capital, Innovation and Growth: Evidence from Europe. *European Economic Review, 53*(5), 544–567.

Bapna, S. (2017). Complementarity of Signals in Early-Stage Equity Investment Decisions: Evidence from a Randomized Field Experiment. *Management Science, 65*(2), 933–952.

Batjargal, B., & Liu, M. (2004). Entrepreneurs' Access to Private Equity in China: The Role of Social Capital. *Organization Science, 15*(2), 159–172.

Belleflamme, P., Lambert, T., & Schwienbacher, A. (2014). Crowdfunding: Tapping the Right Crowd. *Journal of Business Venturing, 29*(5), 585–609.

Berggren, N., & Jordahl, H. (2006). Free to Trust: Economic Freedom and Social Capital. *Kyklos, 59*(2), 141–169.

Bowles, S., & Gintis, H. (2002). Social Capital and Community Governance. *The Economic Journal, 112*(483), F419–F436.

Burtch, G., Ghose, A., & Wattal, S. (2014). Cultural Differences and Geography as Determinants of Prosocial Lending. *MIS Quarterly, 38*(3), 773–794.

Cai, W., Polzin, F., & Stam, E. (2019). *Crowdfunding and Social Capital: A Systematic Literature Review*. SSRN Scholarly Paper ID 3361748. Rochester, NY: Social Science Research Network. Retrieved from https://papers.ssrn.com/abstract=3361748.

Calderón, C., Chong, A., & Galindo, A. (2002). Development and Efficiency of the Financial Sector and Links with Trust: Cross-Country Evidence. *Economic Development and Cultural Change, 51*(1), 189–204.

Camagni, R. (2017). Regional Competitiveness: Towards a Concept of Territorial Capital. In R. Capello (Ed.), *Seminal Studies in Regional and Urban Economics: Contributions from an Impressive Mind* (pp. 115–131). Cham: Springer International Publishing.

Chen, D., Lai, F., & Lin, Z. (2014). A Trust Model for Online Peer-to-Peer Lending: A Lender's Perspective. *Information Technology and Management, 15*(4), 239–254.

Chen, X., Zhou, L., & Wan, D. (2016). Group Social Capital and Lending Outcomes in the Financial Credit Market: An Empirical Study of Online Peer-to-Peer Lending. *Electronic Commerce Research and Applications, 15*, 1–13.

Colombo, M. G., Franzoni, C., & Rossi-Lamastra, C. (2015). Internal Social Capital and the Attraction of Early Contributions in Crowdfunding. *Entrepreneurship Theory and Practice, 39*(1), 75–100.

Crisp, C. B., & Jarvenpaa, S. L. (2013). Swift Trust in Global Virtual Teams: Trusting Beliefs and Normative Actions. *Journal of Personnel Psychology, 12*(1), 45–56.

Cumming, D. J., & Zhang, Y. (2018). *Are Crowdfunding Platforms Active and Effective Intermediaries?* SSRN Scholarly Paper ID 2882026. Rochester, NY: Social Science Research Network. Retrieved from https://papers.ssrn.com/abstract=2882026.

Cumming, D. J., Vanacker, T., & Zahra, S. A. (Forthcoming). Equity Crowdfunding and Governance: Toward an Integrative Model and Research Agenda. *Academy of Management Perspectives.*

Dushnitsky, G., & Fitza, M. A. (2018). Are We Missing the Platforms for the Crowd? Comparing Investment Drivers Across Multiple Crowdfunding Platforms. *Journal of Business Venturing Insights, 10,* e00100.

Dushnitsky, G., Guerini, M., Piva, E., et al. (2016). Crowdfunding in Europe: Determinants of Platform Creation Across Countries. *California Management Review, 58*(2), 44–71.

Eiteneyer, N., Bendig, D., & Brettel, M. (2019). Social Capital and the Digital Crowd: Involving Backers to Promote New Product Innovativeness. *Research Policy, 48*(8), 103744.

Estrin, S., Gozman, D., & Khavul, S. (2018). The Evolution and Adoption of Equity Crowdfunding: Entrepreneur and Investor Entry into a New Market. *Small Business Economics, 51*(2), 425–439.

Feldman, M., & Zoller, T. D. (2012). Dealmakers in Place: Social Capital Connections in Regional Entrepreneurial Economies. *Regional Studies, 46*(1), 23–37.

Financial Conduct Authority. (n.d.). *FCA Handbook*. Retrieved May 21, 2019, from https://www.handbook.fca.org.uk/handbook/COBS/.

Ge, R., Feng, J., Gu, B., et al. (2017). Predicting and Deterring Default with Social Media Information in Peer-to-Peer Lending. *Journal of Management Information Systems, 34*(2), 401–424.

Giudici, G., Guerini, M., & Rossi-Lamastra, C. (2018). Reward-Based Crowdfunding of Entrepreneurial Projects: The Effect of Local Altruism and Localized Social Capital on Proponents' Success. *Small Business Economics, 50*(2), 307–324.

Greiner, M. E., & Wang, H. (2010). Building Consumer-to-Consumer Trust in E-Finance Marketplaces: An Empirical Analysis. *International Journal of Electronic Commerce, 15*(2), 105–136.

Grilli, L., Latifi, G., & Mrkajic, B. (2016). *Institutional Determinants of Venture Capital Activity: A Survey of the Literature and a Research Agenda*. SSRN Scholarly Paper ID 3105441. Rochester, NY: Social Science Research Network. Retrieved from https://papers.ssrn.com/abstract=3105441.

Guiso, L., Sapienza, P., & Zingales, L. (2004). The Role of Social Capital in Financial Development. *American Economic Review, 94*(3), 526–556.

Hornuf, L., & Schwienbacher, A. (2016). Crowdinvesting: Angel Investing for the Masses? In H. Landström & C. Mason (Eds.), *Handbook of Research on Business Angels* (pp. 381–398). Cheltenham: Edward Elgar.

Hornuf, L., & Schwienbacher, A. (2017). Should Securities Regulation Promote Equity Crowdfunding? *Small Business Economics, 49*(3), 579–593.

Karlan, D. S. (2007). Social Connections and Group Banking. *The Economic Journal, 117*(517), F52–F84.

Kim, P. H., Wennberg, K., & Croidieu, G. (2016). Untapped Riches of Meso-Level Applications in Multilevel Entrepreneurship Mechanisms. *Academy of Management Perspectives, 30*(3), 273–291.

Kirby, E., & Worner, S. (2014). *Crowd-Funding: An Infant Industry Growing Fast*. Staff Working Papers. IOSCO Research Department.

Knack, S., & Keefer, P. (1997). Does Social Capital Have an Economic Payoff? A Cross-Country Investigation. *The Quarterly Journal of Economics, 112*(4), 1251–1288.

Kshetri, N. (2018). Informal Institutions and Internet-Based Equity Crowdfunding. *Journal of International Management, 24*(1), 33–51.

La Porta, R., Lopez-de-Silanes, F., Shleifer, A., & Vishny, R. W. (1997). Legal Determinants of External Finance. *The Journal of Finance, 52*(3), 1131–1150.

La Porta, R., Lopez-de-Silanes, F., & Shleifer, A. (2006). What Works in Securities Laws? *The Journal of Finance, 61*(1), 1–32.

Li, Y., & Zahra, S. A. (2012). Formal Institutions, Culture, and Venture Capital Activity: A Cross-Country Analysis. *Journal of Business Venturing, 27*(1), 95–111.

Liu, J. (2018). The Dramatic Rise and Fall of Online P2P Lending in China. *TechCrunch* (blog). Retrieved May 24, 2019, from http://social.techcrunch.com/2018/08/01/the-dramatic-rise-and-fall-of-online-p2p-lending-in-china/.

Liu, D., Brass, D. J., Lu, Y., et al. (2015). Friendships in Online Peer-to-Peer Lending: Pipes, Prisms, and Relational Herding. *MIS Quarterly, 39*(3), 729–7A4.

Lukkarinen, A., Teich, J. E., Wallenius, H., et al. (2016). Success Drivers of Online Equity Crowdfunding Campaigns. *Decision Support Systems, 87*, 26–38.

Malecki, E. J. (2012). Regional Social Capital: Why It Matters. *Regional Studies, 46*(8), 1023–1039.

Martínez-Climent, C., Zorio-Grima, A., & Ribeiro-Soriano, D. (2018). Financial Return Crowdfunding: Literature Review and Bibliometric Analysis. *International Entrepreneurship and Management Journal, 14*(3), 527–553.

Mayer, R. C., Davis, J. H., & Schoorman, D. F. (1995). An Integrative Model of Organizational Trust. *Academy of Management Review, 20*(3), 709–734.

Nahapiet, J., & Ghoshal, S. (2000). Social Capital, Intellectual Capital, and the Organizational Advantage. In *Knowledge and Social Capital* (pp. 119–157). Boston: Butterworth-Heinemann.

North, D. C. (1991). Institutions. *Journal of Economic Perspectives, 5*(1), 97–112.

Peng, M. W., & Heath, P. S. (1996). The Growth of the Firm in Planned Economies in Transition: Institutions, Organizations, and Strategic Choice. *Academy of Management Review, 21*(2), 492–528.

Porta, R., Lopez-de-Silanes, F., Shleifer, A., & Vishny, R. W. (1998). Law and Finance. *Journal of Political Economy, 106*(6), 1113–1155.

Rau, P. R. (2017). *Law, Trust, and the Development of Crowdfunding. Cambridge Centre for Alternative Finance Conference*. Cambridge, UK.

Rossi, A., & Vismara, S. (2018). What Do Crowdfunding Platforms Do? A Comparison Between Investment-Based Platforms in Europe. *Eurasian Business Review, 8*(1), 93–118.

Shane, S., & Cable, D. (2002). Network Ties, Reputation, and the Financing of New Ventures. *Management Science, 48*(3), 364–381.

Sørheim, R. (2003). The Pre-Investment Behaviour of Business Angels: A Social Capital Approach. *Venture Capital, 5*(4), 337–364.

Uzzi, B. (1999). Embeddedness in the Making of Financial Capital: How Social Relations and Networks Benefit Firms Seeking Financing. *American Sociological Review, 54*(4), 481–505.

Vismara, S. (2016). Equity Retention and Social Network Theory in Equity Crowdfunding. *Small Business Economics, 46*(4), 579–590.

Vismara, S. (2018). Information Cascades Among Investors in Equity Crowdfunding. *Entrepreneurship Theory and Practice, 42*(3), 467–497.

Wang, W., Mahmood, A., Sismeiro, C., et al. (2019). The Evolution of Equity Crowdfunding: Insights from Co-investments of Angels and the Crowd. *Research Policy, 48*(8), 103727.

Westlund, H., & Bolton, R. (2003). Local Social Capital and Entrepreneurship. *Small Business Economics, 21*(2), 77–113.

Wu, W., Huang, X., Li, Y., et al. (2018). Optimal Quality Strategy and Matching Service on Crowdfunding Platforms. *Sustainability, 10*(4), 1–17.

Xu, J. J., & Chau, M. (2018). Cheap Talk? The Impact of Lender-Borrower Communication on Peer-to-Peer Lending Outcomes. *Journal of Management Information Systems, 35*(1), 53–85.

Yoon, Y., Li, Y., & Feng, Y. (2019). Factors Affecting Platform Default Risk in Online Peer-to-Peer (P2P) Lending Business: An Empirical Study Using Chinese Online P2P Platform Data. *Electronic Commerce Research, 19*(1), 131–158.

Yum, H., Lee, B., & Chae, M. (2012). From the Wisdom of Crowds to My Own Judgment in Microfinance Through Online Peer-to-Peer Lending Platforms. *Electronic Commerce Research and Applications, 11*(5), 469–483.

Zheng, H., Li, D., Wu, J., et al. (2014). The Role of Multidimensional Social Capital in Crowdfunding: A Comparative Study in China and US. *Information & Management, 51*(4), 488–496.

Ziegler, T., Shneor, R., Wenzlaff, K., Odorovic, A., Johanson, D., Hao, R., & Ryll, L. (2019). *Shifting Paradigms: The 4th European Alternative Finance Benchmarking Report.* Cambridge, UK: Cambridge Centre for Alternative Finance.

Part II

Crowdfunding: A Historical Perspective

10

Crowdfunding Development and the Financial Industry

Aki Kallio and Lasse Vuola

Introduction

Crowdfunding is a means of raising finance for projects from the crowd often through an internet-based platform where project owners pitch their idea to potential backers, who are typically not professional investors, although increasing activity by institutional investors has been recorded. Crowdfunding takes many forms and sometimes without any potential for a financial return. Crowdfunding in its current context is relatively young and business models are evolving at a fast pace. Crowdfunding platforms have emerged recently since internet technology evolved in such a way as to allow easy and simple two-way

A. Kallio (✉)
Danske Bank A/S Finland Branch, Helsinki, Finland
e-mail: aki.kallio@danskebank.fi

L. Vuola
Fundu Ltd., Helsinki, Finland
e-mail: lasse.vuola@fundu.fi

communication. This enables interaction between the members of the crowd of investors, as well as between the crowd and the project owners pitching their specific projects (European Securities and Markets Authority 2014).

In 2017, alternative finance volumes from across Europe grew by 36%, from 7.67 billion euros to 10.44 billion euros (Ziegler et al. 2019). Overall, the major share of European volume still originates from the UK (68%). However, excluding the UK, the European online alternative finance market grew at nearly double the UK's year-on-year growth rate—63% in comparison to 35% in 2017. While this growth was not as strong as in 2016 (101%), there was visible growth in each sub-region of continental Europe. As a whole, the market grew by just over 1.3 billion euros to 3.369 billion euros in 2017 (Ziegler et al. 2019). While there was an overall growth, the rate of growth seems to have cooled in some more mature markets even though it is continuing (Ziegler et al. 2019).

The growth of crowdfunding as a new complementary and alternative form of financing is indisputable, and its importance to businesses both domestically and internationally is already remarkable (Ziegler et al. 2019). With the ever-increasing advent of digitalization combined with tightening regulation for banks, alternative finance has become an important part of the present financial markets. The alternative of today may turn out to be the mainstream of tomorrow. It is therefore important to evaluate the role of crowdfunding as part of the history of the financial markets. This is particularly relevant in the context of what is currently happening in financial markets via the transformation brought about by digitalization and ever-increasing regulatory burden imposed especially towards banks while restricting their ability to finance small and medium-sized enterprises (SMEs). Crowdfunding, at least for the time being, can be considered one of the most viable examples of the gradual transformation of financial markets caused by emergence of financial technology (fintech). Thus, crowdfunding joins an important group of innovations, which have changed, formed, and developed the financial markets through time like credit cards, stocks, mutual funds, and online banking, all of which have been influential innovations and disruptors of their time (Atack and Neal 2009).

However, as a phenomenon, there is nothing new in crowdfunding and similar ways to access finance have been utilized in the past. Currently crowdfunding is increasingly establishing itself as an integral part of the finance industry especially for start-ups and early phase companies that have traditionally been funded by "family, friends, and fools" in order to develop and gradually attract more interest (by direct investments and/or other collaboration) from sophisticated investors and venture capital funds (Kallio and Vuola 2018; Ziegler et al. 2019). This chapter focuses on those forms of crowdfunding, which have the most relevance to the financial markets, namely debt- and investment-based crowdfunding, and aims to give an analysis why, what, and how crowdfunding has become the phenomenon we are witnessing today and at the same time contextualize it as one of the continuous innovations in the history of ever-changing modern financial markets.

Fundamentals of the Financial System

The financial system is a complex environment comprising of different markets that use various financial instruments, such as equities and bond markets, and includes a number of different institutions such as pension funds, banks, insurance companies, funds, large companies, and retail investors (Drake and Fabozzi 2010). The purpose and functioning of financial markets from an economical perspective is based on a fairly simple point of view: markets channel money from surplus sectors to deficit sectors. This mechanism leads, in theory, to the allocation of capital in a most efficient and profitable way for the economy as a whole. Well-functioning financial markets and financial system in general are a prerequisite for the economic activity and growth we are familiar with. In market driven economies, general welfare is strongly connected to efficiency of the markets (Drake and Fabozzi 2010; Kallio and Vuola 2018).

Main functions of the financial markets are (i) providing information to and between market participants, which at best makes the market work transparently and allows the information available to be immediately, equally, and correctly reflected in the prices of the financial instruments; (ii) enabling efficient allocation of funds from the surplus sector to the deficit sector often through intermediaries such as banks so that funding for necessary investments can be acquired at the lowest possible cost and without delay; (iii) risk management aimed at proportionate spread of the risk inherently built into financial markets to be divided among different investments quantitatively over time; and (iv) providing liquidity, the purpose of which is to enable an investment acquired from the financial markets to be cheaply, easily, and quickly liquidated to cash (Atack and Neal 2009; Drake and Fabozzi 2010).

The usual cause of acquiring financing is rooted in a situation where a company's (or private person's) own capital is not sufficient to carry out the necessary or targeted investments, cover running costs, or overcome unexpected costs. In these cases, equity or debt financing become the most viable option. Financing is a way to mobilize resources quicker compared to collection of such resources by cash flow, which would take a considerable amount of time. The leverage function of new capital enables faster growth, but it involves a cost. In practice, the company is always forced to pay compensation for the use of the capital it has acquired. Equity financing is in practice direct equity investments into the company in which the investor receives an ownership share equalling the value of his investment in the company. The return on equity investment consists of the profit distributed by the company as well as profits re-invested into the company. These may increase at par if the valuation of the holding in the company increases, so the return on equity investment is theoretically unlimited. Similarly, the risk is at most equal to the invested equity (not more, not less) (Ferran 2008; Drake and Fabozzi 2010).

Debt financing is both short term (i.e. for a period of less than one year), such as trade payables and overdrafts, and long term (i.e. over a period of one year or more), such as bonds and bank loans. Debt financing is always external financing, and, as such, there is always an underlined obligation to repay on fixed terms compared to equity. On the other hand, debtor also carries the credit risk and the risk of the company having sufficient cash flow, which the lender must carefully consider when making a financing decision in addition with the evaluation of potential collaterals. The risk of an unsecured debt investment is at most equal to the borrowed capital and overdue, accrued and unpaid interest related thereto (Ferran 2008). Often an investor seeks to secure his position contractually, but also by using various collateral arrangements that secure status of the creditor in the event of a serious default and ultimately in the event of insolvency of the company (Ferran 2008). Debt financing takes precedence in the ranking of the payment order in case of an insolvency of the company compared to equity financing (Ferran 2008). Since profit is a reward for risk taken in business, the lower rank of equity means more risk compared to debt. Therefore, the profit expectancy in equity is generally higher than in debt (Drake and Fabozzi 2010).

The board and the management of a company have a fiduciary duty towards the owners. Rational companies aim to optimize their financing seeking for the best available capital structure. With debt financing the company can, from the owners' perspective, often lower the total cost of capital because investors usually require higher risk premium in relation to equity investments than for debt investments (Drake and Fabozzi 2010). In general, owners of the company try to protect themselves against dilution of ownership making debt finance often a lucrative way to grow through leverage (Ferran 2008). In addition, liability to pay interest in relation to debt financing might provide opportunities to optimize corporate taxation of the company in some jurisdictions (Drake and Fabozzi 2010). With the current stagnating low interest rate era, high leverage ratio may well seem lucrative from owners' perspective.

Setting the Scene

The history of financial markets and finance are united by continuous fluctuations between economic cycles from bull markets to bear markets or bubbles to recessions as well as crises usually caused by structures that enable opportunism and moral gambling. Every crisis contains the seeds of a change, but also risks for regulative overreactions, as well as drastic market reactions. One example is the Great Depression of the US in

1929, which was caused by virtually free speculative trading of stocks and derivatives to the general public and the loss of trust through separation of ownership, as explained by Berle & Means in *The Modern Corporation and Private Property* in 1932. Another and more modern example is the subprime crisis that began in 2007, which was caused by securitization of speculative mortgages and secondary markets related thereto, which at first stage caused widespread credibility gap between banks (i.e. credit crunch), and then later spread across the financial markets as a whole. This latter crisis gradually grew into a worldwide financial crisis eventually leading to the European sovereign debt crisis when several European countries experienced the collapse of major financial institutions, bankrupts of numerous of the countries' biggest companies, high government debt, and rapidly rising bond yield spreads in government securities (Bradley 2013; Chambers and Dimson 2016).

The European sovereign debt crisis also heavily influenced later changes to functioning of and initiatives taken by the European Central Bank (ECB) such as (i) the long-term refinancing operation (LTRO), which is an enhanced credit support measure to support bank lending and liquidity in the euro area announced in 2011, (ii) the targeted longer-term refinancing operations (TLTROs), which are euro system operations that provide financing to credit institutions announced 2014, 2016, and 2019, respectively, and (iii) the asset purchase programme (APP), which is part of a package of non-standard monetary policy measures that also includes targeted longer-term refinancing operations initiated in mid-2014 including corporate sector purchase programme (CSPP), public sector purchase programme (PSPP), asset-backed securities purchase programme (ABSPP), and third covered bond purchase programme (CBPP3). The aim of the ECB with abovementioned programmes was on the one hand to offer banks long-term funding at attractive conditions in order to preserve favourable borrowing conditions for banks and stimulate bank lending to the real economy and on the other to support the monetary policy transmission mechanism and provide the amount of policy accommodation needed to ensure price stability (European Central Bank 2020). In addition, the crisis acted as a catalyst to a still persisting zero-level (or even negative) interest rate environment in Europe.

The former (i.e. Great Depression) led to the implementation of two important acts in the US. First, the Banking Act (i.e. the Glass–Steagall Act), which prohibited any one bank from both accepting deposits and underwriting securities, in order to ensure that if a bank made significant losses underwriting securities, deposits would not be adversely affected. And, second, the extremely tight Securities Act of 1933, representing the first major federal legislation to regulate the offer and sale of securities in the US in order to ensure that buyers of securities receive complete and accurate information before they invest in securities, which is still in force in the US with only some relief from the original statute (Cassis 2017; Mitchener 2005). Both Acts restricted banks' business opportunities largely for the benefit of the general public and society as a whole.

The latter caused tightening of bank regulation, such as risk-weighted capital requirements, market condition, and investor protection, in the global financial markets (especially in the US and Europe) (Chambers and Dimson 2016, pp. 193–194). The enactment of the Dodd–Frank Act in the US was a response to the subprime crisis and brought about the most significant changes to financial regulation in the US since the 1930s preventing the US government from bailing out failing banks with taxpayers' money and imposing short-selling restrictions. In Europe, similar legislative changes were implemented and, with enactments of, among others, the Capital Requirements Directive IV (CRD IV) and the Markets in Financial Instruments Directive II (MIFID II), many restrictions were imposed on banks' businesses. Actions taken both in the US and Europe have heavily impaired banks' business opportunities, by way of, among others, tying their capital to much higher ratios than before the crisis, preventing or even restricting the use and leverage of their balance sheets as well as increasing regulatory compliance and wider conduct requirements (Zestos 2016).

This restrictive trend, as described, has been particularly strong in Europe, with the result that especially the financing of small and medium-sized enterprises (SMEs) has become more challenging. This has been counterbalanced by large-scale EU-wide financing and guarantee arrangements, whose long-term effects are still unknown. In future, we shall learn whether this partial "socialization" of credit risk to the taxpayers was an effective means to counterbalance the tightening regulation. Examples of these approaches, include a corporate bond purchase programmes started by the ECB (as referred above) and the setting up the European Fund for Strategic Investments, which is an EU budget guarantee that provides a shield for the European Investment Bank covering most risky part of the projects it has funded. In authors' view, once these instruments have been introduced to the markets, it may be hard to withdraw them even in the bull market leading into a long-term partial socialization of SME credit risk to taxpayers.

Like other forms of financing, crowdfunding always works within a particular jurisdiction. The provisions laid down in the regulation, in particular the mandatory ones, must be taken into account when utilizing all forms of financing. Besides understanding the history and functioning of global financial markets, it is always necessary to place the activity within the given operating environment and regulations related thereto (Drake and Fabozzi 2010). At the same time social institutions, such as governments, central banks, market supervisors, and supranational institutions, strive to promote trading to maintain economic growth while contrary to this goal also control the markets and operations therein in order to prevent the emergence and spread of systemic risks. Financial law includes acts, which in many cases point to opposite ways aiming at enabling efficient exchange to support investment, economic growth, and employment, and, at the same time, to prevent actions threatening the basic operation of national economies through avoiding emergence of systemic crises. The goal of financial market legislation is simple: trying to optimize the functioning of the financial market. Efficiency in the financial markets does not mean extreme liberalism. On the contrary, the financial market regulation should be limited to what is necessary so that overall confidence in the financial system remains (Drake and Fabozzi 2010).

Every statute increases complexity of the legal system in a non-linear manner. New regulation may lead to artificial market practices and efficiency losses for all market players. Hence, regulation should, from a market liberal economic perspective, focus on ensuring the functioning of key market mechanisms with minimal interruption. In *Confusion de Confusiones* Joseph de la Vega well stated in 1688 that financial system is at the same time "the fairest and most deceitful business … the noblest and the most infamous in the world, the finest and most vulgar on earth".

Things have not changed so much after de la Vega. The aim for the regulator is to incentivize the fairness and nobleness and de-incentivize the deceitfulness and vulgarness.

Efforts to maximize the interests of different stakeholders in the financial markets, and competition among them, create incentives for moral gambling, which lawmakers seek to counter by creating and imposing counter-incentives as well as effective control and enforcement systems. Financial market regulation always affects competitiveness of stakeholders in the financial markets, and regulation that is too burdensome can be seen detrimental to the whole financial market system. On the other hand, legislation can also help speed up market disruption (PWC 2017). Delays are a challenge for the legislator: decision delay, legislative delay, and implementation delay cause problems for effective and well-functioning legislation. The longer the delays the legislator is facing are, the easier it is for crises to emerge and the deeper they can become.

Similarly, the faster the new forms of financing, innovations, and practices are emerging in the financial markets, the more challenging is the role of the financial market supervisor and the legislator. However, as the legislator and market supervisor seek to control systemic risk by observing and regulating existing phenomena, new forms or models and other financial innovations are evolving at an ever-increasing pace in the financial markets. Of these, crowdfunding is an illustrative example. A considerable amount of new financial regulation has come into effect during the last years affecting those operating in the financial markets by increased costs and complexity. This emphasises the ongoing struggle between the stakeholders operating in the financial markets and the broad, ever-increasing, and multi-level regulation shaping the fundaments of financial ecosystem (Kallio and Vuola 2018).

The Brief History of the Modern Financial System

The development of the international financial system is in every respect a historical, economic, and political process. Because of this, it is essential to briefly outline the past, in addition to the present, in order to be able to assess potential future developments and guidelines of the financial markets. The beginning of the international financial system as we know it today dates back to the 1970s, but, more broadly speaking, a global financial system has existed much longer. This further stresses the importance to understand events, notions and wider developments described in the written financial history, which provides the means to comprehend functioning of modern financial markets. In *On the Genealogy of Morals* Friedrich Nietzsche noted in 1887 that the whole idea of duty and personal obligation is rooted in the oldest and the most primitive relationship there is, the relationship between creditor and debtor. This statement continues to quite accurately describe fundamental relationships in the modern financial markets.

The financial markets tend to operate in cycles, which differ depending on the subject matter (volatility, share prices, etc.) under consideration. For example, it is possible to assess the business cycle or the stock market cycle, which largely differ from each other due to differences in relation to the underlying subject matter in question. Although history may not be said to repeat itself, the cyclicity of the financial markets has largely been scientifically proven (Marmer 2016; Chambers and Dimson 2016; Atack and Neal 2009) although the timing of different cycles cannot be determined with any precision.[1] Therefore, it is not surprising that the financial markets witness both highs and lows, of which the former can in the worst case create a financial bubble[2] and the latter a recession meaning a deeper and longer lasting economic downturn.[3] Previous major changes in the financial markets may be categorized in many ways (Atack and Neal 2009). They can be approached through economic bubbles in relation to their impact on the real economy.

One way to outline the most important financial market development stages is to divide them into five phases. In the first phase in the nineteenth century, the leading European industrialized countries and the colonized non-European regions they ruled moved to a gold-denominated currency system that collapsed during World War I. There were sincere efforts to return the gold-denominated currency system in the 1920s, but they failed. This can be considered the second phase of the financial markets' development. In the third phase, the Great Depression of the US, followed by significant tightening of the US financial market regulation and eventually World War II caused international financial markets to shut down almost completely. The fourth stage of the international financial system began after World War II based on gradual dismantling of the post-war regulated economy and opening of the international financial markets, which lasted up to the oil crisis of the 1970s. After the 1970s, we have more or less lived in the current historical era comprising building of the global financial system based on neoclassical theoretical approach and characterized by ever-increasing globalization. This can be called the fifth stage, which we are still in (Kari 2016). The end of the 2010s has been marked by a certain degree of inward turning tendency, during which even many influential parties have openly denied functioning of the open and global financial system. The future will show whether we are in the middle of changing paradigm and living the beginning of the new sixth stage in which the international financial system is being gradually overtaken by separate national and inward-looking systems such as we are currently, at least to some degree, witnessing in the US, Brazil, and Russia to a greater extent. Recent outbreak of COVID-19 virus might further accelerate such inward-looking tendencies on a global level.

Understanding of historical changes of both the financial market and the financial system as a whole will help to put new financial innovations, such as crowdfunding and, more broadly, fintech into perspective (Chambers and Dimson 2016). The change in the financial markets is an extremely wide and complex matter influenced by technological advances and digitalization. Also, the current political, economic, and ideological conditions affect the financial system as a whole. While international development seems to be moving towards an increasingly global financial market (despite some inward-looking tendencies), diverse corporate cultures, differences in politics, as well as legislation between countries remain prevalent.

The Modern Emergence of Crowdfunding

There is nothing new in sourcing money from the crowds. However, crowdfunding, as a concept, is a modern financial service enabled by advanced digitalization. The underlying technology of which has the potential to help investors to find ventures and projects, which need financing and, accordingly, allows the ventures or projects to find investors and backers to finance their growth and development (Dresner 2014, p. 3). Based on one definition "crowdfunding" refers to the ability of pooling small amounts of capital from a potentially large pool of interested funders and supporters (Short et al. 2017). This definition, however, is close to the definition of an initial public offering (IPO). The ability of pooling in IPO is mainly based on the marketing efforts of investment banks acting as "underwriters" whereas in crowdfunding it is based on the digital online platform and its functionalities. In recent years, we have witnessed hybrid models where IPOs have also been executed through crowdfunding platforms.

A crowdfunding platform is "an internet application bringing together project owners and their potential backers, as well as facilitating exchanges between them, according to a variety of business models" (Shneor and Flåten 2015, p. 188). The crowdfunding platforms act as intermediaries between investors and companies (or other projects) and facilitate opportunities for investors to find and support the projects they are interested in (Spacetec 2014). The platform's core value proposition is in taking down the transaction costs and lowering the bar to start a fundraising campaign effort. Just a decade ago, it was basically impossible for an early stage venture to reach out to tens of thousands of potential investors in a cost-efficient way.

Thus far, crowdfunding has been gaining ground very rapidly (European Commission 2016). Major contributing factors to this growth and spread of crowdfunding are both the international crisis in the financial markets in 2008 that has led, inter alia, tightening the capital adequacy and solvency requirements for credit institutions, and the explosion of internet usage and usability, which together have made it possible to reach large crowds of potential funders in a cost-effective manner (IOSCO 2015).

In the near future, crowdfunding may become an increasingly important source of non-bank financing. Worldwide crowdfunding market has been estimated to reach 371 billion euros in 2017 and based on market data strong growth in recent years has been continued (Ziegler et al. 2019), although the rate of growth seems to have cooled in some more mature markets (Ziegler et al. 2019). Crowdfunding is increasingly establishing itself as an integral part of the finance industry especially for start-ups and early phase companies that have traditionally been funded by "family, friends, and fools". Furthermore, crowdfunding provides a feasible alternative to unsecured bank loans that have, for the time being, been one of the most important sources of external financing for SMEs in some jurisdictions, while being almost non-existent in others (European Commission 2018b).

A Brief History of Crowdfunding

Crowdfunding as a form of financing is not a new phenomenon (Spacetec 2014). A similar approach has been used to manage investment risks before internet time (Dresner 2014). For example, in shipping, one of the oldest forms of risk management are guarantee agreements between traders and shipping companies, in which upon the event of loss of cargo all pay part of such loss, but when cargo arrives safely, all parties to the contract (i.e. the guarantors) will receive their proportional share of the profits. This approach has provided the necessary financing to carry out high-risk projects and at the same time enabled successful diversification of the risk associated with the project between the parties.

The basic principles of the crowdfunding business go back to the early eighteenth-century Ireland, where "forefather of microcredits" Jonathan Swift[4] founded the Irish Loan Fund. The Fund offered small loans to low-income rural families who did not have the collateral required by large banks or proper credit history. By the nineteenth century, more than 300 schemes were implemented in Ireland in all of which small amounts were lent by private investors to individuals who needed a loan for short periods.

One of the early contemporary crowdfunding campaigns was carried out in the US in 1885 when the project of the Statue of Liberty on Liberty Island off New York had run into severe financial difficulties. When other means had proven ineffective, Joseph Pulitzer decided to launch a fundraising campaign to fund the erection of a pedestal for the Statue of Liberty in his own newspaper, *The New York World*. In exchange for a donation, he promised to publish the names of all donors in his magazine regardless of the amount. Over 160,000 donors in about five months had donated more than US $100,000 to erect the pedestal. Most of the donations were quite small—from a few cents to one dollar (Dresner 2014). However, while possibly the most famous and most often cited, the Statue of Liberty project was not the first crowdfunding campaign.

Even earlier examples of crowdfunding are evident. One example is when poet Alexander Pope set out to translate Greek poetry into English in 1713, an effort that included the translation of Homer's epic poem, "The Iliad", and asked donors to pledge two gold guineas to support his work in exchange for having the donors' names published in the acknowledgements of an early edition of the book. Another example is that in the end of the eighteenth century, the famous composer Mozart took a similar path. He wanted to perform three piano concertos in a concert hall in Vienna and published an invitation to prospective backers offering manuscripts to those who agreed to donate funds for this purpose. This approach mirrors the way in which Kickstarter operates today, where campaigners offer backers the first chance to get access to new products offered in campaigns. However, while Mozart failed to reach his funding goal on his first attempt, he succeeded a year later in a second attempt, where 176 backers donated enough funds to bring his concerto tour alive and they were all mentioned in his concertos' manuscript.

Muhammad Yunus further developed Jonathan Swift's idea on microcredits and microfinance by founding the Grameen Bank in 1976 (being authorized in 1983 by national legislation to operate as an independent bank in Bangladesh). The goal was to grant loans for entrepreneurs too poor to qualify for traditional bank loans. The bank's funding has come from different sources, and the main contributors have shifted during times from bulk agencies to central bank of Bangladesh. Grameen Bank is founded on the principle that loans are better than charity to interrupt poverty: they offer people the opportunity to take initiatives in business or agriculture, which provide earnings and enable them to pay off the debt and start a social climb. The Bank has offered credit to classes of people formerly outscoped: the poor, women, illiterate, and unemployed people. Access to credit is based on reasonable terms, such as the group lending system and weekly instalment payments, with reasonably long terms of loans, enabling the poor to build on their existing skills to earn better income in each cycle of loans. He and Grameen Bank were jointly awarded the Nobel Peace Prize in 2006 for their efforts through micro-credit to create economic and social development from below (Grameen Bank 2006).

Between 1996 and 1997, the British rock band Marillion funded its tour in the US by collecting US $60,000 from its fans via the internet. This project and other successful fan-based funding rounds that followed gave a boost to the increasing popularity of contemporary crowdfunding from the beginning of twenty-first century. Wider utilization of the form of financing and the spread thereof was made possible by the ever-increasing accessibility to the internet and its growing use by both businesses and households, which in turn made it possible to cost-effectively reach a large crowd at the same time. ArtistShare was one of the first modern crowdfunding services when it was released in the US in 2003. Through its service the artists had, and still have, the opportunity to seek funding to cover their recording costs from a wide audience such as their own supporters and fans. Here, supporters making financial contributions receive the right to download the artist's album (or song) once it is completed. The success of ArtistShare has also attracted other players to the market, of which perhaps the best known and most successful are reward-based platforms Indiegogo since 2008 and Kickstarter from 2009.

When donation and reward-based crowdfunding started to become widespread successes, it was relatively clear that a similar approach would also be used in the capital markets to raise investment-oriented finance. During the last decade, the market started to see platforms seeking to enable capital raising from investors by utilizing opportunities offered by the internet to collect and share investment information in an easier and faster manner, while simplifying the process and using standard terms. Here, the goal was to simplify, to the extent possible, the acquisition of finance from previously heavy and burdensome processes by using modern technology. In the past, acquisition of finance from angel investors lasted at least a number of months, but by using the internet the same funding could be secured within days or at most within a few weeks. One of the most successful pioneers in the industry are the US-based peer-to-peer and business-to-business lending platform—Lending Club, founded

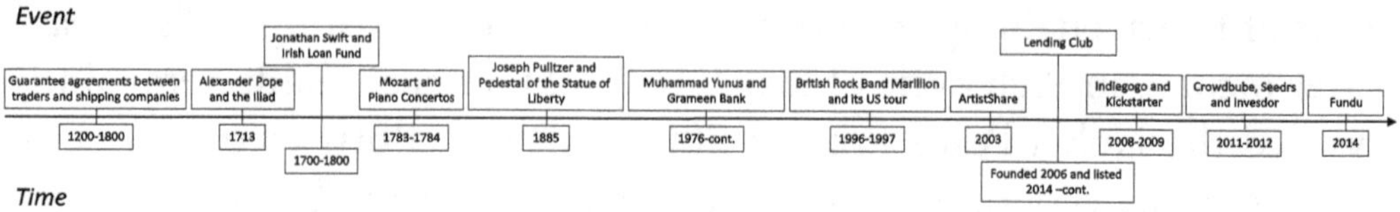

Fig. 10.1 Timeline—Brief history of crowdfunding

in 2006 in San Francisco and listed in December 2014 on the New York Stock Exchange (Freedman and Nutting 2015), and UK-based Zopa, which was launched in 2005 (Kupp and Anderson 2007) as well as Finnish-based equity platform Invesdor, which was founded in 2012, and being the first MIFID II licensed crowdfunding platform to operate cross-border in Europe (Fig. 10.1).

Crowdfunding and Its Significance in the Modern Era

Starting in 2007 from the overheated housing market in the US, and reaching full speed in 2008, the financial crisis has significantly changed the functioning of international financial markets. Increased regulation, and in particular the tightening of capital requirements for banks, has contributed to the need to find new sources of finance for businesses. Tighter regulation, especially the risk-weighted capital requirements has limited the number of companies that banks could provide debt finance for, and, in turn, led to increased borrowing costs. Therefore, it can be argued that at least to a certain extent, the changes described here have reduced the capacity of credit institutions to meet the financing needs of companies. In addition, a weak and precarious economic situation, which has only recently turned for better, has increased the risk of credit losses and thereby reduced banks' risk appetite (European Commission 2013). The situation has had a particularly strong impact on European SMEs, which have, due to historical reasons, been dependent on bank financing and, hence, resorted to alternative sources of financing (European Commission 2013, 2015). This is expected to affect the diversification of financial markets in the future. In particular, changes in the regulation of financial institutions can be seen as a limiting factor on the effective functioning of financial markets for entrepreneurial finance and growth companies.

The financial position and access to finance for growth companies and SMEs have weakened to some extent globally. As a result, companies have not always been able to meet the funding needs for their projects from existing sources of finance, which has in certain situations led to a financing gap (European Commission 2018b). Of course, not all the companies are fundable by any means of finance. However, statistics published by European Central Bank have shown evidence of a decline in access to finance for growth companies and SMEs especially in Europe in the aftermath of financial crisis even though situation has gradually improved in recent years. Based on surveys, also covenants (i.e. special conditions) as well as the security requirements of corporate loans have been tightened and interest for corporates, but especially SMEs risen (European Central Bank 2019). Although the situation in Europe is relatively good in comparison to other continents, it has developed for the worse since the financial crisis. Structural deficiencies, overcapacity, low/negative interest rates, and the absence of a pan-European banking regulatory agency have all likely contributed to European banks experiencing persistent profitability challenges (Deloitte 2019).[5] In Europe, the proportion of SMEs that mention access to finance as one of their main problems, and hence feel that they are not able to drive all potentially profitable projects, has grown (European Central Bank 2019). These findings may well be proof that the EU and national level SME guarantee facilities have not had the expected outcome. In addition, it is uncertain how socialization of credit risk affects the economy as a whole in zero (or even negative) central bank interest environment.

Low interest rates weaken banks' profitability and reduce the transparency of the actual price paid by the customer, which depends on not only each customer's financial status and profitability of the business but also the banks' current fundraising costs and the pursued level of profitability. Based on business and investor surveys (such as European Central Bank

2019) growth companies experience slower growth and higher growth thresholds. Hence, businesses, as they continue to grow, are often lacking access to finance and ability to entice new owners through listings. Low availability of alternative sources of funding, lack of expertise, and the relatively high cost of the listing process, as well as negative attitudes of owners, slow down the growth path of companies.

Therefore, from the perspective of growth-oriented companies, funding opportunities that are complementary or alternative to bank financing, such as risk and equity finance (i.e. bond markets, crowdfunding, venture capital) have increased their importance. Equity crowdfunding is especially important to finance the growth of technology-intensive businesses and innovative companies in general. This is even more relevant when a company is looking for new markets or planning to develop new products. Palmer has concluded in his study that the price of the (crowd) funding (i.e. associated costs) is not the main reason why some companies decide to use crowdfunding instead of traditional sources of finance. The main reason for companies to avoid bank-based financing is, according to Palmer, to avoid the heavy bureaucracy involved in dealing with banks in the first place (Palmer 2016).

The prevailing (zero or even negative interest) market conditions have also forced investors to look into new channels for investments providing high yields with higher risks, which have not been available from traditional sources of finance, such as banks balance sheet financing or capital markets in general. Both loan and investment-based crowdfunding include many opportunities for investors looking for investments with different return-to-risk ratios. From the investors' perspective, crowdfunding also offers a new way to diversify investments and seek higher than average profits with a higher risk profile compared to more general investment products available in the market. However, the several hundred years old banking institution is unlikely to vanish any time soon. On the contrary, there is strong indication that some leading business banks have established successful partnerships with crowdfunding platforms and other fintech companies (Nordea 2018; BBVA 2019; Deloitte 2019).

What Next?

The Fourth Industrial Revolution is underway. According to Statista—a German online portal for statistics, which makes data collected by market and opinion research institutes and data derived from the economic sector and official statistics available—there were about 26 billion devices connected to the internet around the world in 2019. The total installed base of internet connected devices is projected to amount to 75.44 billion worldwide by 2025, a fivefold increase in ten years. The internet of things, enabled by the already ubiquitous internet technology, seems to be the next major step in delivering internet's promise of making the world a connected place (Statista 2019). Currently it seems that artificial intelligence, machine learning, and the internet of things will have the most effect on the financial sector (Deloitte 2019). Digitalization is currently shaping the financial market sector with a force that has not been experienced in this scale before (Chambers and Dimson 2016). The disruption we are currently witnessing means a development during which many existing policies might be abandoned, and new ones adopted within a relatively short term. This has become even more evident after the outbreak of COVID-19 virus and how it has forced governments, institutions and companies to adopt to new and digitalized ways of working.

The financial market has, throughout its history, experienced tremendous economic and functional breakthroughs and changes, but basic operating models have remained largely unchanged, unlike, for example in industrial and service sectors (Atack and Neal 2009; Chambers and Dimson 2016). However, digitalization and technological advancement have significantly changed people's behaviour since the beginning of the twenty-first century. The virtual world has entered into all aspects of human life, and modern devices (such as tablets, mobile phones, smart watches, etc.) and applications (such as Facebook, Instagram, WhatsApp, WeChat, Skype, different e-mail applications, etc.) allow people to be continuously reached and contacted. This has given people many new opportunities to improve their living conditions and use of time, but, at the same time, mixed and overlapped time between work and leisure.

In parallel, social interaction is increasingly moving into the internet and its complex social media networks (Joinson et al. 2009; Kallio and Vuola 2018).

Not surprisingly, in the same context, people's expectations towards (financial) service providers have changed. This naturally influences financial markets, which are not a separate fort from the rest of society. People's expectations as consumers require ongoing development work from the financial markets so that financial market participants are better equipped to meet people's ever-growing expectations. Nascent technology creates numerous new business opportunities in all business sectors.[6] In the financial markets of the near future, it is likely that besides existing incumbent market operators, such as banks, also big technology companies like Amazon, Facebook (especially with its proposed cryptocurrency project Libra), Apple, Google, Tencent, or Alibaba, who are already integrating payment services on a large scale to their own services, will take a big share of the markets (Deloitte 2019).

Advances in technology seem to ensure that internet, and other sharing networks, will become more significant and take a larger part of our living environment, which will also inevitably change the financial markets as well, while enabling new service concepts and forms of financing (Morel et al. 2018). This poses challenges for current financial market participants, especially for banks (Deloitte 2019) but also creates a correspondingly high potential to newcomers (disruptors), investors, and companies seeking finance. Lawmakers and market supervisors are facing challenging times, though it is essential to keep in mind that the biggest and often most amazing things happen in a period of big breakthroughs or changes that can at this stage only be expected to accelerate through technological development. With these developments, the role of central banks may be changing rapidly. For instance, ECB is examining whether to develop a digital currency as an alternative to cash (Financial Times 2019). To further support and derive from the project, a body of six central banks (the Bank of England, Bank of Canada, BOE, the Bank of Japan, the European Central Bank, the Riksbank, and the Swiss National Bank, along with the Bank for International Settlements) have been set in order to "share experience as they assess the potential cases for central bank digital currency in their home jurisdictions" (Bloomberg 2020).

Fintech refers to those technological innovations in the field of financial services that may lead to new business models, applications, processes, or products and have a significant ancillary effect on financial markets and institutions in the way financial services are provided. The history of the financial market is full of financial innovations, but the importance of these innovations has grown and market transformation accelerated by technological advances (European Commission 2018a). Accordingly, the market is, at an accelerating pace, deploying various fintech solutions that leverage digital identification, mobile applications, cloud services, big data analysis, artificial intelligence, blockchain, and distributed ledger technologies. New technologies are changing the financial industry and the way consumers and businesses buy services. This creates opportunities for fintech-based solutions that improve access to finance and financial inclusion of digitally networked consumers (PWC 2017).

Today, crowdfunding is used to finance business growth at an accelerated pace. Until recently, it has generally been considered to be appropriate during the seed and growth stages for start-ups and especially small businesses (Spacetec 2014) involving financing from non-professional investors often reaching sums between ten thousand euros to a few million euros. In the financial markets, crowdfunding is typically seen as a high-risk mezzanine as well as debt or equity financing. However, the paradigm might be shifting. The crowdfunding market has already seen institutional interest, which may further accelerate growth of this form of financing (Ziegler et al. 2019). This trend is partly supported by regulation making crowdfunding part of regulated financial markets, as well as governments' continuous will to impose ever-stricter regulation to existing financial market players.

There may well be an underlying risk that the crowds will be pushed back in the most successful platforms, which are able to show long-term track record especially in debt crowdfunding. If this happens, the credit rating models of platforms would have been battle-tested by the non-professional crowds, but eventually the professional investors will come and harvest the fruit. In addition, deepening deflation in the financial markets seems to push more and more institutional investors to alternative finance in order to pursue profits, which are less available from traditional sources. However, recent research has shown that institutionalization across all crowdfunding model types has actually decreased between 2016 and 2017. This includes funding from pension funds, mutual funds, asset management firms, and banks (Ziegler et al. 2019).

Conclusion

The size of the crowdfunding market, and hence the importance of this form of financing, has grown rapidly (European Commission 2016) and continues to grow based on recent studies (Ziegler et al. 2019). Crowdfunding transactions taking place digitally on different technological platforms via the internet is a concrete demonstration of how digitalization and business models applying new technological solutions can influence access to finance. Subsequently, such solutions also channel and allocate the limited resources of society to benefit a larger pool of companies, investors, and consumers, and hence supporting the society as a whole.

Nevertheless, crowdfunding is not immune to risks, immorality, opportunism, and moral hazard, which have been witnessed in the financial sector from the start. Here, although the systemic risk may be quite low for the economy as a whole, it is for the benefit of all stakeholders in crowdfunding that some level of governmental control is being exercised. So far, it may be fair to argue that there are no crowdfunding platforms that are "too big to fail". The business model of crowdfunding involves the ability to seek instant profits from and at the expense of investors, for example, by loosening the service platform's customer selection. Here, it may be argued that less-informed investors may take risks which better informed investors may not. This risk is highlighted by a fact that crowdfunding platform operators are often start-ups themselves struggling with adequate cash flows and may be pressed to onboard campaigns and investors less selectively. This argument defends reasonable minimum capital requirements.

In the end, the markets naturally repair themselves when investors start to avoid those crowdfunding platforms, which price the risks of their projects and operations poorly or indifferently. For a young and developing industry, the market-based correction mechanism may not necessarily be sufficient, because the industry's overall reputation can significantly weaken already from one bigger moral gambling case. This is true especially in the current situation where advanced self-regulation of the industry has not yet formed, but competition on market shares and customers has constantly been growing and tightening. The biggest risk for crowdfunding industry and its long-term success would seem to be the industry itself if it does not take these signs of danger seriously enough.

The history of the financial markets is full of innovations, starting from the invention of money and using it as a medium of exchange, the exit from the gold-denominated currency system, and all the way to the increasing popularity of online payment systems. Crowdfunding as a form of financing is part of this series of innovations in the general history of financial markets. Crowdfunding has in quite short period acquired a small but significant position in the international financial markets making it important and accessible funding channel especially for start-ups and SMEs. It can also be stated that crowdfunding has democratized the process of commercialization and financing by making investing in start-ups more widespread and easier to access for all people, instead of being accessible to only high-net-worth individuals, business angels, or venture funds (Ziegler et al. 2019). This has also given new opportunities for companies seeking financing and diversified the functioning of existing financial markets.

The evolution of financial markets or corporate finance naturally will not end in crowdfunding. For example, blockchain technology can, if sufficiently advanced, enable completely new business models that can challenge, when scaled adequately enough, traditional corporate finance as well as crowdfunding as we know it today. Blockchain technology, like other fintech innovations, can have a significant impact on the development of financial markets in the future (Deloitte 2019). This also relates to cyber security and data privacy in general, which are issues that need to be addressed globally in order to capitalize on the benefits of digitalization not just for the good of financial markets, but for the society as a whole (European Commission 2018a). The big challenge for the regulators in this rapidly changing financial environment is to maintain an attitude of "mend it, don't end it".

In the future, it is necessary for researchers to further study the historical evolution and development of crowdfunding markets in the wider context of financial markets. The relevance of crowdfunding as a new form of financing to market participants (i.e. investors, companies, and established operators like banks) would be worthwhile researching. This is especially true in the current exceptional financial market environment, which is characterized by zero or even negative interest rates, as well as continuous liquidity injections by central banks and government-led projects or initiatives (especially in Europe), such as the European Fund for Strategic Investments and its local counterparts. An alternative historical approach may be comparisons between the development of crowdfunding and other innovations in financial markets, highlighting common and different drivers and barriers to such developments, and the actors behind them. There is also a need for more (historical) study on both the positive and negative implications of financial innovations (including crowdfunding), the determinants of risk taking by institutional and individual investors, the governance problems (including conflict of interest between different stakeholders), and the causes of volatility in financial markets in relation to emergence of fintech. All these issues have practical implications to the success and implementation speed of new financial innovations to practice and everyday service offering and use by individual banks, companies, and households.

Also increasing regulatory burden, which has mostly fallen on the shoulders of established financial institutions like banks, might distort the functioning of financial markets even further and create more concerns among investors and in the public, which can have unprecedented effects to the financial markets of today. Big shifts in current paradigm in the financial markets can make crowdfunding more attractive to institutional investors in the future. The relationship between institutional investors and crowdfunding platforms is a particularly interesting research opportunity, as it may have profound effects on industry development, and the extent to which it will remain loyal to its grass-root ideals.

Further, more research is needed on the effects on and implications of the crowdfunding industry on systemic risk especially if the growth of the industry continues as strong as it has to date. It will also be interesting to follow how quickly and agile crowdfunding platforms will adapt innovations of fintech (blockchain, AI, cloud computing, etc.) into their everyday operations compared to, for example, banks, as well as what effects will that have on the future position and service portfolios of platforms and banks respectively. In growing markets, there also seems to be an increasing pressure for consolidation of the crowdfunding platforms as well as expansion of their current product lines and ability to adapt to new and more scalable business models (e.g. setting up alternative investment funds in order to ensure steadier cash flow as well as expanding from solely lending-based crowdfunding to cover other crowdfunding forms). In addition, it is interesting to study the increasing syndication and cooperation activities between traditional banks and crowdfunding platforms.

In conclusion, we are living in interesting times of constantly evolving financial markets. In order to be able to predict future trends and directions, we must understand the past and derive from the teachings of history; and in this particular case-financial history. In order to understand history, it is essential not to highlight only similarities between historical episodes such as the Great Depression of 1929 and the subprime crisis of 2007 but also differences.[7] Such an approach shows us that history does not always have such a conclusive predictive power than we would probably like it to have (Chambers and Dimson 2016). However, history has always provided invaluable guidance to those willing to learn from events, and especially mistakes, of the past. At the finalizing phase of this chapter we are witnessing an outbreak of COVID-19 virus that hammers the global economy at forces rarely seen before. The outcomes of such crises are hard to predict. We might be entering into a beginning of a new era of disintegration in EU and rising levels of nationalisation. On the other hand, the solidarity may even strenghten among EU states, and the level of global co-operation and transparency might increase and improve.

From practical standpoint, it is useful to contextualize crowdfunding—a modern and digitalized form of financing—as part of financial markets, its rules, and mechanics. In order to achieve such a goal, it is essential to understand fluctuations between economic cycles driven by historical, economic, and political processes. Crowdfunding and fintech in general will definitely offer many interesting research topics for researchers in the financial markets for years to come.

Notes

1. Although the economic history of the past 300 years has shown many instances of financial crises and bank failures, their effects on asset values and on the real economy have been quite varied. Much depends on how the authorities react to these events. Although we understand from history the factors that lead to and exacerbate crises, the attempts to make such crises less frequent and less virulent have been largely misguided (Chambers and Dimson 2016, p. xvi).
2. "Economic bubble" means a situation in the economy where a price of a trading object (e.g. a stock or other commodity) differs from the balanced price defined by the fundamentals of the market (based on availability, valuation, supply, etc.). The bubble may form, for example, to the prices of stocks or house prices (Chambers and Dimson 2016, pp. 149–168 and 174–175). One of the traditional and frequently used examples of "economic bubble" is the so-called tulip mania, which was an investment bubble in the Netherlands between 1634 and 1637, where prices of tulip bulbs entering the markets most recently rose to record levels and eventually collapsed. The highest price of tulips was in 1637. Tulip mania is considered one of the first economic bubbles in the modern financial markets.
3. Economic cycles affect, among others, (i) the number of loan transactions, (ii) the size of the loan facilities, (iii) pricing for the loans, (iv) default rates, and (v) institutional demand for secondary trading. A buoyant economy with low default rates encourages lenders to commit to large loans and more frequently, whereas a contracting economy usually results in a more cautious approach in the number of transactions and the terms on which the loans are made. A deteriorating economy with high default rates spurs the secondary market in distressed loans (Mugasha 2007, p. 6).
4. Jonathan Swift is better known as an author of a well-known prose satire; Gulliver's Travels, or Travels into Several Remote Nations of the World. In Four Parts. By Lemuel Gulliver, First a Surgeon, and then a Captain of Several Ships.

5. US banks, compared to their European counterparts, are ahead on multiple measures. Aggressive policy interventions and forceful regulations helped propel US banks to health more quickly. And more recently, favourable GDP growth, tax cuts, and rising rates have further bolstered the state of the industry. Total assets in the US reached a peak of $17.5 trillion. Capital levels are up as well, with average tier 1 capital ratio standing at 13.14%. Return on equity (ROE) for the industry is at a post-crisis high of 11.83%. Efficiency ratios also are at their best. Similarly, on other metrics, such as non-performing loans and number of failed institutions, the US banking industry is robust (Deloitte 2019, p. 1).
6. For example: (i) video rentals (Blockbusters) have gone online (Netflix, Viaplay, HBO), (ii) instead of CDs, music is listened online via web streaming services (Spotify), (iii) instead of travel agencies, most trips and accommodations are booked directly through internet platforms (e-aggregators) (Trivago, Ebookers), and (iv) instead of visiting branches, banking is handled through online banking channels or, increasingly, via banking applications on mobile phones.
7. For example, complex and highly automatized/digitalized structured financial products—non-existent during crisis of the 1930s—were vastly used in global financial markets prior to the subprime crisis. The use of as well as lack of understanding related to these products has been identified as one of the major contributing factors to the subprime crisis (Chambers and Dimson 2016, pp. 272–276).

References

Atack, J., & Neal, L. (2009). *The Origins and Development of Financial Markets and Institutions—From the Seventeenth Century to the Present*. Cambridge: Cambridge University Press.

BBVA. (2019). *BBVA-backed Holvi Announces Plan to Expand in Europe*. Press Release, May 16. Retrieved December 1, 2019, from https://www.bbva.com/en/bbva-backed-holvi-announces-plan-to-expand-in-europe/.

Berle, A., & Means, G. (1932). *The Modern Corporation and Private Property*. New York: The Macmillan Company.

Bloomberg. (2020). *Central Banks Team Up to Study Case for Digital Currencies*. Retrieved January 1, 2020, from https://www.bloomberg.com/news/articles/2020-01-21/central-banks-team-up-to-study-case-for-digital-currencies.

Bradley, C. M. (2013). From Global Financial Crisis to Sovereign Debt Crisis and Beyond: What Lies Ahead for the European Monetary Union? *Transnational Law and Contemporary Problems, 22*(9), 9–39.

Cassis, Y. (2017). *Regulatory Responses to the Financial Crises of the Great Depression: Britain, France and the United States.* Retrieved December 1, 2019, from https://archive.kenan.ethics.duke.edu/wp-content/blogs.dir/2/files/2013/10/Regulatory-responses_cassis.pdf.

Chambers, D., & Dimson, E. (2016). *Financial Market History—Reflections on the Past for Investors of Today.* Cambridge: Cambridge University Press.

de la Vega, J. (1688). *Confusion de Confusiones: Portions Descriptive of the Amsterdam Stock Exchange* (H. Kellenbenz, Trans., Harvard University, 1957). Retrieved December 1, 2019, from https://www.gwern.net/docs/economics/1688-delavega-confusionofconfusions.pdf

Deloitte Touche Tohmatsu Limited. (2019). *Banking and Capital Markets Outlook—Reimagining Transformation.* Retrieved December 1, 2019, from https://www2.deloitte.com/cy/en/pages/financial-services/articles/gx-banking-industry-outlook.html.

Drake, P. P., & Fabozzi, F. J. (2010). *The Basics of Finance: An Introduction to Financial Markets, Business Finance, and Portfolio Management* (Vol. 192). John Wiley & Sons.

Dresner, S. (2014). *A Guide to Raising Capital on the Internet.* Hoboken, New Jersey: John Wiley & Sons.

European Central Bank. (2019). *Survey on the Access to Finance of Enterprises—April to September 2019.* Retrieved December 1, 2019, from https://www.ecb.europa.eu/stats/ecb_surveys/safe/html/index.en.html

European Central Bank. (2020). *Asset Purchase Programmes.* Retrieved January 1, 2020, from https://www.ecb.europa.eu/mopo/implement/omt/html/index.en.html

European Commission. (2013). Green Paper: Long-Term Financing of the European Economy. *COM,* 150. Brussels, March 25. Retrieved December 1, 2019, from https://eur-lex.europa.eu/legal-content/EN/TXT/PDF/?uri=CELEX:52013DC0150&from=EN

European Commission. (2015). Green Paper: Building a Capital Markets Union. *COM,* 63. Brussels, February 18. Retrieved December 1, 2019, from https://eur-lex.europa.eu/legal-content/EN/TXT/PDF/?uri=CELEX:52015DC0063&from=EN.

European Commission. (2016). Commission Staff Working Document: Crowdfunding in the EU Capital Markets Union. *SWD,* 154. Brussels, May 3. Retrieved December 1, 2019, from https://ec.europa.eu/transparency/regdoc/rep/10102/2016/EN/10102-2016-154-EN-F1-1.PDF.

European Commission. (2018a). Communication from the Commission to the European Parliament, the Council, the European Central Bank, the European Economic and Social Committee and the Committee of the Regions on FinTech Action Plan: For a More Competitive and Innovative European Financial Sector. *COM*, 109. Brussels, March 8. Retrieved December 1, 2019, from https://eur-lex.europa.eu/resource.html?uri=cellar:6793c578-22e6-11e8-ac73-01aa75ed71a1.0001.02/DOC_1&format=PDF

European Commission. (2018b). Proposal for a Regulation of the European Parliament and of the Council on European Crowdfunding Service Providers (ECSP) for Business. *COM*, 113. Brussels, March 8. Retrieved December 1, 2019, from https://eur-lex.europa.eu/resource.html?uri=cellar:0ea638be-22cb-11e8-ac73-01aa75ed71a1.0003.02/DOC_2&format=PDF.

European Securities and Markets Authority. (2014). Opinion. Investment-based Crowdfunding. ESMA/2014/1378, December 18. Retrieved December 1, 2019, from https://www.esma.europa.eu/sites/default/files/library/2015/11/2014-1378_opinion_on_investment-based_crowdfunding.pdf.

Ferran, E. (2008). *Principles of Corporate Finance Law*. Oxford: Oxford University Press.

Financial Times. (2019). *ECB Explores Development of a Digital Currency*. Retrieved December 1, 2019, from https://www.ft.com/content/56db1f62-104b-11ea-a7e6-62bf4f9e548a.

Freedman, D., & Nutting, M. R. (2015). *A Brief History of Crowdfunding Including Rewards, Donation, Debt, and Equity Platforms in the USA*, Updated November 5. Retrieved December 1, 2019, from https://www.freedman-chicago.com/ec4i/History-of-Crowdfunding.pdf

Grameen Bank. (2006). *The Nobel Peace Prize 2006*. Retrieved December 1, 2019, from http://www.grameen.com/the-nobel-peace-prize-2006/.

International Organization of Securities Commissions. (2015). *Crowdfunding*. Survey Responses Report. FR29/2015, December 12. Retrieved December 1, 2019, from https://www.iosco.org/library/pubdocs/pdf/IOSCOPD520.pdf.

Joinson, A., McKenna, K., Postmes, T., & Reips, U. D. (Eds.). (2009). *Oxford Handbook of Internet Psychology*. Oxford: OUP.

Kallio, A., & Vuola, L. (2018). *Joukkorahoitus*. Liettua (in Finnish—Abstract in English).

Kari, M. (2016). *Suomen rahoitusmarkkinoiden murros 1980-luvulla*. Oikeushistoriallinen tutkimus (in Finnish—*Transformation of the Finnish financial markets in the 1980s*).

Kupp, M., & Anderson, J. (2007). Zopa: Web 2.0 Meets Retail Banking. *Business Strategy Review., 18*(3), 11–17.

Marmer, Harry S. (2016). *Lessons from Capital Market History—Popular Beliefs and Stylized Facts*. Retrieved December 1, 2019, from https://www.cfainstitute.org/en/research/cfa-magazine/2016/lessons-from-capital-market-history-expanded.

Mitchener, K. J. (2005). Bank Supervision, Regulation, and Instability During the Great Depression. *Journal of Economic History, 65*(1), 152–185.

Morel, P., Teschner, C., Paoli, P., Vialaron, F., Bertali, V., Mikroulis, K., & Lavrov, B. (2018). *Fintech in Capital Markets 2018: Boosting Productivity Through Technology Innovation*. The Boston Consulting Group. Retrieved December 1, 2019, from http://image-src.bcg.com/Images/BCG_2018_Capital_Markets_Fintech_White_Paper_March_16_tcm108-187378.pdf.

Mugasha, A. (2007). *The Law of Multi-Bank Financing—Syndicated Loans and the Secondary Loan Market*. Oxford: Oxford University Press.

Nietzsche, F. (1887). *On the Genealogy of Morality Friedrich—A Polemic*.

Nordea Bank Abp. (2018). *Nordea and Invesdor to Initiate Collaboration in Digital Financing for Finnish Growth Companies*. Press Release, May 30. Retrieved December 1, 2019, from https://www.nordea.com/fi/media/uutiset-ja-lehdistotiedotteet/press-releases/2018/05-30-07h00-nordea-and-invesdor-to-initiate-collaboration-in-digital-financing-for-finnish-growth-companies.html

Palmer, A. (2016). *Smart Money. How High-Stakes Financial Innovation is Reshaping Our World for the Better*. New York: Basic Books.

PWC. (2017). *Global Fintech Report 2017: Redrawing the Lines: FinTech's Growing Influence on Financial Services*. Retrieved December 1, 2019, from https://www.pwc.com/gx/en/industries/financial-services/assets/pwc-global-fintech-report-2017.pdf

Shneor, R., & Flåten, B.-T. (2015). Opportunities for Entrepreneurial Development and Growth through Online Communities, Collaboration, and Value Creating and Co-Creating Activities. In H. R. Kaufmann & S. M. R. Shams (Eds.), *Entrepreneurial Challenges in the 21st Century*. Basingstoke: Palgrave Macmillan.

Short, J. C., Ketchen, D. J., McKenny, A. F., et al. (2017). Research on Crowdfunding: Reviewing the (Very Recent) Past and Celebrating the Present. *Entrepreneurship Theory and Practice, 41*(2), 149–160.

SpaceTec Capital Partners GmbH. (2014). *Crowdfunding Innovative Ventures in Europe—The Financial Ecosystem and Regulatory Landscape*. Brussels: European Commission, Directorate-General of Communications Networks, Content & Technology.

Statista. (2019). *Internet of Things (IoT) Connected Devices Installed Base Worldwide from 2015 to 2025*. Statista Research Department, November 14. Retrieved December 1, 2019, from https://www.statista.com/statistics/471264/iot-number-of-connected-devices-worldwide/

Zestos, G. K. (2016). *The Global Financial Crisis—from US Subprime Mortgages to European Sovereign Debt*. London: Routledge.

Ziegler, T., Shneor, R., Wenzlaff, K., et al. (2019). *Shifting Paradigms—The 4th European Alternative Finance Benchmarking Report*. Cambridge, UK: Cambridge Centre for Alternative Finance.

11

ICT Development and the Financial Services Sector

Paul Griffiths

Introduction

The last three decades of the twentieth century witnessed the adoption of information and communications technology (ICT) by business corporations at an increasing rate and banks were leaders and trendsetters in this process. However, this leadership role of banking in the development of corporate ICT was lost in the second half of the first decade of this millennium. This chapter intends to shed light on the process that led to this. In so doing, it addresses the questions: Why did FinTech emerge as an industrial sector, independent of banking?

The author is strongly connected to the world of ICT transformation and of banking as an information intensive industry. He entered the business world as a young graduate during the mainframe-based, bespoke systems age; he then oriented his career towards management consulting, where he carried out and led technology-enabled business transformation

P. Griffiths (✉)
EM Normandie Business School, Métis Lab, Oxford, UK
e-mail: pgriffiths@em-normandie.co.uk

projects in the enterprise resource planning (ERP) era and the customer relationship management (CRM) and e-commerce solutions era; he replaced legacy core-banking systems by more modern client-server platform ones. On the academic side, he went back to university and enrolled on a doctoral programme that he researched into strategy-technology alignment in banks from which he graduated in 2005. He then became a full time academic and for the last three years has been researching the industrial organization of the FinTech sector. So, it is from this broad background that bridges across the practitioner and academic worlds in banking and technology that he sets out to address the above questions.

The rest of this chapter is organized in the following way. Section "Twentieth Century: ICT Emerging and Evolution" will give an overview, based on the author's professional experience, of the evolution of ICT in the last three decades of the twentieth century. From the specific perspective of banks, it will show that the financial sector in general, and banking in particular, was a driver of the ICT evolution during that period, until the mid-2000s. Section "Advent of the Tipping Point: Why Did Banks Lose Control?" will, based on current literature, identify three root-causes for banks to have lost control over the ICT agenda in the financial sector. In having lost control of the evolution of ICT, Section "A New Industrial Sector: The Emerging of FinTech" will give a framework to understand how the FinTech sector is structured based on a classification of the players according to the functional services they offer and the types of technology they apply. It will emphasize the role of crowdfunding in this landscape. Section "Discussion" will offer a discussion on the findings, and Section "Conclusions" will draw some conclusions.

Twentieth Century: ICT Emerging and Evolution

The last three decades of the twentieth century witnessed the adoption of information and communications technology (ICT) by business corporations at an increasing rate. During the 1970s and 1980s it was large systems developed and running on mainframe computers, with bespoke applications of narrow functional scope and weak integration with other functional applications. ICT was essentially about number-crunching large volumes of flat files, initially fed in by perforated cards and later in the period by magnetic tapes and discs. It was a domain restricted to the largest corporations, prominent amongst them the big banks, government institutions and universities. Systems were all corporate and managed by large IT departments with battalions of in-house programmers, analysts and systems engineers complemented by professional staff belonging to the large systems companies (that later called themselves 'integrators') such as IBM, Honeywell-Bull, ICL, Unysis. The technology platforms on which these corporate applications were developed were proprietary, with no convertibility from one vendor's platform to another vendor's: Client lock-in was the name of the game.

Democratization of ICT and its access to the smaller corporations and companies came in the mid-to-late 1980s and early 1990s with the advent of the mini-computer, the table-top personal computer, local area networks, handheld devices and, very importantly, the relational database. Democratization turned into revolution with the access to, and popularization of, the Internet.

The until then reigning mainframe computer and its centralized architecture ceded part of its domain to the distributed client-server architecture. The mainframe did not completely go away as those organizations who had them tended to keep the mainframe as database server due to its low cost per transaction for large volumes of transactions.

In parallel with client-server a significant change in the 1990s was the advent of the enterprise resource planning (ERP) systems with a new key player that with time became the dominant player in the corporate applications world, breaking the until then hegemony of the Anglo-Saxon companies: SAP from Waldorf, Germany. Being the four founders of SAP ex-IBM engineers, the first versions of their ERP ran on mainframes, but they really took off with their first client-server version that they called R/3. There were competing providers such as Oracle (with its Financials), JDEdwards, and PeopleSoft. This wave responded to a significant change in philosophy and the name of the game now had two dimensions: (a) it was all about packaged solutions, that is solutions that did not need code developed from scratch for each corporation, but that would be standard with the possibility of configuring parameters for limited adaptation to each company; and (b) integration was dominant over best-of-breed solutions, that is that now it was more important to have integration across functional applications than to have the best individual and isolated application.

Integrated packaged solutions brought with them another significant change: the concept of 'leading practices' in business processes. While the bespoke systems of the mainframe era were modelled in line with the processes of each company, in the ERP era the company would adapt its processes to the leading practices in-built in the solution. The implications of this is that the implementation of an ERP system would lead to significant changes in processes that, in turn, radically changed people's jobs. Thus, change management became an important component of implementation projects, with a focus on stakeholder management and training of people in entire processes, not just their specific task in a large process as was the case before.

Another change that came with the ERP wave is how projects were organized. The configuration of a systems project team was no longer a team of highly technical analysts and programmers, but people who were versed in business processes. The bulk of the work was not in coding but in parameter configuration and change management activities. So, the project teams were integrated mainly by non-technical systems people. ERP projects were not referred to as systems or technology projects anymore, but as business transformation projects enabled by technology.

Ripples of ERP in 1991–1993 became waves in 1994–1998 and turned into tsunamis approaching 2000 and the generalized policy of implementing 'vanilla' ERPs to sort the Y2K problem (this term was coined by Gartner Group and refers to the fact that the early mainframe systems had only two-digits for the year in dates, so it was suspected that they would all fail with the advent of the new millennium). With the advent and establishment of ERPs, came the reduction in the size of the IT departments in corporations. In effect, what adopting and implementing ERP meant was that the development of new functionalities to adapt to changes in the legal and tax environment, or to the need for new functionalities, was outsourced to the ERP vendors.

Of course, ERP were not the panacea that appears at first sight. Significant amount of coding to ensure integration with legacy systems or vertical industry-specific applications were still necessary. Although 'big bang' projects were highly promoted, common sense and risk management led to many projects being piloted and phased in, which meant that temporary interfaces had to be developed. And although the ERP vendors did produce their solutions with specific flavours for different industries, this was still not enough and corporations demanded having some of their vertical functionality developed outside of the ERP. For example, SAP achieved a highly competent footprint in the consumer packaged goods (CPG) and in the utilities industries, but never managed to produce convincing solutions for the core-banking functionalities despite having invested heavily in its solution for that sector. In other words, coding and development effort for integration did not entirely go away.

After the ERP binge running up to Y2K came the hangover in the form of a relative slowdown in the ERP market, but that did not stop the corporate-systems business as a whole. At around the time that ERP slowed down e-commerce and client relationship management (CRM) solutions emerged with force. E-commerce was the hottest product but it was severely impacted by 9/11 and the implosion of dot.com, recovering afterwards but growing at a more moderate pace.

With the slowdown of the ERP market and of the global economy after 9/11, came a consolidation within the corporate ICT solutions industry. SAP expanded its functionality into CRM, e-commerce and business intelligence through internal developments but later broke this tradition by entering the acquisitions path. Oracle, on the other hand, acquired PeopleSoft, Siebel (the leading CRM provider), JDEdwards, and many others, with significant pains in converting all these independent applications into a coherent, seamless offering to its clients. Oracle also moved into the hardware space by acquiring SUN Microsystems and SAP moved into Oracle's traditional realm, the database layer, through acquisition, too. Oracle articulated the concept of 'stack', from hardware to enterprise application, through operating systems, databases, integration layers and others. Oracle publicized itself as being able to offer the whole stack or just some of the layers.

The strong narrative of ERP vendors in terms of the importance of integration started weakening with the advent of intelligent middleware communications platforms that made unnecessary the dreaded point-to-point, or one-to-one, interface development. The nightmarish spaghetti-style interfaces that haunted CIOs and kept them awake at night, could now be substituted by simpler to understand middleware layers into which applications could easily be plugged in. Another highly significant concept that was materializing and coming of age at the turn of the century was the API (application programming interface—term that was coined decades before by Cotton and Greatorex 1968), a set of subroutine definitions, communications protocols and tools for building software. As will be seen in Section "Discussion", APIs would play an important role in the FinTech world.

The prior paragraphs give an overview of how corporate ICT in general developed from the 1970s to the early 2000s. The effect on business transformation of the adoption of ICT was highly significant, but nowhere more than in banking. Banking is an information-intensive industry, by which it is meant that differentiation comes exclusively from their intellectual capital and information or, in other words, their people, processes, relationships, and technology (Clayton and Waldron 2003; Griffiths 2003, 2005; McKeen and Smith 1996; OECD 2003, pp. 65–66).[1]

Driven by this dependence on information, banks played very much of a leading role in adoption and development of ICT, and the trajectory they followed differed from the mainstream CPG, retail, industrial products, and utilities corporations. Banks were clearly ahead of the pack in the early phase of that period, that of the bespoke systems running on mainframe computers. They were so heavily vested in those technologies and had such high numbers of transactions compared to the other industries, that they could not make the business case for moving to client-server. This, together with the fact that banking processes and applications had become highly sophisticated and business critical at an extreme, disincentivized the ERP vendors to develop vertical solutions for banking in the early days of ERP. Eventually SAP did propose a banking-solution, but its adoption was disappointingly slow and hardly ever with an end-to-end footprint but limited to fragmented pieces of the business.

Essentially, the largest banks are trapped, to this day, in their legacy systems.

Indeed, banks have adopted standard packaged solutions in many parts of their business, particularly the highly technical middle office, but the back office remains on the legacy systems. That is not to say that there have not been any client-server solutions for banks, but the more successful ones have been developed by specialized companies and not the leading ERP vendors. For example, Citi co-developed a client-server core banking system with a company called i-Flex in India, to implement in its smaller operations around the world (it later divested from i-Flex and a few years later i-Flex was absorbed by Oracle). So, essentially, banks did not participate in the ERP part of the prior narrative.

Notwithstanding their attachment to the legacy mainframe systems, banks did make some memorable breakthroughs, of which the ATM is a notable example. The generalization of ATMs in the 1980s enabled banks to give 24 × 7 service and significantly lower their banking transaction costs. This led the self-service kiosk technology that is still in the process of being adopted by other corporations in most other industries and government.

The ATM was followed by the waves of phone banking, home banking, and Internet banking. They all had in common pushing their clients out of the branch office and lowering further the costs of banking transactions and brought with them the need for omni-channel, that is the need to show the same face to the client independently of what channel the client chose to interact with her bank. So, the big banks that had departed from mainstream in the ERP age, took leadership again in the CRM phase. With this came the transformation of the banking branch office, that until the 1990s was a mini-bank in its own right with all functionalities in the branch. From the turn of the century banks took all the back-office and middle-office functionalities (e.g., bookkeeping and accounting, credit scoring, loan origination) from the branch to the head office, and most of the transactional activity out of the branch to remote channels. The branch office became far smaller and focused on value-added client services.

This narrative brings us to the mid-2000s when a tipping-point with several fronts was reached in the ICT world as will be developed in later sections. As has briefly been outlined in this section, ICT in business and government went from a rarity in the 1970s to complete infiltration and dissemination in the early 2000s. What this story is telling us is that during this period of study the world, or at least what we generally refer to as the Western world, almost unperceptively migrated from an industrial economy of predominantly tangible assets, to a knowledge one where intangible ones overwhelmingly predominate over the tangible. This is a new era where the application of ICT radically changed, and where banks lost their grip on its development.

The importance that ICT took on in the business world in general, but especially so in such an information-intensive sector as is banking, makes the research question stated in Section "Introduction" of the utmost relevance both to the practitioner and to the academic world. The process through which this happened is described in the next section.

Advent of the Tipping Point: Why Did Banks Lose Control?

Overview

A thorough review of the literature on the emerging of the FinTech sector was carried out—the emphasis was put on academic papers from 2012 onwards, as it is thought that before then would be too close to the events for clarity and that it has been found by Zavolokina et al. (2016, p. 9, fig. 1) that article publication numbers started growing that year. Based on that search this section identifies three root-causes that, although unrelated to each other, happened to coincide in time and lead banks to have lost control over the ICT agenda in the financial sector. The narrative in Section "Twentieth Century: ICT Emerging and Evolution" brings us to the mid-2000s and it announces that around that time several major events happened in the banking, the ICT world and society in general that led to the emerging of a new industrial sector that we nowadays call FinTech as a contraction of financial technology. The Basel Committee on Banking Supervision (BCBS) defines FinTech quite broadly as

> *[t]echnologically enabled financial innovation that could result in new business models, applications, processes or products with an associated material effect on financial markets and institutions and the provision of financial services.* (Claessens et al. 2018; Palazzeschi 2018)

So for BCBS FinTech is a form of innovation, but a very broad one at that, as it includes business models, applications, processes, or products. Dorfleitner et al. (2017) while admitting that there is no universally accepted definition of FinTech, take a more cautious approach and refrain from proposing a definition based on that while accepting that most companies in the FinTech sector share certain features, there are always enough exceptions to render them inadequate for producing a general definition. They opt to give a summary description of the different service domains of FinTechs, that they group in four: (a) financing, (b) asset management, (c) payments (in which they include cryptocurrencies), and (d) other FinTechs. The latter includes a hotchpotch of things such as insurance; search engines and comparison sites; technology, IT and infrastructure; plus 'other FinTechs'. Both approaches have limitation: BCBS stay at a conceptual level, and Dorfleitner et al. (2017) are far too broad and encompassing, which unsurprisingly gives place to so many exceptions.

In this chapter we will overcome those problems and propose and adopt a definition. We will overcome the BCBS limitation by defining FinTech as a company/organization, and we will narrow the service offering domain. We will limit the services to banking services, that is services where the core competence is managing credit risk, market risk, or banking operational risk. So, by FinTech in this chapter we understand *not the technology itself, but a digital technology-enabled entrepreneurial initiative that offers services to clients that would traditionally be considered within the domain of banks; or that are an innovative service in the natural business domain of banks; or that help banks develop their back-office processes.*

So, returning to the research question—*Why did FinTech emerge as an industrial sector, independent of banking?*—and to focus the mind we will address it by responding to four subquestions:

- What caused banks to lose leadership in the development of corporate ICT systems?
- What enabled the FinTech sector to emerge with such vitality in a business dominated by behemoths?
- What encouraged entrepreneurs to move into the service domain traditionally served by banks?
- How is the FinTech industry organized and where does crowdfunding fit in?

Arner et al. (2017) divide the co-evolution of finance and technology into three stages, namely:

(a) The *analogous age* prior to the late twentieth century,
(b) the *digitalization era* that goes from the late twentieth century until 2008, and
(c) the *diverging era* with the advent of new financial providers based on advanced technologies.

As is mostly the case, there is not a single cause for the advent of the tipping point that moved the evolution of finance and technology into the *diverging era*. This research identifies three unrelated causes that happened in the 2007–2008 point in time; it is quite probable that none of these causes alone would have caused such a disruption, but their coincidence in time enabled them to feed into each other and cause havoc in the banking industry. The first is the global financial crisis known as the Great Recession that is generally accepted as having been caused by the banking system and its greed in the mortgage segment. The second is several nearly simultaneous major breakthroughs in the technology sector that led to a drastic drop in entry barriers to the banking services sector. And finally, significant social changes with the coming of age of the millennial generation and their growing role in the business world and in relationship to banking. The rest of this section will flesh out these three causes.

The Effect of the Great Recession

The 2007–2008 recession put banks in the US, the UK, and several countries on the European continent at the brink of collapse leading to systemic failure which, in turn, led banking authorities in those markets to bail them out with public funds. Subsequent investigation into the events detected that banks accelerated their growth by taking on excessive risk that they partially transferred to other organizations through financial engineering devises concocted by their investment banking arms. In conjunction with this, the population became extremely critical of banks and there was general distrust in these institutions. These three factors led national authorities to react, and in many cases over-react, with the result of far more stringent banking regulations that caused great regulatory challenges to the banks (European Central Bank 2016; Haddad and Hornuf 2019; Kotarba 2016). These more stringent regulations worked in two directions (see Fig. 11.1).

The first was in the sense of demanding banks to significantly increase their regulatory capital so that never again would they need to be rescued with public money. Because as a result of the crisis capital was costly to acquire by banks, they reacted by reducing the denominator of the capital adequacy ratio, that is by reducing their exposure to risk. They did this by pruning those clients of higher-risk profile, and by letting go the less

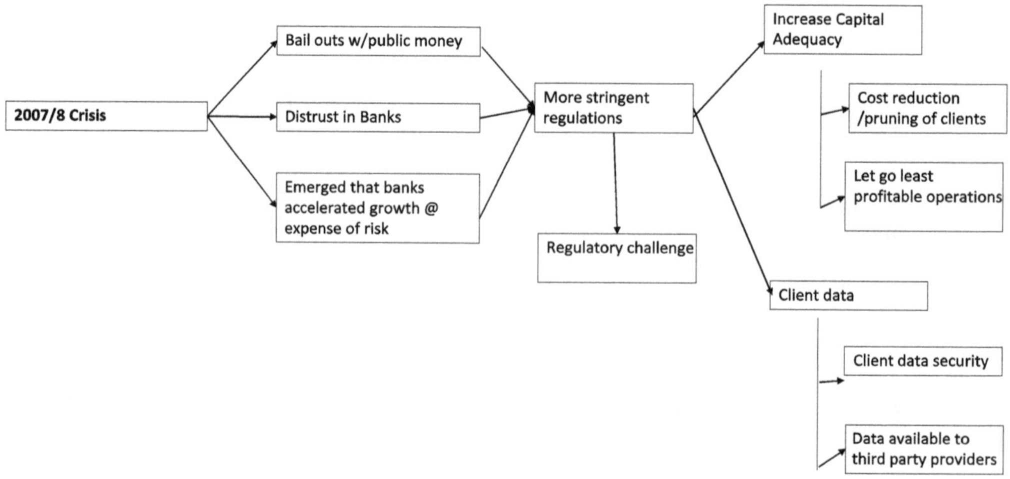

Fig. 11.1 The effect of the 2007–2008 crisis

profitable operations (e.g., certain products and geographic markets). The resulting reduction in scale in turn led them to embark on cost reduction initiatives (European Central Bank 2016; Kotarba 2016).

The other way in which more stringent regulations worked was related to client data. On the one hand the authorities put emphasis on client data security, and on the other hand bank regulators demanded that client data be made available to third-party providers in order to break the oligopoly of incumbent banks and increase competition in banking service (European Commission 2014, 2015; Tammas-Hastings 2017).

The Effect of Major Technological Breakthroughs

At the time the banks focused all their senses inside to cope with the regulatory changes that came because of the crisis, three key technology phenomena were happening. The first is incremental and refers to the continuing of Moore's law that translated into lower prices and thus giving more and more people access to devices (Lundstrom 2003; Waldrop 2016).

The second was the swift coming of age of Cloud computing with a change in mind-frame in the business community in the sense that moving from on-premise applications to cloud ones did not bring extra risks in terms of data security, and that adopting an on-demand model for technology appropriation had significant operational and balance sheet advantages (Ambrust et al. 2010; Rimal et al. 2009).

The third phenomenon was surely disruptive and is the advent of the first i-Phone and from there all the forms of smartphones that came after it. Moreover, the smartphone had the effect of enabling the development of social networks and, thus, the side effect of the advent of the data tsunami usually understated as Big Data (Barkhuus and Polichar 2011; Lee and Shin 2018; Smolan and Erwitt 2012).

These three phenomena had effect on what was to be the emerging FinTech sector, and on incumbent banks. The effects on these two groups initially developed quite independently of each other, but as will be seen opportunities for cross-fertilization emerged in later stages (EY 2018, p. 28; Gai et al. 2018; Lee and Shin 2018).

Looking at the FinTech sector first, it is found that the conjunction of the three technological phenomena had the effect of both lowering entry barriers for small new players to offer components of financial services and giving many more people access to devices and thus become potential clients for these new entrants to the financial services market offering. As opposed to entrepreneurial technology-based start-ups in other sectors, in general these new players in the FinTech sector did not have cash to burn at outrageous rates, so they developed two characteristics. On the one hand they are limited in the scope of their service, and on the other they take incremental opportunities in relatively mature markets that offer them quick cash-flow. These two characteristics translate into them focusing on niche but profitable parts of the incumbent banks' business, causing strong reaction from the banks who denounce them as avoiding regulations to take the icing of their cake (Lacasse et al. 2016).

The conjunction of taking the more profitable pieces of the banks' business and being able to serve many more people who were then possessing digital devices, converted into great opportunities for the emerging FinTechs. But their increasing visibility and the protests of the incumbent bankers led banking regulators to observe this new sector and extend at least part of the regulations to them.

From the perspective of incumbent banks, these three technological phenomena and their derivations (i.e., social networks and Big Data) had a significant impact on their own operations. Bank clients were demanding new channels such as mobile and generating massive data flows that offered significant potential if properly exploited. However, they also posed unsurmountable challenges in terms of cybersecurity, of data analytics issues and of data visualization complexities to incumbent banks that were constrained by their legacy systems as described above. This led the banks to start seeing FinTechs as potential enablers for their own processes in this new era of financial services (EY 2018; Gai et al. 2018).

Particularly on continental Europe where FinTechs were being funded more by banks than venture capital (Lee and Shin 2018), risk management challenges emerged quickly and were addressed by regulators which erected barriers for FinTechs to operate as independent client-facing service providers, but opened opportunities in the banks that were funding them. So, in general, the antagonistic atmosphere between incumbent

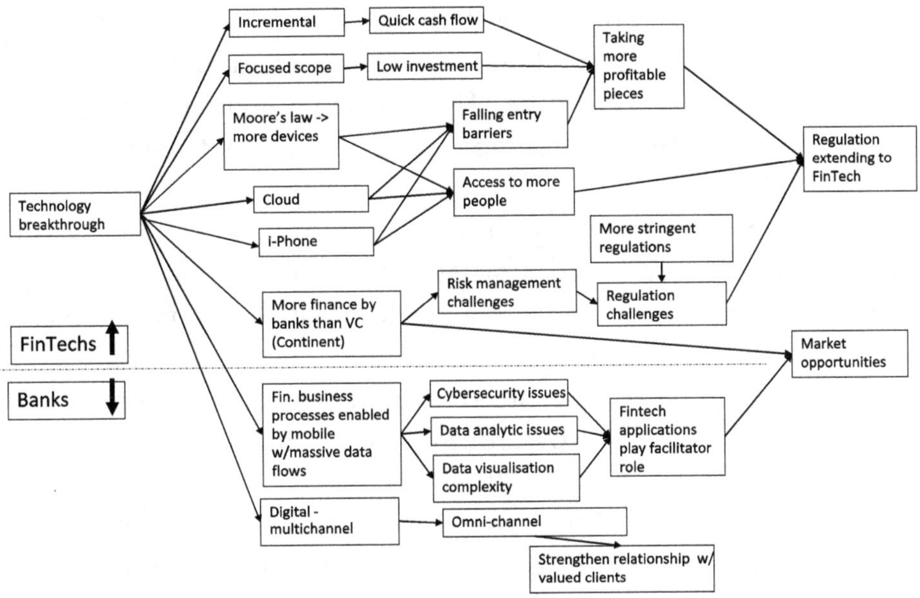

Fig. 11.2 The effect of major technological breakthroughs on FinTech and banks

banks and FinTechs that prevailed in the early post-2008 years gave way to a more collaborative spirit between both sectors. This effect of the technological breakthroughs is depicted graphically in Fig. 11.2.

The Effect of Social Changes

At the time of the financial crisis and the advent of the technological phenomena described above, the business world was going through major social transformations in terms of power as depicted by Naim (2013), of the changes in mindset that came with Generation Y taking a growing role in the workforce and of the advent of social entrepreneurs and entrepreneurship.

The Generation Y are avid adopters of mobile banking as long as it is easy to use and it poses no excessive risks in terms of data security. Both these conditions were hard to meet for incumbent bankers due to their legacy platforms, but straight forward for the FinTechs. On the other hand, due to the capital constraints mentioned above banks put effort into developing CRM processes and solutions that enabled them to strengthen their relationship with their 'valued' (i.e., the older more affluent) customers, and let go their less profitable and higher risk ones, as the Generation Y were seen to be. This opened a segment of great potential to the FinTechs (Boonsiritomachai and Pitchayadejanant 2017; Lee and Shin 2018).

In parallel with the above and especially in the Anglo-Saxon world, there emerged a new breed of what were to be called social entrepreneurs whose projects did not pursue a predominantly financial objective and thus were unfit to be assessed in terms of the banks' traditional credit scoring criteria. This new breed of entrepreneurs resort to alternative finance sources such as crowdfunding so became another market opportunity for FinTechs (Kotarba 2016).

On continental Europe it was found that while people do not trust banks much more than in the Anglo-Saxon world, they have less incentive to leave their banks and trust FinTechs even less than banks. So that becomes a barrier for FinTechs on the continent.

The effects of social changes are depicted and summarized in Fig. 11.3.

As a result of these three external forces (i.e., the Great Recession and subsequent regulatory changes, the technology breakthroughs, and the social changes) acting nearly simultaneously, banks lost control of the

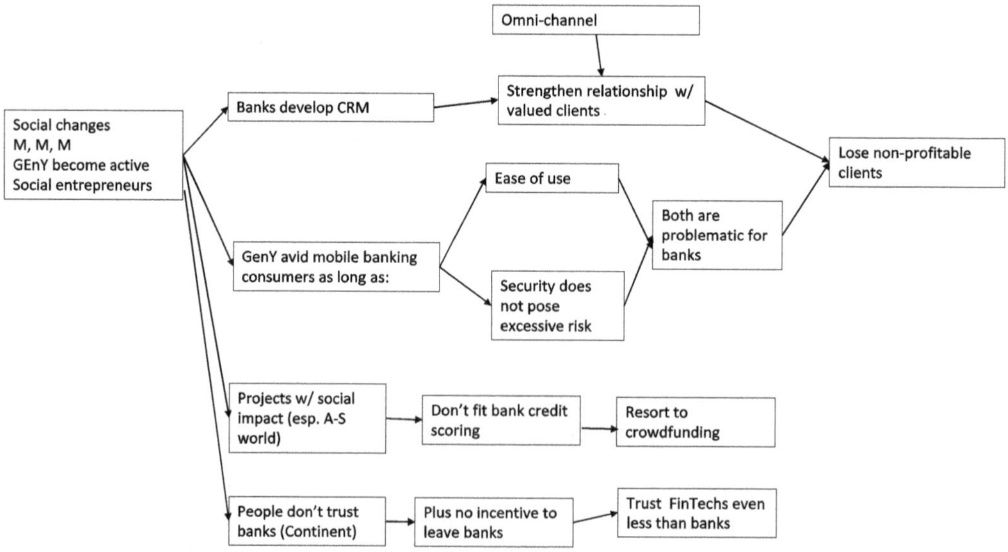

Fig. 11.3 Effects of social changes on banks and FinTech

evolution of ICT and left the door wide open for technology entrepreneurs to set up independently and eat away at the icing of their cake. The next section gives an overview of the industrial organization of this new sector.

A New Industrial Sector: The Emerging of FinTech

As mentioned above the FinTech sector is quite different from other technology-driven entrepreneurial or start-up sectors in the sense that it did not access massive funding and therefore its companies had to be focused in terms of service scope, and it did not produce great new markets but rather served extant markets that were until then poorly or underserved by banks. While, due to the latter, initially the relationship between traditional banks and FinTechs was notoriously antagonistic, with the passage of time banks realized that their constraints from legacy systems would obstruct them entering the digital era, so started to see FinTechs as possible collaborators to help overcome those barriers. This is particularly so in the data-oriented, security and privacy, and compliance spaces (Duan and Da 2012; Gai et al. 2018; Roumani et al. 2016).

Growth of the FinTech sector in terms of investment is literally exponential, going from \$1.8 billion in 2010 to \$19 billion in 2015 according to some sources (Citi 2016 cited by Leong et al. 2017) or from \$1.5 billion in 2010 to \$22 billion in 2015 according to others (Shuttlewood et al. 2016) and there are indications of steep growth in 2016 (Lee and Shin 2018). Within this context, seven banking-service areas emerge as the domains where FinTechs carry out their offering. These are: alternative finance, transactions, investment markets, banking back office, financial inclusion, cryptocurrencies, and business partner integration.

Alternative finance refers to services that supersede the traditional lending function of banks. They include personal finance, consumer finance, small and medium enterprise lending, and prominent in this category is *crowdfunding* in its four formats: reward-based, donation-based, equity-based and loan-based. Examples of reward-based crowdfunding companies include Kickstarter, Indiegogo, CrowdFunder, and RocketHub; of donation-based are GoFundMe, GiveForward, and FirstGiving; of equity-based crowdfunding companies are AngelList, Early Shares, and Crowdcube; finally, of loan-based crowdfunding companies are Funding Circle and Cumplo (Lee and Shin 2018; Shneor and Munim 2019 citing Ziegler et al. 2018).

Transactions refers to one of the most active areas of FinTech as are payments and remittances. These two areas were traditionally controlled by banks but are now giving way—in the case of payments by offering layers of service overlaying those of traditional banks and biting away at parts of the fees that banks charge in this space. In the case of remittances, it is about offering channels that circumvent bank services and fees altogether (Lee and Shin 2018).

Investment markets include services such as equity financing, retail investment, institutional investment, fund management and crowdfunding as an opportunity for investing (Lee and Shin 2018; Shneor and Munim 2019).

Banking back office is about FinTechs supplying banks agile services such as banking infrastructure, financial security services, identity verification, compliance, business tools, financial research, and energy efficiency in regard to achieving green finance. Prominent amongst these are RegTech, a flavour of FinTech aimed at helping banks comply with the demands of regulators and assist banking supervisors in keeping track of the banks under their watch (Gai et al. 2018; Puschmann 2017; Tammas-Hastings 2017).

Financial inclusion means reaching out to the unbanked and offering financial services at an extremely low cost and fill a gap that banks have never tackled, with well thought through and low-cost service offerings; micro-finance is prominent amongst this category (Lacasse et al. 2016).

Cryptocurrencies emerged as an initiative to circumvent banks altogether in the payments space but have not materialized as such; up to now they have served more as investment than payment instruments, and with doubtful outcomes at that. However, the distributed ledger technology that underlies them could be of application in many other areas such as trading and 'smart contracts' (Chen 2018; Hawlitschek et al. 2018).

Business partner integration is about FinTech offering services that bridge across the traditional offerings of banks and of other sectors with large business-to-consumer operations, such as telecommunications, retailers and airlines (Kumar et al. 2006; Rosingh et al. 2001; Schmitt and Gautam 2016).

To deliver these services FinTechs will apply one or multiple emerging technologies such as the DANCE acronym (Data, Algorithm, Networks, Cloud, Exponential) proposed by McAfee and Brynjolfsson (2017) and others including mobile, distributed ledgers, bioinformatics and behavioural biometrics, robots, all-in-one smartcards, and others.

It is helpful to understand the industry to present this in the form of a double entry table and map the FinTech companies onto the cells of this matrix (see Table 11.1).

The rest of the chapters in this book will develop the contents that will fit into the columns under alternative finance and investment markets of this framework. Those are the two service domains in the FinTech I/O framework where crowdfunding plays a key role. In the first case in its funding role, and in the second in its investment opportunities role. Just as an example of how this works, Table 11.2 reproduces the contents of one cell in this framework: The cell corresponding to Alternative Finance as a service domain, and data analytics and the exploiting of Big Data as a predominant enabling technology for those services.

It should be noted that in the Table 11.2 there are the four kinds of crowdfunding companies described above, but there are also other companies such as Touch Bank, which is a retail bank, or Retail Capital, which lends through partnership with banks, and do not conform to the crowdfunding principles but nevertheless are FinTechs in the alternative finance space.

With all this information in mind, the next section will extract some insights into how the FinTech sector emerged and evolved, and it will address the research question.

Discussion

Many interesting insights emerge from this analysis of the FinTech sector, of which four will be mentioned in this section. The first is that technological breakthroughs are all important but are only a necessary but not a sufficient condition for the advent of FinTech. Cultural-based influences

Table 11.1 The FinTech I/O framework

	Alternative Finance: Profitable Finance; Consumer banking; SME lending; Crowd-funding	*Transactions*: Payments; Remittances	*Investment Markets*: Equity financing; Retail investment Institutes. Investment; Crowd-funding	*Back Office*: Banking Infrastructure: Fin. Security; Business tools; Financial research; Regtech	*Financial Inclusion*: Reaching out: Fees and Profitability; Micro-finance	*Cryptocurrencies*: Payment or investment instrument? ICO.	*Business Partner integration*: Telcos, Retail, Airlines
Data: Exploiting 'Big Data'							
Algorithms: AI and Cognitive Computing							
Networks: 5G, faster data accumulation							
Cloud: Lower entry barriers; local vs central computation							
Exponential improvement in digital h/w; Moore's law effect							
Mobile							
Robotics							
Bioinformatics & behavioural biometrics							
Distributed Ledgers							
All-in-One smartcards							
VR, interactive & AR							

Table 11.2 Sample from the repository of FinTechs

Company's name	Country	Activity	Notes	Website
Lendingkart	India	Business loan for small business	Co-lending with banks	www.lendingkart.com
KredX	India	Business loan for small- and medium-sized businesses	Investors/applied for an Non-Banking Financial Company (NBFC) licence	www.kredx.com
Wefinance	USA	Lending to particular by funding from particulars		www.wefinance.com
Upstart	USA	Bring together high-potential borrowers and investors	Calculate credit score based on borrower's background	www.upstart.com
SoFi	USA	P2P lending for students		www.sofi.com
Rocket Mortgage	USA	Loans and mortgages	Focus on millennials	www.rocketmortgage.com
C2fo	UK	Short-term loans		C2fo.com
Zopa	UK	P2P lending	Founded in 2005, one of the first sites directly bringing together borrowers and savers, cutting out financial institutions from the lending process (NYT)	www.zopa.com
Touch bank	Russia	Retail banking	Online credits, loans, card, account management without paperwork, saving management	www.touchbank.com

(continued)

Table 11.2 (continued)

Company's name	Country	Activity	Notes	Website
Smart asset	USA	Advices throughout database (find best credit, loan solution among all propositions in the market	Tax, retirement, bank, account comparison tool	Smartasset.com
Simple finance	Russia	Micro lending	Asset-based loans, unsecure loans	www.ewdn.com

have also been essential and probably the most important was the Millennium generation taking their place in the labour and consumer markets. The incumbent bankers disregarded them to focus on more affluent baby-boomers, particularly in asset management services. What the banks did not anticipate is that Millennials are not individually affluent yet but that they are on the way to being the largest demographic group and as a group they hold over $1 trillion in wealth (Pitchbook).[2] This group is not interested in investing in active management funds and having costly financial advisors; they want passive management funds that can be monitored through their mobile phone. What is even of more impact is that the older generations learn to trust technologies that are embraced by the Millennials, so disregarding this generation exposes them to losing their senior relations.

A second insight is that according to some sources of the seven service categories of FinTechs, the most highly funded (Venture Scanner 2019) are lending to consumers and to businesses, (meaning small- and medium-sized enterprises, SMEs). Most of this is based on the peer-to-peer business model thus constructing links between borrowers and investors. Some of the FinTechs in this space are co-lending with banks and loan criteria vary across companies, but most want to avoid the classic credit scoring criterion in favour of seeking the highest potential borrowers and the most interesting personal projects. Based on keeping a low operating cost, these FinTechs can offer lower rates to borrowers and higher returns to lenders or investors. This insight is saying that crowdfunding is in a highly relevant position within FinTechs.

The third insight, as anticipated, is that banks have departed from their original antagonistic view of FinTechs to start finding potential in them as start-up venture opportunities and, more importantly, as resources for internal projects to make their operation more responsive, secure, compliant and efficient (EY 2018; Lee and Shin 2018). Typically, they look at FinTechs to help them reduce operational costs, provide more personalized services through data, and respond to customer behaviour changes. As a result of this, FinTechs have extended their role from retail customer facing to the back office or middle office of banks. Although it is mentioned above that alternative lending is the most funded domain, this can be contested based on the massive resources that are increasingly going into security and privacy initiatives (Gai et al. (2018), citing Gartner, says that the cybersecurity market reached $75 billion in 2015 and is projected to reach $170 billion by 2020; a significant share of this will go to financial services).

Finally, it has been said that in the UK, following the 2007–2008 financial crisis and the tarnished image with which established banks came out of it, the regulators proactively promoted FinTechs in the hope that challenger banks would emerge from them. And in effect this did happen as several challenger banks have emerged (e.g., Monzo, Metro) but their real impact on the market concentration has been marginal with the five big banks still firmly in control. What is even more disappointing is that some of these challenger banks have had to have their business models closely scrutinized by the banking supervisors under suspicion of adopting aggressive lending practices and even manipulating of balance sheets to avoid increased demand for fresh regulatory capital (FT 2019). It is hoped that the implementation of open banking supported by regulations such as Payment Services Directive 2 (PSD2) will enable FinTechs and the most agile and forward-looking mainstream banks to offer more API-enabled services and thus change the oligopolistic structure of the banking business. Traditional banks will not go away but they will most likely become a component of a more fragmented industry in the form of a network of hyperspecialists (Malone et al. 2011).

This evolution of the evolving relationship of banks and FinTechs is summarized in Fig. 11.4.

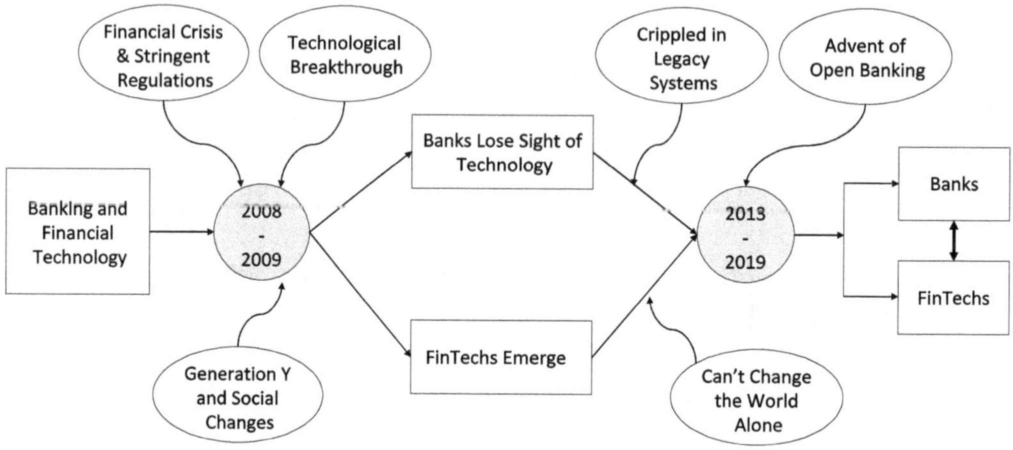

Fig. 11.4 Evolution of the relationship between banks and FinTechs

So, returning to the research question, *Why did FinTechs emerge as an industrial sector, independent of banking?* A combination of factors happening nearly simultaneously led banks to get distracted from the transformations that were happening around them. Just as the banks were looking inside their own organization to deal with the severe regulatory changes being imposed upon them as a result of the Great Recession, bankers did not perceive the importance that new technologies such as the smartphone were having, nor did they understand the cultural changes that were starting to happen with the coming of age of Gen-Y.

The effect of the smartphone and thus accessibility to devices of a mass market of relatively low income individuals, combined with the lowering of barriers to entry into the banking business of agile entrepreneurs that came with the maturing of cloud computing, enabled FinTech companies to roar into activity.

What encouraged entrepreneurs to move into the multiple banking services domains was the fact that they could detect a great number of underserved banking customers, with a young mindset, to whom they could approach with a narrow service offering driven by technology. That the offering was narrow meant that investment in developing application was relatively low; and the fact that the market was already there meant that cash flow would start coming in quickly. The combination of these two factors meant that the amount of working capital required was relatively low.

The fact that the FinTech companies developed relatively focused service offerings within a far reaching service industry as is banking, and that their services are enabled by a large spectrum of technologies that either emerged or matured in the second half of the last decade when this sector was emerging, has led the FinTech sector to encompass a large number of companies with quite different configurations. The framework presented in Table 11.1 as a double-entry table, with seven service-offering domains in one dimension, and over ten technology categories in the other, helps to understand how the sector is organized and where each company plays.

Conclusions

In summary this research has found that, distracted by the 2007–2008 crisis and its immediate regulatory changes, the banking industry lost sight of the technological breakthroughs and social changes that were happening around it. As a result, after decades of having been a driver and leader for technological change, the industry left windows wide open for nimble companies based on ground-breaking technologies to emerge and 'eat its lunch'.

It is extraordinary that in such a closely regulated industry as banking, these FinTech entrepreneurs could have found gaps in regulations to eat away at some of the most profitable icing on the banking industry's cake. It is also extraordinary that in such a short period of time FinTechs could open into so many different business domains, enabled by the emerging of such an unprecedented number of different game-changing technologies.

The FinTechs managed this feat with little capital in comparison with the deep pockets of the institutions they were outpacing. They achieved this precisely by focusing on niches where the market was already there and waiting for a solution. So, in a way, it was more a pull by social changes than a push by the FinTechs (this is quite different from other areas of technology-based entrepreneurship where the pioneers created a market). However, FinTechs should not become complacent as regulation is creeping in. Approximately one-third of the FinTech business in the Eurozone is not regulated, but going forward, FinTechs should count on the fact that banking regulations will move further into their space.

Crowdfunding and other forms of alternative finance occupy a position of relevance within the FinTech sector and together have the greatest fraction of investment as compared to the other six business domains included in the FinTech industrial organization framework. Clearly banks have great difficulty in financing the SME segment, where its traditional credit scoring techniques are not appropriate. There is, thus, a promising opportunity for crowdfunding to grow in this space.

Banks have found it hard to keep up as selecting a new technology that will drive its processes is no minor decision for a bank and in times when so many technologies are emerging, it is hard to predict which will be the winning ones. This is not a level field: Clearly banks as incumbents have far more to lose than FinTechs so the question we need to ask ourselves is this: Do extant strategy-technology alignment models apply to banks in times of so much disruption? Banks need to address this issue.

This review of the FinTech sector as a framework to give context to the theme of crowdfunding that is the focus of the rest of this book, is necessarily generic and bridges across the different markets. But clearly the process of emerging of the FinTech sector and the evolution of its relationship to banks, as synthesized in the process described in Fig. 11.4, will change from market to market. As a result of the stage of economic development, the regulatory environment, the quality of the technological infrastructure, the different attitudes towards the financial sector, and many others, the FinTech sector has evolved differently in each market. There is scope to do comparative analyses of this evolution between markets and thus arrive at a more granular knowledge on its evolution.

Finally, another question for future research is why, despite the advent of the FinTech sector with all its diverse set of players, has the market structure in terms of market control by a small number of traditional players, remained essentially unchanged. Will open banking be the answer to this problem?

Notes

1. OECD (2003, pp. 65–66) finds that financial intermediation organizations '*are intensive users of information and thus have the greatest scope to benefit from ICT*'.
2. https://pitchbook.com/news/articles/blend-becomes-latest-fintech-startup-to-bank-a-mega-round-in-2019

References

Ambrust, M., Fox, A., Griffith, R., Joseph, A. D., Katz, R., Konwinski, A., Lee, G., Patterson, D., Rabkin, A., Stoica, I., & Zaharia, M. (2010, April). A View of Cloud Computing. *Communications of the ACM, 53*(4), 50–58. https://doi.org/10.1145/1721654.1721672.

Arner, D. W., Barberis, J., & Buckley, R. P. (2017). FinTech, RegTech, and the Reconceptualization of Financial Regulation. *Northwestern Journal of International Law and Business, 37*(3), 371–382.

Barkhuus, L., & Polichar, V. E. (2011, August). Empowering Through Seamfulness: Smart Phones in Everyday Life. *Journal Personal and Ubiquitous Computing, 15*(6), 629–639. https://doi.org/10.1007/s00779-010-0342-4.

Boonsiritomachai, W., & Pitchayadejanant, K. (2017). Determinants Affecting Mobile Banking Adoption by Generation Y Based on the UTAUTM Modified by the TAM Concept. *Kasetsart Journal of Social Science*. https://doi.org/10.1016/j.kjss.2017.10.005.

Chen, Y. (2018). Blockchain Tokens and the Potential Democratization of Entrepreneurship and Innovation. *Business Horizons, 61*(4), 567–575.

Claessens, S., Frost, J., Turner, G., & Zhu, F. (2018). Fintech Credit Markets Around the World: Size, Drivers and Policy Issues. *BIS Quarterly Review*, September, pp. 29–49.

Clayton, T., & Waldron, K. (2003). *E-Commerce Adoption and Business Impact, A Progress Report, in Economic Trends, ICT and Economic Growth: Evidence from OECD Countries, Industries and Firms*. OECD Publications.

Cotton, I. W., & Greatorex, F. S. (1968). Data Structures and Techniques for Remote Computer Graphics. *Proceedings of the AFIPS '68 (Fall, Part I) Joint Computer Conference*, December 9–11, San Francisco, California, pp. 533–544. https://doi.org/10.1145/1476589.1476661.

Dorfleitner, G., Hornuf, L., Schmtt, M., et al. (2017). Definition of FinTech and Description of the FinTech Industry. In G. Dorfleitner, L. Hornuf, M. Schmitt, & M. Weber (Eds.), *FinTech in Germany*. Cham: Springer International Publishing.

Duan, L., & Da, X. (2012). Business Intelligence for Enterprise Systems: A Survey. *IEEE Transactions on Industrial Informatics Information, 8*(3), 679–687.

European Central Bank. (2016). *ECB Banking Supervision: SSM Priorities 2016* [online]. Retrieved from https://www.bankingsupervision.europa.eu/ecb/pub/pdf/publication_supervisory_priorities_2016.en.pdf?024a0072fe923441556e5bba7251dd6d.

European Commission. (2014). Investment Services and Regulated Markets (MiFID 1 & MiFID 2). Retrieved June 2, 2019, from https://ec.europa.eu/info/law/markets-financial-instruments-mifid-ii-directive-2014-65-eu_en.

European Commission. (2015). Payment Services (PSD 2)—Directive (EU) 2015/2366. Retrieved June 2, 2019, from https://ec.europa.eu/info/law/payment-services-psd-2-directive-eu-2015-2366_en.

EY. (2018). *ASEAN FinTech Census 2018*. Retrieved June 19, 2019, from https://www.ey.com/Publication/vwLUAssets/EY-asean-fintech-census-2018/$FILE/EY-asean-fintech-census-2018.pdf.

Financial Times. (2019). *BoE Raises Alert Over 'Aggressive' New Lenders,* June 16.

Gai, K., Qiu, M., & Sun, X. (2018). A Survey on Fintech. *Journal of Network and Computer Applications, 103*, 262–273.

Griffiths, P. D. R. (2003). *A Literature Review: Converting Information Technology Investments into Shareholder Value in Financial Services Organisations*. Henley Working Papers, HWP 0315, ISBN. 1861811780.

Griffiths, P. D. R. (2005). *The Application of Market Power Theory as a Value Driver for Information Technology Investment Decisions: A Study of Six Chilean Banks*. Doctoral thesis, Henley Management College/Brunel University.

Haddad, C., & Hornuf, L. (2019). The Emergence of the Global Fintech Market: Economic and Technological Determinants. *Small Business Economics, 53*(1), 81–105.

Hawlitschek, F., Notheisen, B., & Teubner, T. (2018). The Limits of Trust-Free Systems: A Literature Review on Blockchain Technology and Trust in the Sharing Economy. *Electronic Commerce Research and Applications, 29*, 50–63.

Kotarba, M. (2016). New Factors Inducing Changes in the Retail Banking Customer Relationship Management (CRM) and Their Exploration by the Fintech Industry. *Foundations of Management, 8*. ISSN 2080-7279. https://doi.org/10.1515/fman-2016-0006.

Kumar, A., Nair, A., Parsons, A., & Urdapiletta, E. (2006). *Expanding Bank Outreach through Retail Partnerships: Correspondent Banks in Brazil.* World Bank Working Papers, https://doi.org/10.1596/978-0-8213-6702-5

Lacasse, R. M., Lambert, B. A., Osmani, E., Couture, C., Roy, N., Sylvain, J., & Nadeau, F. (2016). A Digital Tsunami: Fintech and Crowdfunding. *Proceedings of International Scientific Conference on Digital Intelligence*, April 4–6, UQAR, Quebec, Canada.

Lee, I., & Shin, Y. J. (2018). Fintech: Models, Investment Decisions, and Challenges. *Business Horizons, 61*, 35–46. https://doi.org/10.1016/j.bushor.2017.09.003.

Leong, C., Tan, B., Xiao, X., Tan, F. T. C., & Sun, Y. (2017). Nurturing a Fintech Ecosystem: The Case of a Youth Microloan Startup in China. *International Journal of Information Management, 37*, 92–97.

Lundstrom, M. (2003). Moore's Law Forever? *Science, 299*(5604), 210–211. https://doi.org/10.1126/science.1079567.

Malone, T. W., Laubacher, R., & Johns, T. (2011). The Age of Hyperspecialisation. *Harvard Business Review, 89*, 56–65.

McAfee, A., & Brynjolfsson, E. (2017). *Machine Platform Crowd: Harnessing our Digital Future*. New York: Norton.

McKeen, J. D., & Smith, H. A. (1996). *Assessing the Value of Information Technology: A Focus on Banking and Insurance*. Working Paper #94-27, Queens University.

Naim, M. (2013). *The End of Power*. New York: Basic Books.

OECD. (2003). *ICT and Economic Growth: Evidence from OECD Countries, Industries and Firms*. OECD Publications.

Palazzeschi, E. (2018) *Fintech: Why and What Is in the Regulatory Pipe*. Presentation at Fintech Conference, EM-Normandie & Oxford Fintech & Smart Law Society, March 15.

Puschmann, T. (2017). Fintech. *Business & Information Systems Engineering, 59*(1), 69–76. https://doi.org/10.1007/s12599-017-0464-6.

Rimal, B. P., Choi, E., & Lumb, I. (2009). A Taxonomy and Survey of Cloud Computing Systems. *Proceedings of the 2009 Fifth International Joint Conference on INC, IMS and IDC*, August 25–27, Seoul. https://doi.org/10.1109/NCM.2009.218.

Rosingh, W., Seale, A., & Osborn, D. (2001). *Why Banks and Telecoms Must Merge to Surge*. Strategy+Business (Technical & Innovation, Q2 2001, Issue 23). Retrieved June 22, 2019, from https://www.strategy-business.com/article/17163?gko=4cda6.

Roumani, Y., Nwankpa, J., & Roumani, Y. (2016). Examining the Relationship Between Firm's Financial Records and Security Vulnerabilities. *International Journal of Information Management, 36*(6), 987–994.

Schmitt, M. G., & Gautam, T. (2016). Transformation of Banking Institutions: Comparing Germany and India. In H. Ellermann, P. Kreutter, & W. Messner (Eds.), *The Palgrave Handbook of Managing Continuous Business Transformation*, (pp. 151–171). Palgrave-Macmillan.

Shneor, R., & Munim, Z. H. (2019). Reward Crowdfunding Contribution as Planned Behavior: An Extended Framework. *Journal of Business Research, 103*, 56–70.

Shuttlewood, P., Volin, M., & Wozniak, L. (2016). Global fintech investment growth continues in 2016 driven by Europe and Asia, accenture study finds. https://newsroom.accenture.com/news/global-fintech-investment-growth-continues-in2016-driven-by-europe-and-asia-accenture-study-finds.htm.

Smolan, R., & Erwitt, J. (2012). *The Human Face of Big Data*. Sausalito, CA: Against All Odds Productions.

Tammas-Hastings, D. (2017) The Exploding Popularity of RegTech. *LSE Review*. Retrieved December 12, 2018, from http://blogs.lse.ac.uk/business-review/2017/07/07/the-exploding-popularity-of-regtech/.

Venture Scanner. (2019). Fintech Q1 Update [Online]. Retrieved June 3, 2019, from http://insights.venturescanner.com/category/financial-technology/.

Waldrop, M. M. (2016). The Chips Are Down for Moore's Law: The Semiconductor Industry Will Soon Abandon Its Pursuit of Moore's Law. *Nature, 530*, 144–147. https://doi.org/10.1038/530144a.

Zavolokina, L., Dolata, M., & Schwabe, G. (2016). The FinTech Phenomenon: Antecedents of Financial Innovation Perceived by the Popular Press. *Financial Innovation, 2*(1), 1–16.

Ziegler, T., Shneor, R., Garvey, K., Wenzlaff, K., Yerolemou, N., Zhang, B., & Hao, R. (2018). *Expanding Horizons: The 3rd European Alternative Finance Industry Report*. Cambridge: Cambridge Centre for Alternative Finance.

Permissions

All chapters in this book were first published by Springer; hereby published with permission under the Creative Commons Attribution License or equivalent. Every chapter published in this book has been scrutinized by our experts. Their significance has been extensively debated. The topics covered herein carry significant information for a comprehensive understanding. They may even be implemented as practical applications or may be referred to as a beginning point for further studies.

The contributors of this book come from diverse backgrounds, making this book a truly international effort. We would like to thank all the contributing authors for lending their expertise to make the book truly unique. They have played a crucial role in the development of this book. Without their invaluable contributions this book wouldn't have been possible. They have made vital efforts to compile up to date information on the varied aspects of this subject to make this book a valuable addition to the collection of many professionals and students.

This book was conceptualized with the vision of imparting up-to-date and integrated information in this field. To ensure the same, a matchless editorial board was set up. Every individual on the board went through rigorous rounds of assessment to prove their worth. After which they invested a large part of their time researching and compiling the most relevant data for our readers.

The editorial board has been involved in producing this book since its inception. They have spent rigorous hours researching and exploring the diverse topics which have resulted in the successful publishing of this book. They have passed on their knowledge of decades through this book. To expedite this challenging task, the publisher supported the team at every step. A small team of assistant editors was also appointed to further simplify the editing procedure and attain best results for the readers.

Apart from the editorial board, the designing team has also invested a significant amount of their time in understanding the subject and creating the most relevant covers. They scrutinized every image to scout for the most suitable representation of the subject and create an appropriate cover for the book.

The publishing team has been an ardent support to the editorial, designing and production team. Their endless efforts to recruit the best for this project, has resulted in the accomplishment of this book. They are a veteran in the field of academics and their pool of knowledge is as vast as their experience in printing. Their expertise and guidance has proved useful at every step. Their uncompromising quality standards have made this book an exceptional effort. Their encouragement from time to time has been an inspiration for everyone.

The publisher and the editorial board hope that this book will prove to be a valuable piece of knowledge for students, practitioners and scholars across the globe.

Index

L

M

P

R

S

V

Printed in the USA
CPSIA information can be obtained
at www.ICGtesting.com
LVHW082202201023
761596LV00009B/1542

9 798888 360187